INTRODUCTION TO CONSTRUCTION

MARK HUTH

*This book is dedicated
to my wife, Marjorie,
whose patience and
devotion made it possible.*

INTRODUCTION TO CONSTRUCTION

MARK HUTH

DELMAR PUBLISHERS
COPYRIGHT © 1980
BY LITTON EDUCATIONAL PUBLISHING, INC.

LIBRARY OF CONGRESS CATALOG CARD NUMBER: 78-60838
ISBN: 0-8273-1737-9

10 9 8 7 6 5 4 3 2 1

Printed in the United States of America
Published simultaneously in Canada by
Delmar Publishers, a division of
Van Nostrand Reinhold, Ltd.

Consulting Editor
James E. Good,
President A.I.A.A.

DELMAR PUBLISHERS • ALBANY, NEW YORK 12205
A DIVISION OF LITTON EDUCATIONAL PUBLISHING, INC.

PREFACE

Construction comprises a major part of modern industry, both in terms of output and the work force employed. A recent study by the U.S. Department of Labor indicates that more than 3.4 million skilled workers are employed in construction, which is approximately 3 out of every 10 skilled workers. In addition, the construction industry employs great numbers of unskilled workers, technicians, and professionals. INTRODUCTION TO CONSTRUCTION discusses these occupations and the structures they build. The knowledge and experience gained through the use of this textbook is valuable in choosing a career and in preparing for careers in the construction industry.

In general, the sequence of topics in this book is the same as the sequence of events in construction. Early units discuss design and the design professions; later units cover materials, tools, and finally, construction techniques and related occupations.

Each unit begins with a statement of what is to be learned – objectives. This informs the student what to expect and allows the teacher to plan the instruction.

The body of the unit explains how the topic applies to the construction industry and what occupations are involved. Where appropriate, the units describe how a structure is built. A large number of illustrations show materials, methods, and people at work in construction.

Following the body of each unit, there are activities for experiencing a part of the field of construction. These activities are outlined with specific procedural steps. The teacher may alter these procedures to fit a particular course or classroom situation. However, INTRODUCTION TO CONSTRUCTION is an activity-based textbook and each unit should be reinforced by hands-on experiences.

The final element of each unit is a series of review questions. These review questions are useful in measuring the student's comprehension of the unit content. They may be used by the student for self-evaluation or assigned by the teacher as quizzes.

ABOUT THE AUTHOR

Mark Huth has experience in the construction industry as a carpenter and a contractor. He has taught industrial arts on the junior-high and high-school level. He is a member of numerous professional organizations, including the American Industrial Arts Association, American Vocational Association, American Institute for Design and Drafting, and the Society for Technical Communication.

CONTENTS

SECTION V HEAVY CONSTRUCTION

SECTION VI NONSTRUCTURAL SYSTEMS

SECTION VII MANUFACTURED CONSTRUCTION

SECTION 1
SECTION 1
SECTION 1
SECTION 1

CONSTRUCTION PLANNING AND DRAWING

UNIT 1.
PURPOSES AND TYPES OF CONSTRUCTION

OBJECTIVES

After completing this unit, the student will be able to:

- discuss the importance of technological advancement in areas related to the construction industry.

- recognize how the economy affects the construction industry.

- describe the various occupations in the construction industry.

- explain the differences between light, heavy, industrial, and civil construction.

THE DEVELOPMENT OF TECHNOLOGY

One of the most noticeable traits of civilization is the use of tools and materials to create things. This is called *technology*. One of the first uses of technology was to improve shelter. This may have been as simple as using a pole as a lever to pry large stones out of a cave.

From the early beginnings, civilization continued to develop better tools and discover new ways of using available materials. Technology fulfilled a wide range of needs. Among the most ancient archeological finds are constructions for shelter, recreation, worship, and even for the further advancement of technology, figure 1-1.

For at least 2 1/2 million years, technology was limited to the raw materials that were readily available. Tools were primitive devices made of wood and stone. The materials of construction were grasslike plants, wood, clay, and stone. About 4000 B.C., it was discovered that copper could be extracted from the earth. After copper, tin and zinc were found. These metals produced better tools and materials that, in turn, made more complex and permanent construction possible.

With each new discovery, technology advanced. Metal fittings, for example, produced sturdier animal-drawn carts and wagons that could move material more efficiently. Transportation could now handle heavier loads over longer distances. This made larger and more sophisticated construction easier to build. From the first use of the earth's raw materials to the Industrial Revolution (circa 1800 A.D.), each new discovery led to others and civilization expanded.

During the Industrial Revolution, technology advanced at an incredible rate. Almost

1

Fig. 1-1 Ancient temple built around 500 B.C. *(Richard T. Kreh, Sr.)*

at once new methods were discovered for extracting raw materials from the earth. New machinery modernized the industrial world and new industries were created. Better sources of power and materials with more desirable properties produced even more advances and the whole technological chain snowballed. This rapid advancement still continues today.

INTERDEPENDENCE OF INDUSTRIES

All areas of technology have a great impact on one another. In the preceding examples of the development of tools, tool manufacturing and the discovery of metals played an important part in the advancement of construction practices.

In the modern world this interdependence of one industry on another is even more striking. When the automobile was developed around the turn of the century, better roads had to be built. These roads were built by the construction industry. With better roads, transportation became quicker and safer. People began to depend on automobiles and highway travel. To support this growing demand for motor vehicles, the manufacturing industry had to open new factories and offices, figure 1-2.

The construction industry affects every other sector of industry and vice versa. All manufactured goods are produced in factories built by construction workers, stored in warehouses

Fig. 1-2 **This automobile manufacturing plant is a product of the construction industry.** *(Chrysler Corp.)*

built by construction workers, transported over roads built by construction workers, and sold in stores built by construction workers. In return, the construction industry relies on other modern industries. For example, construction materials are transported in trucks, trains, and ships built by the manufacturing industry.

When all industries have the resources for new projects, a country can develop and advance. This is only possible when the economy is healthy. When the economy of a country is failing, all industries suffer. Because of the interdependence of industries, when one sector of industry is doing poorly, it affects all other sectors. Without money to build roads, there is no reason to make more autos or find new methods of transporting materials. On the other hand, when the economy is healthy, resources are available for every industry. Economy greatly affects the development of a country in this way.

CONSTRUCTION PERSONNEL

The construction industry encompasses many occupations. It employs approximately one-sixth of the working people in the United States. These people have varying levels of training, ranging from the unskilled laborer to those with college educations. Some work in air-conditioned offices, while others work on construction sites that may be in tropical heat or subzero cold.

Architects, engineers, drafters, specification writers, surveyors, and building code officials work on construction projects from the very beginning. *Architects* consider the surrounding environment and the needs of the people who will use the building when designing structures. The architect acts as the owner's representative at the construction site. *Engineers* specializing in mechanical, electrical, and structural systems design those systems into the building. There are also *civil engineers* who design structures, such as roadways, bridges, dams, and airports. *Surveyors* measure land and locate the buildings on the land. *Building code officials* write and enforce federal, state, and local *building codes.* These building codes govern the safety and quality of construction. *Specification writers* describe the materials and construction practices used on a particular project.

All of these people must work very closely with one another to design a construction project. To communicate this design to those who must construct the project, drawings are prepared of every detail of the design. These drawings are drawn by the architectural drafters, figure 1-3.

The occupations involved with producing materials for the construction industry are numerous. Some of the more obvious of these

Fig. 1-3 Drafters at work in a large company. *(The Boeing Co.)*

occupations are involved with lumbering and milling lumber, making cement and masonry materials, producing plastics, and distributing these materials to the construction industry, figure 1-4.

The actual construction of a project involves the building trades – carpenters, electricians, ironworkers, plasterers, masons, painters, plumbers, operating engineers, etc. Construction also requires the efforts of many related fields, such as construction superintendents, estimators, expeditors, and unskilled laborers.

The *construction superintendent* is responsible for overseeing the work on all phases of a construction project. Construction superintendents must have some formal education in construction technology and management, as well as experience in the construction industry. *Estimators* work with calculators, catalogs, and tables to predict the cost in time and money required to complete a project. The *expeditor* is responsible for ordering materials so they are

Fig. 1-4 Salesperson at a counter in a retail lumber outlet *(Richard T. Kreh, Sr.)*

Fig. 1-5 Light construction refers to houses and other small buildings. *(Weyerhaeuser Co.)*

available when needed and scheduling the work of various trades so there are no conflicts. *Unskilled laborers* help the workers in all of the building trades. There are masonry laborers, carpentry laborers, etc.

All of these phases of the construction industry require office workers. The secretary for the general contractor, the file clerk for the architect, and the typist for the specification writer are all members of the construction family.

TYPES OF CONSTRUCTION

Construction may be broadly defined as the assembly or erecting of structures which cannot be readily moved once completed. This definition includes structures that fit into four categories: light, heavy, industrial, and civil.

Light construction is the building of homes and other small buildings, figure 1-5. These may be single-family dwellings, small apartment buildings, offices, stores, etc. Larger structures are not normally included in this category because the materials and techniques are quite different from those used in light construction.

Heavy building construction includes the construction of large buildings that are used for commercial purposes, figure 1-6. Heavy building

Fig. 1-6 This office building is an example of heavy construction. *(Portland Cement Assoc.)*

Fig. 1-7 Industrial construction includes structures other than buildings that are used for industrial purposes.

construction includes larger apartment buildings, schools, churches, office buildings, and warehouses. This type of construction involves larger equipment, a greater financial investment, and more time than light construction.

Industrial construction includes structures other than buildings that are erected for industrial purposes, figure 1-7. Such things as dry

docks for shipbuilding, nuclear power plants, and steel mills cannot be considered buildings. Many construction companies specialize in one type of industrial construction, such as oil refineries.

Civil construction is more closely linked with the land than other areas of construction, figure 1-8. Civil construction generally

Fig. 1-8 This modern highway is an example of civil construction. *(Portland Cement Assoc.)*

benefits the public as a whole more directly than other types. Examples of civil construction are airport runways, highways, dams, and bridges.

CONSTRUCTION CAREERS

With so many of the world's working force employed in the construction industry, there are excellent opportunities for people with a wide range of interests. The occupations directly related to construction can be grouped into four levels:

- Professionals
- Technicians
- Skilled laborers
- Unskilled laborers

Professionals

For those who plan to attend college after high school, there are a number of career opportunities in the construction professions. Most of the professions related to construction are involved with the design of buildings, highways, bridges, and other structures. These professions include architects, mechanical engineers, civil and structural engineers, and land-use planners. In addition to these design professions, industrial education teaching employs many construction professionals.

It takes at least four years of college to become an assistant engineer or architect. These assistants work on the staff of design companies with senior engineers or architects. Usually several years experience as a practicing professional are required before the engineer or architect is prepared for full professional status or to own a company. For those who choose to teach industrial education as a profession, a minimum of four years of college is required. Teachers are normally required to continue their education to at least the Master's degree level. Although the educational requirements are rigid, the construction professions provide good job security and above average professional salaries.

Technicians

Construction technicians work with full professionals as a part of a team. Most technicians are employed in the design stages of

Fig. 1-9 Construction technicians, such as the estimator, work with full professionals as part of a team. *(Richard T. Kreh, Sr.)*

construction. They provide a link between the professions and the skilled and unskilled laborers working in the field. Technicians may be employed as estimators, drafters, surveyors, and design assistants, figure 1-9.

Junior colleges and technical institutes provide courses of study for construction technicians. These courses usually concentrate on drafting, estimating, construction management, surveying, or general construction technology. Following two years of study in construction technology the technician is employed by an architectural design company, engineering company, construction company, or government agency.

The level of the construction technician is the newest of the construction career levels and also the fastest growing. The starting salary of a construction technician is usually approximately the same as that of a skilled worker. However, this group of careers offers exceptionally good advancement opportunities and good job security.

Skilled Laborers

The careers that are directly involved with working with tools and materials to erect structures are the construction trades (often called the *building trades*). The people employed in the construction trades are highly skilled in a particular phase of construction. These trades include carpenters, electricians, plumbers, masons, ironworkers, operating engineers (heavy equipment operators), painters, etc.

The skill necessary to be employed in the construction trades is usually learned in an *apprenticeship program.* Apprentices attend classes a few hours a week to learn the necessary theory. The rest of the week they work on a construction project under the supervision of a *journeyman* (skilled laborer who has completed the apprenticeship). Apprentices receive a percentage of the regular salary for the trade during their apprenticeship. Some skilled laborers receive their training through vocational school and informal on-the-job training. However, classroom training and construction

experience are still required to attain the necessary skill.

The construction trades are among the highest paying of all skilled occupations in the world when considered on an hourly basis. However, construction trades work is apt to depend on the weather and may move from one location to another. During winter months in the north many construction workers are unemployed and must rely on income earned during the summer months. When a major construction project is underway, there may be an excess of construction work; but when the project is completed, construction workers may have to look to other geographical locations for work. This should not be too much of a threat to the person interested in a career in construction. The construction industry is growing at a high rate nationwide and there is generally plenty of work available to provide a comfortable living for a sincere worker.

Unskilled Laborers

Most of the construction trades require the assistance of workers with less skill in a particular trade, figure 1-10. This provides a plentiful source of employment for persons who

Fig. 1-10 Unskilled laborers are needed in every phase of construction. *(ARB, Inc.)*

have not obtained a particular skill. Some unskilled laborers specialize in working with a specific trade, such as carpenters' helpers and mason tenders. However, most unskilled laborers in construction are general laborers who do whatever work is assigned.

ACTIVITIES

A. TYPES OF CONSTRUCTION

1. List at least two examples of each of the four types of construction in your community.

2. Choose one example from each category and explain how it has affected other industries in the area.

B. INFLUENCE OF OTHER INDUSTRIES

1. Name one important industry in your community.

2. Explain how this industry has affected the local construction industry.

C. CONSTRUCTION PLANNING

1. List three new construction projects that would benefit your community.

2. Compare your list with two to four other students. From all the projects listed, choose the three that would be most beneficial.

3. Discuss the resources of the community that would be used to complete and operate each of these construction projects.

D. OCCUPATIONS

1. Name one occupation in the construction industry that interests you and describe the education and training necessary to enter that field.

REVIEW

A. Matching

Choose which kind of construction in the right-hand column is indicated by each item listed in the left-hand column.

1. Bus terminal
2. Eighty-unit apartment building
3. Single home
4. Hospital
5. Water tower
6. Housing development
7. Grain elevator
8. Subway

(a) Civil construction
(b) Industrial construction
(c) Light construction
(d) Heavy building construction

B.   **Matching**

Choose the occupation in the right-hand column which performs each duty in the left-hand column.

1. Overseas construction of an office building
2. Designs machinery for operating a drawbridge
3. Designs the approach to a major highway
4. Handles materials at a construction site
5. Owner's representative during construction
6. Inspects new homes for compliance with city ordinances

(a)   Mechanical engineer
(b)   Laborer
(c)   Architect
(d)   Building code official
(e)   Construction superintendent
(f)   Civil engineer

UNIT 2.
ARCHITECTURAL DRAWINGS

OBJECTIVES

After completing this unit, the student will be able to:

- identify the factors to consider when designing a structure.

- demonstrate how to draw architectural plans and make models from those drawings.

- locate dimensions of components and overall sizes on architectural drawings.

- identify common symbols used on architectural drawings.

- measure scale drawings with an architect's scale.

DESIGN CONSIDERATIONS

Before work begins on the construction site, an extensive process of designing takes place. The number of people and amount of time involved in the design of a project depends on its size and impact on the community. Most communities have *zoning boards* to study the needs of the community and make recommendations for development. Zoning board members consider the size of the community, resources on hand, and location and condition of existing structures. New construction must comply with the regulations developed by the zoning board.

The first step in designing a construction project is for the architect or engineer to discuss the needs of the client (prospective owner). The designer of a building must know what the building will be used for; how much space is required, at present and in the future; what the existing site conditions are; how much money the client has available for the project; what community regulations must be followed; and what special requirements the client has.

One of the most important considerations in any design problem is *function*. A building fulfills the need for function if its occupants can carry out their activities efficiently. A bridge is functional if traffic can travel smoothly in both directions, without interferring with conditions below, figure 2-1.

Another important consideration in most construction is form. *Form* is the shape and appearence of the structure, figure 2-2. In deciding on the form of a structure, the architect considers the surroundings. A well-designed structure fits in with its surroundings.

Fig. 2-1   This functional pedestrian bridge provides safety, protection from the weather, and free flow of traffic below. *(Weyerhaeuser Co.)*

Fig. 2-2   The form of this airline terminal building is one of its most outstanding characteristics. *(Portland Cement Assoc.)*

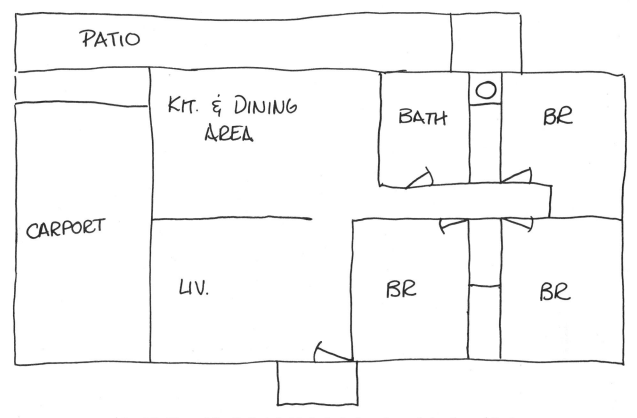

Fig. 2-3 The architect's first sketch in designing a home helps the architect and client understand each other's ideas.

Cost is always an important consideration in designing a project. Size, materials, and special features all affect the cost of a structure. It is often necessary to find an appropriate balance between cost and other considerations, but a well-designed project never sacrifices quality. For example, the prospective owner of a residence may at first desire a house with 3000 square feet of living space and stone siding. When cost is considered, however, it may prove wiser to construct a 2200 square-foot house with redwood siding. The quality of the 2200 square-foot house can still be equal to that of the larger house.

As the design develops, the architect makes rough sketches and notes to describe the proposed structure, figure 2-3. As changes are made in the developing design, new sketches are drawn, old ones are changed, and new notes are made on the sketches. The sketches become more detailed as the design takes shape. When the final design is reached, architectural drafters make accurate, detailed *scale drawings*. The drawings for a house in this unit were developed from the sketch in figure 2-3.

SCALES

It is not possible to make architectural drawings actual size, so they are drawn to scale. The dimensions of all parts are reduced to a size that can be drawn on a sheet of paper. For example, floor plans for most residential construction are drawn 1/48th of actual size. At this scale, 1/4 inch on the drawing represents 1 foot 9 inches on the actual construction site. This scale is written 1/4″ = 1′-0″. When it is necessary to draw a large object, small-scale drawings are used. Smaller objects and detail drawing use a larger scale. The detail drawing in figure 2-4 is drawn to a scale of 1/2″ = 1′-0″.

An *architect's scale* is used to work with these scale drawings. The triangular scale,

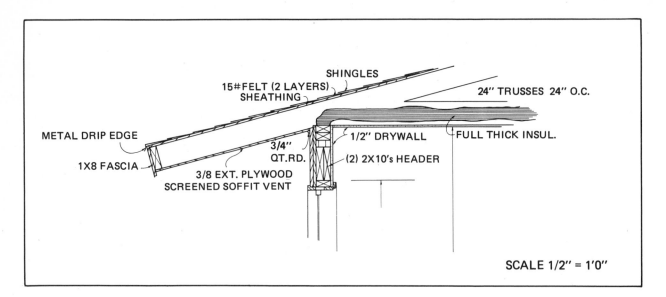

Fig. 2-4 **This detail drawing is done in a scale of 1/2″ = 1′-0″.** *(Home Planners, Inc.)*

shown in figure 2-5, combines eleven frequently used scales. The architect's scale is *open divided*. This means the scales have the main units undivided and a fully subdivided extra unit placed at the zero end of the scales. The eleven scales found on the architect's triangular scale are:

Full scale

1/8″	= 1′-0″	1/4″	= 1′-0″
3/8″	= 1′-0″	3/4″	= 1′-0″
1/2″	= 1′-0″	1″	= 1′-0″
1 1/2″	= 1′-0″	3″	= 1′-0″
3/32″	= 1′0″	3/16″	= 1′-0″

Two scales are combined on each face, except for the full-size scale which is fully divided into sixteenths. The combined scales are compatible because one is twice as large as the other and their zero points and extra-divided units are on opposite ends of the scale.

The fractional number near the zero at each end of the scale indicates the unit length in inches that is used on the drawing to represent one foot of the actual building. The extra unit near the zero end of the scale is subdivided into twelfths of a foot, or inches, as well as fractions of inches on the larger scales.

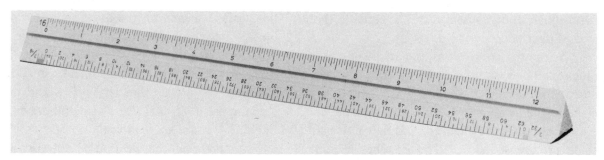

Fig. 2-5 **Triangular architect's scale** *(Keuffel & Esser Co.)*

Metrics in Construction

As the nation changes to the use of metric units of measure instead of inches and feet, it will become necessary for construction workers to change also. Most sectors of industry are undergoing this change at the present time. However, because of the standardization of material sizes and the permanence of much older construction, the construction industry relies mainly on inches and feet for units of measure. When metric materials and designs are used, metric scales are used on drawings.

Reading the Architect's Scale

Most house plans and small buildings are drawn to the 1/4-inch scale. This means that each quarter of an inch on the plans equals one foot of the actual size of the building. The scale of the drawing is noted on the plans and is usually given in the title box on each page. Sometimes, when special details are given, the scale is indicated directly under the detail.

To read the triangular architect's scale, turn it to the 1/4-inch scale. The scale is divided on the left from the zero towards the 1/4 mark so that each line represents one inch. Counting the marks from the zero toward the 1/4 mark, there are twelve lines marked on the scale. Each one of these lines is one inch on the 1/4" = 1'-0" scale.

The fraction 1/8 is on the opposite end of the same scale. This is the 1/8-inch scale and is read from the right to the left. Notice that the divided unit is only half as large as the one on the 1/4-inch end of the scale. Counting the lines from the zero toward the 1/8 mark, there are only six lines. This means that each line represents two inches at the 1/8-inch scale.

WORKING DRAWINGS

To provide all of the information necessary to construct what the architects and engineers have designed, several kinds of drawings are required. These drawings include plans, elevations, sections, and special details. There are primarily two methods used to draw three-dimensional objects: pictorial drawings and orthographic-projection drawings.

A *pictorial drawing* represents how an object looks to the eye. It is shown in only one position. A pictorial drawing may be used to show a client what the proposed structure will look like, figure 2-6.

An *orthographic-projection* drawing shows three views of an object: looking down at the

Fig. 2-6 A pictorial drawing of an office building

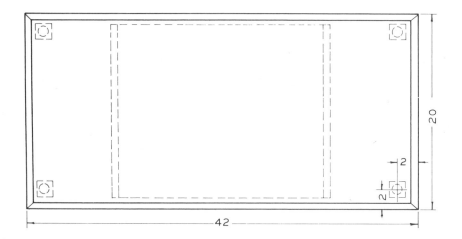

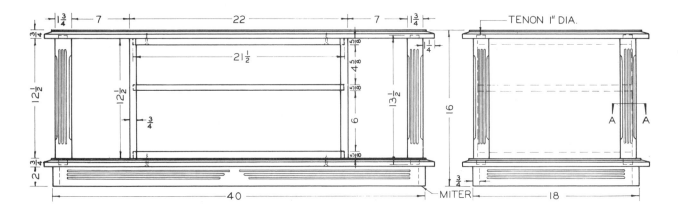

Fig. 2-7 Orthographic-projection drawing and a photograph of the same table

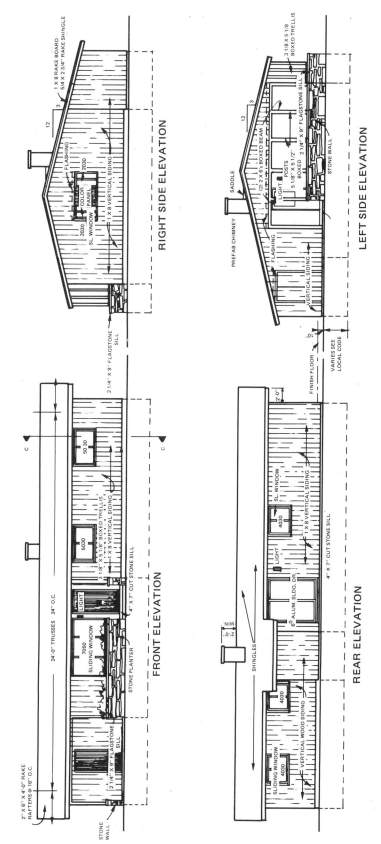

Fig. 2-8 Elevations from a set of working drawings *(Home Planners, Inc.)*

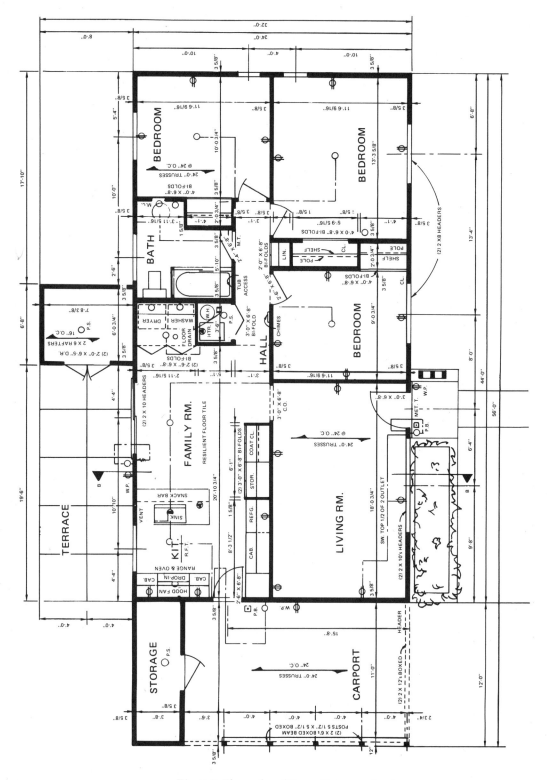

Fig. 2-9 Floor plan *(Home Planners, Inc.)*

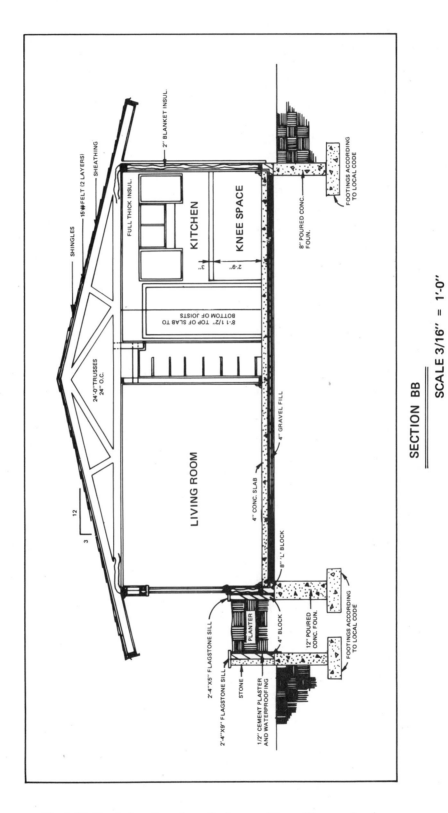

SECTION BB

SCALE 3/16" = 1'-0"

Fig. 2-10 Typical section view of a house. *(Home Planners, Inc.)*

top of the object, looking directly at the front of the object, and looking at one side of the object, figure 2-7, page 16. Orthographic projection is used for all architectural working drawings.

Elevations

Elevations are drawn as one looks at the building. Different elevations are indicated by different names. The front of a building is drawn as the front elevation, the right-hand side is drawn as the right-side elevation, the side on the left is drawn as the left-side elevation, and the back of the building is drawn as the rear elevation, figure 2-8, page 17.

Plan Views

Assume that a horizontal cut is made through the building, about three feet from the floor, and the top section is removed. Looking straight down from the top at the remaining part of the building is what is seen on the *floor plan*, figure 2-9, page 18. The cut through the building is made at the proper height so that it passes through doors, windows, and other wall openings. The floor plan shows the location of the walls, all door and window openings, and their sizes. A separate plan is drawn for the basement and each floor.

Section Views

Think of the original building as it was before the horizontal line was cut through it to make the floor plans. Now assume that a vertical cut is made through the building and one part is removed. Looking into the building, one sees a *section view*, figure 2-10, page 19.

Where sufficient detail cannot be shown on regular plans, elevations, and section views, special *detail drawings* are made. These are drawn to a larger scale and include complete information about the construction of that part of the project, figure 2-11.

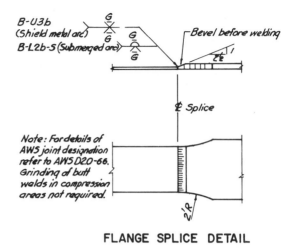

FLANGE SPLICE DETAIL

Fig. 2-11 Special detail drawing of a splice in structural members of the bridge *(U.S. Dept. of Transportation)*

STRUCTURAL DRAWINGS

Structural drawings can be plan views, elevations, or section views. These drawings show the structural parts of the project, figure 2-12. These drawings include information about the size and kind of material to be used, the location of parts, and how the parts are to be fastened.

CIVIL DRAWINGS

Most construction projects involve a certain amount of earth work. For residential construction this may be excavating (digging) for the basement and foundation. Civil constructions, such as highways, require considerably more cutting and filling to produce the desired contour. *Topographical drawings* indicate the contour and layout of the land. The elevation (rise and fall of the land) and layout is measured at various points by surveyors, figure 2-13, page 22.

When very large areas are involved, the survey may be made from aerial photographs, figure 2-14, page 22. Through the use of stereoscopic instruments, variations in elevation can be accurately measured on aerial photographs. The surveyor's notes are then converted into drawings. On topographical drawings, sometimes called contour drawings, *contour lines* show the

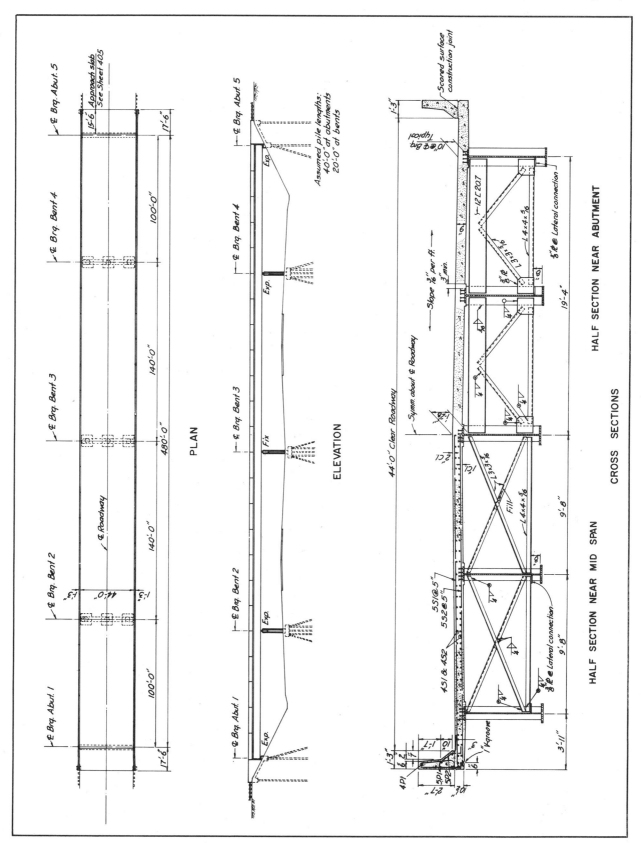

Fig. 2-12 Structural drawings show weld symbols, size and kind of material, and placement of structural parts.

Fig. 2-13 Surveyors measure the slope and area of land and determine boundaries. *(Tompkins-Cortland Community College)*

Fig. 2-14 Aerial photographs show large areas and can be used to prepare topographical drawings.

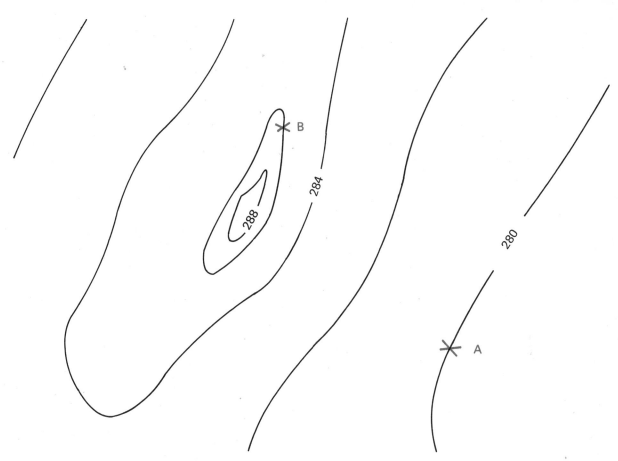

Fig. 2-15 Topographical drawing with vertical contour interval of 2 feet

elevation in feet above sea level. The difference in elevation from one contour line to the next is called the *vertical contour interval* and is usually given on the drawing. For example, if the vertical contour interval in figure 2-15 is 2 feet, the elevation at "B" is 286 feet (three contour lines or 6 feet above "A").

SYMBOLS AND ABBREVIATIONS

It is not practical to show every detail of some features of a construction project by drawing them. Architectural symbols have been developed to show many parts, kinds of construction, and materials, figure 2-16, pages 24 and 25. These symbols are placed on the drawings to provide more complete information. They are standardized, as are many other drawing practices, by the American National Standards Institute

(ANSI). This standardization is necessary so that each symbol means the same thing to everyone.

MODELS

Models are sometimes built of large construction projects. These models are built to scale and may be complete in every detail. They may be made of paper, cardboard, wood, clay, and plastic. Models effectively show the client what the architect has designed, figure 2-17, page 26. When it is necessary to test the solutions to engineering problems, engineering models can be used. Engineering models, made with the actual construction materials and design, can be used to test the wind resistance of tall structures, the operation of mechanical devices, and the strength of bridges, figure 2-18, page 26.

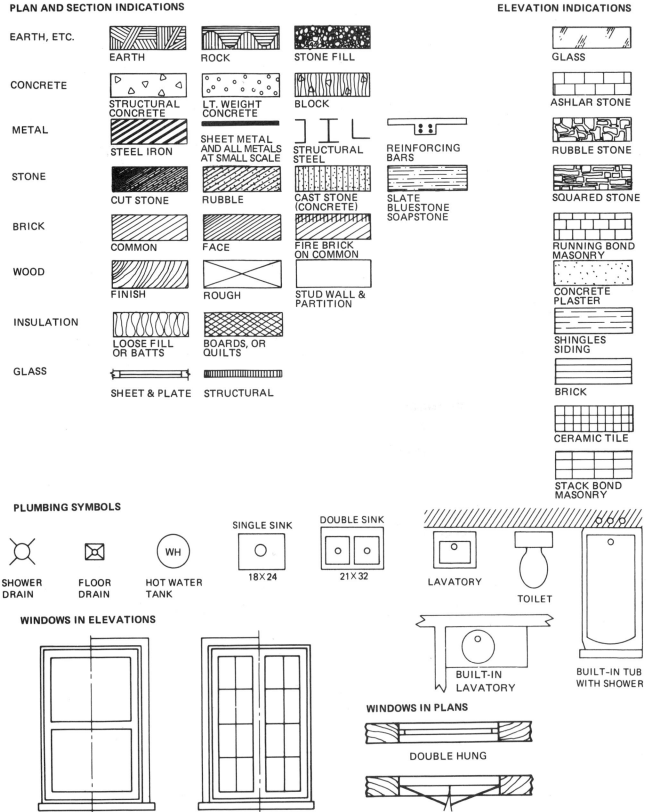

Fig. 2-16 Architectural symbols and abbreviations.

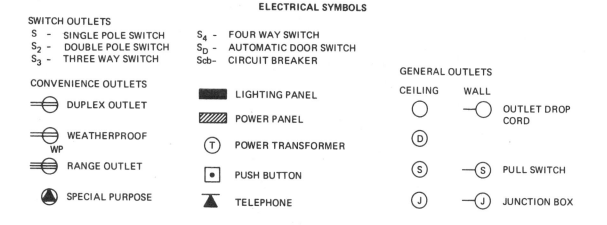

ELECTRICAL SYMBOLS

SWITCH OUTLETS

S   -   SINGLE POLE SWITCH
S_2 -   DOUBLE POLE SWITCH
S_3 -   THREE WAY SWITCH

S_4 -   FOUR WAY SWITCH
S_D -   AUTOMATIC DOOR SWITCH
Scb-   CIRCUIT BREAKER

CONVENIENCE OUTLETS

DUPLEX OUTLET

WEATHERPROOF

RANGE OUTLET

SPECIAL PURPOSE

LIGHTING PANEL

POWER PANEL

POWER TRANSFORMER

PUSH BUTTON

TELEPHONE

GENERAL OUTLETS

CEILING   WALL

OUTLET DROP CORD

PULL SWITCH

JUNCTION BOX

ABBREVIATIONS USED ON WORKING DRAWINGS

AWG	American Wire Gauge	GL	Glass
B	Bathroom	HB	Hose Bibb
BR	Bedroom	C	Hundred
BD	Board	INS	Insulation
BM	Board Measure	INT	Interior
BTU	British Thermal Unit	KD	Kiln Dried
BLDG	Building	K	Kitchen
CLG	Ceiling	LAV	Lavatory
C to C	Center to Center	LR	Living Room
CL or ₵	Centerline	MLDG	Molding
CLO	Closet	OC	On Center
COL	Column	REF	Refrigerator
CONC	Concrete	R	Riser
CFM	Cubic feet per minute	RM	Room
CU YD	Cubic Yard	SPEC	Specification
DR	Dining Room	STD	Standard
ENT	Entrance	M	Thousand
EXT	Exterior	T & G	Tongue and Groove
FIN	Finish	UNFIN	Unfinished
FL	Floor	WC	Water Closet
FTG	Footing	WH	Water Heater
FDN	Foundation	WP	Waterproof
GA	Gauge	WD	Wood

Fig. 2-16 Architectural symbols and abbreviations. (continued)

Fig. 2-17 Architectural models show a client what a structure will look like. *(Northwestern Mutual Life Insurance Co.)*

Fig. 2-18 Engineers sometimes build engineering models to test structural and mechanical design. *(Engineering Graphics)*

—— ACTIVITIES ——

A. DESIGNING A SMALL STORE

After considering the client's needs and other factors, an architect makes rough sketches and notes to describe the proposed structure. From this information, an architectural drafter makes a finished set of plans for the project.

In this activity, assume you are an architect for a client who wants a small auto parts store designed. Visualize the project, making rough sketches and notes. Use these notes as an architectural drafter would to draw a floor plan, front elevation, and side elevation.

Equipment and Materials

17″ x 22″ paper
Architect's scale
Drafting triangle
6H and 2H pencils
Eraser

Procedure

Draw a floor plan, front elevation, and side elevation. Use a scale of 1/4″ = 1′-0″. The total area of the store is between 1400 and 1800 square feet. It must include the following:

1. Front and rear entrances

2. Customer/display area

3. Counter

4. Storage (stock) area of at least 1000 square feet

5. Office

6. Furnace room of at least 60 square feet

7. Lavatory

Drafting Suggestions

1. Architects and drafters use T squares and triangles to draw straight lines and square corners. Use the plastic triangle as a straightedge and as a guide for making square corners if no T square is available.

2. It is considered bad practice to use an architect's scale as a straightedge.

3. Lay out all lines with the 6H pencil, then darken with the 2H pencil.

4. Refer to illustrations in this unit frequently for symbols and drawing style.

B.   MODEL MAKING

After designing a project, an architect or engineer sometimes constructs a model of the proposed structure. This shows the client exactly what it will look like.

Equipment and Materials

Cardboard
Tape
Glue
Knife
Poster paints
Balsa wood

Procedure

Construct an architectural model of the building described in Activity A. This should appear as much like the exterior of the building as possible.

REVIEW

Questions

Give a brief answer for each question. These questions are based on the drawings in figures 2-8 and 2-9.

1.   How far beyond the end walls of the house does the roof overhang?

2.   What is the exterior of the house covered with?

3.   How high does the chimney project above the top of the roof?

4.   What are the overall dimensions of the living room?

5.   What size is the bathroom door?

6.   How many electrical outlets are located in the carport?

7.   How many windows does the house have?

8.   How far is the center of the main entrance from the outside wall of the carport?

9.   What is the overall length and width of the house?

10.   Where is the water heater located?

UNIT 3.
SPECIFICATIONS AND CONTRACTS

OBJECTIVES

After completing this unit, the student will be able to:

- describe the purpose and organization of construction specifications.

- explain the importance of construction contracts to owners, designers, and contractors.

- define fixed-sum contracts and cost-plus contracts

SPECIFICATIONS

Working drawings contain as much information as possible about the materials to be used, the location of parts, and the size of parts for a construction project. However, it is impossible to include all of the information that is necessary. For example, it is impractical to show the grade of lumber to be used for the roof framing of a house on the drawings. *Construction specifications*, commonly called *specs*, are written documents that give detailed information not shown on the working drawings. Specs describe the quality and type of material to be used, and the method for putting the materials together.

Specification writing requires a great deal of knowledge about construction practices and construction materials. Thorough knowledge of building codes and regulations governing construction is also required. On smaller projects the specifications may be written by the architect who designed the structure. However, on larger projects and in large architectural firms, *specification writers* with a background in architectural engineering and experience in the construction industry perform this task.

The amount of detail described by the specifications can vary depending on the size of the construction project. On small jobs, and where the reputation of the contractor is known, the specifications may be brief. The Federal Housing Administration's (FHA) *Description of Materials*, figure 3-1, pages 30 thru 34, is an example of a brief form of specifications. In 1966, the construction industry adopted the Construction Specification Institute's (CSI) *Format for Construction Specification*. This format uses a

U. S. DEPARTMENT OF HOUSING AND URBAN DEVELOPMENT
FEDERAL HOUSING ADMINISTRATION

FHA Form 2005
VA Form 26-1852
Rev. 2/75

For accurate register of carbon copies, form
may be separated along above fold. Staple
completed sheets together in original order.

Form Approved
OMB No. 63–R0055

☐ Proposed Construction

DESCRIPTION OF MATERIALS

No. _____
(To be inserted by FHA or VA)

☐ Under Construction

Property address _____ City _____ State _____

Mortgagor or Sponsor _____ _____
(Name) (Address)

Contractor or Builder _____ _____
(Name) (Address)

INSTRUCTIONS

1. For additional information on how this form is to be submitted, number of copies, etc., see the instructions applicable to the FHA Application for Mortgage Insurance or VA Request for Determination of Reasonable Value, as the case may be.

2. Describe all materials and equipment to be used, whether or not shown on the drawings, by marking an X in each appropriate check-box and entering the information called for in each space. If space is inadequate, enter "See misc." and describe under item 27 or on an attached sheet. THE USE OF PAINT CONTAINING MORE THAN ONE HALF OF ONE PERCENT LEAD BY WEIGHT IS PROHIBITED.

3. Work not specifically described or shown will not be considered unless

required, then the minimum acceptable will be assumed. Work exceeding minimum requirements cannot be considered unless specifically described.

4. Include no alternates, "or equal" phrases, or contradictory items. (Consideration of a request for acceptance of substitute materials or equipment is not thereby precluded.)

5. Include signatures required at the end of this form.

6. The construction shall be completed in compliance with the related drawings and specifications, as amended during processing. The specifications include this Description of Materials and the applicable Minimum Property Standards.

1. EXCAVATION:

Bearing soil, type _____

2. FOUNDATIONS:

Footings: concrete mix _____; strength psi _____ Reinforcing _____

Foundation wall: material _____ Reinforcing _____

Interior foundation wall: material _____ Party foundation wall _____

Columns: material and sizes _____ Piers: material and reinforcing _____

Girders: material and sizes _____ Sills: material _____

Basement entrance areaway _____ Window areaways _____

Waterproofing _____ Footing drains _____

Termite protection _____

Basementless space: ground cover _____; insulation _____; foundation vents _____

Special foundations _____

Additional information: _____

3. CHIMNEYS:

Material _____ Prefabricated (make and size) _____

Flue lining: material _____ Heater flue size _____ Fireplace flue size _____

Vents (material and size): gas or oil heater _____; water heater _____

Additional information: _____

4. FIREPLACES:

Type: ☐ solid fuel; ☐ gas-burning; ☐ circulator (make and size) _____ Ash dump and clean-out _____

Fireplace: facing _____; lining _____; hearth _____; mantel _____

Additional information: _____

5. EXTERIOR WALLS:

Wood frame: wood grade, and species _____ ☐ Corner bracing. Building paper or felt _____

Sheathing _____; thickness _____; width _____; ☐ solid; ☐ spaced _____" o. c.; ☐ diagonal; _____

Siding _____; grade _____; type _____; size _____; exposure _____"; fastening _____

Shingles _____; grade _____; type _____; size _____; exposure _____"; fastening _____

Stucco _____; thickness _____"; Lath _____; weight _____ lb.

Masonry veneer _____ Sills _____ Lintels _____ Base flashing _____

Masonry: ☐ solid ☐ faced ☐ stuccoed; total wall thickness _____"; facing thickness _____"; facing material _____

Backup material _____; thickness _____"; bonding _____

Door sills _____ Window sills _____ Lintels _____ Base flashing _____

Interior surfaces: dampproofing, _____ coats of _____; furring _____

Additional information: _____

Exterior painting: material _____; number of coats _____

Gable wall construction: ☐ same as main walls; ☐ other construction _____

Fig. 3-1 Brief specification form

6. FLOOR FRAMING:

Joists: wood, grade, and species _____ ; other _____ ; bridging _____ ; anchors _____

Concrete slab: ☐ basement floor; ☐ first floor; ☐ ground supported; ☐ self-supporting; mix _____ ; thickness _____ ";

reinforcing _____ ; insulation _____ ; membrane _____

Fill under slab: material _____ ; thickness _____ ". Additional information: _____

7. SUBFLOORING: *(Describe underflooring for special floors under item 21.)*

Material: grade and species _____ ; size _____ ; type _____

Laid: ☐ first floor; ☐ second floor; ☐ attic _____ sq. ft.; ☐ diagonal; ☐ right angles. Additional information: _____

8. FINISH FLOORING: *(Wood only. Describe other finish flooring under item 21.)*

LOCATION	ROOMS	GRADE	SPECIES	THICKNESS	WIDTH	BLDG. PAPER	FINISH
First floor ___							
Second floor ___							
Attic floor ___	___ sq. ft.						

Additional information: _____

9. PARTITION FRAMING:

Studs: wood, grade, and species _____ size and spacing _____ Other _____

Additional information: _____

10. CEILING FRAMING:

Joists: wood, grade, and species _____ Other _____ Bridging _____

Additional information: _____

11. ROOF FRAMING:

Rafters: wood, grade, and species _____ Roof trusses (see detail): grade and species _____

Additional information: _____

12. ROOFING:

Sheathing: wood, grade, and species _____ ; ☐ solid; ☐ spaced _____ " o.c.

Roofing _____ ; grade _____ ; size _____ ; type _____

Underlay _____ ; weight or thickness _____ ; size _____ ; fastening _____

Built-up roofing _____ ; number of plies _____ ; surfacing material _____

Flashing: material _____ ; gage or weight _____ ; ☐ gravel stops; ☐ snow guards

Additional information: _____

13. GUTTERS AND DOWNSPOUTS:

Gutters: material _____ ; gage or weight _____ ; size _____ ; shape _____

Downspouts: material _____ ; gage or weight _____ ; size _____ ; shape _____ ; number _____

Downspouts connected to: ☐ Storm sewer; ☐ sanitary sewer; ☐ dry-well. ☐ Splash blocks: material and size _____

Additional information: _____

14. LATH AND PLASTER:

Lath ☐ walls, ☐ ceilings: material _____ ; weight or thickness _____ Plaster: coats ___ ; finish _____

Dry-wall ☐ walls, ☐ ceilings: material _____ ; thickness _____ ; finish _____ ;

Joint treatment _____

15. DECORATING: *(Paint, wallpaper, etc.)*

ROOMS	WALL FINISH MATERIAL AND APPLICATION	CEILING FINISH MATERIAL AND APPLICATION
Kitchen ___		
Bath ___		
Other ___		

Additional information: _____

16. INTERIOR DOORS AND TRIM:

Doors: type _____ ; material _____ ; thickness _____

Door trim: type _____ ; material _____ Base: type _____ ; material _____ ; size _____

Finish: doors _____ ; trim _____

Other trim *(item, type and location)* _____

Additional information: _____

17. WINDOWS:

Windows: type _____ ; make _____ ; material _____ ; sash thickness _____

Glass: grade _____ ; ☐ sash weights; ☐ balances, type _____ ; head flashing _____

Trim: type _____ ; material _____ Paint _____ ; number coats _____

Weatherstripping: type _____ ; material _____ Storm sash, number _____

Fig. 3-1 Brief specification form. (continued)

Screens: ☐ full; ☐ half; type _____ ; number _____ ; screen cloth material _____

Basement windows: type _____ ; material _____ ; screens, number _____ ; Storm sash, number _____

Special windows _____

Additional information: _____

18. ENTRANCES AND EXTERIOR DETAIL:

Main entrance door: material _____ ; width _____ ; thickness _____". Frame: material _____ , thickness _____"

Other entrance doors: material _____ ; width _____ ; thickness _____". Frame: material _____ , thickness _____"

Head flashing _____ Weatherstripping: type _____ ; saddles _____

Screen doors: thickness _____"; number _____ ; screen cloth material _____ Storm doors: thickness _____"; number _____

Combination storm and screen doors: thickness _____"; number _____ ; screen cloth material _____

Shutters: ☐ hinged; ☐ fixed. Railings _____ , Attic louvers _____

Exterior millwork: grade and species _____ Paint _____ ; number coats _____

Additional information: _____

19. CABINETS AND INTERIOR DETAIL:

Kitchen cabinets, wall units: material _____ ; lineal feet of shelves _____ ; shelf width _____

Base units: material _____ ; counter top _____ ; edging _____

Back and end splash _____ Finish of cabinets _____ ; number coats _____

Medicine cabinets: make _____ ; model _____

Other cabinets and built-in furniture _____

Additional information: _____

20. STAIRS:

STAIR	TREADS		RISERS		STRINGS		HANDRAIL		BALUSTERS	
	Material	Thickness	Material	Thickness	Material	Size	Material	Size	Material	Size
Basement ____										
Main ____										
Attic ____										

Disappearing: make and model number _____

Additional information: _____

21. SPECIAL FLOORS AND WAINSCOT:

	LOCATION	MATERIAL, COLOR, BORDER, SIZES, GAGE, ETC.	THRESHOLD MATERIAL	WALL BASE MATERIAL	UNDERFLOOR MATERIAL
FLOORS	Kitchen ____				
	Bath ____				

	LOCATION	MATERIAL, COLOR, BORDER, CAP. SIZES, GAGE, ETC.	HEIGHT	HEIGHT OVER TUB	HEIGHT IN SHOWERS (FROM FLOOR)
WAINSCOT	Bath ____				

Bathroom accessories: ☐ Recessed; material _____ ; number _____ ; ☐ Attached; material _____ ; number _____

Additional information: _____

22. PLUMBING:

FIXTURE	NUMBER	LOCATION	MAKE	MFR'S FIXTURE IDENTIFICATION NO.	SIZE	COLOR
Sink ____						
Lavatory ____						
Water closet ____						
Bathtub ____						
Shower over tub△ ____						
Stall shower△ ____						
Laundry trays ____						
____						
____						
____						

△☐ Curtain rod   △☐ Door   ☐ Shower pan: material _____

Water supply: ☐ public; ☐ community system; ☐ individual (private) system. ★

Fig. 3-1 Brief specification form. (continued)

Sewage disposal: ☐ public; ☐ community system; ☐ individual (private) system. ★

★ *Show and describe individual system in complete detail in separate drawings and specifications according to requirements.*

House drain (inside): ☐ cast iron; ☐ tile; ☐ other _____ House sewer (outside): ☐ cast iron; ☐ tile; ☐ other _____

Water piping: ☐ galvanized steel; ☐ copper tubing; ☐ other _____ Sill cocks, number _____

Domestic water heater: type _____; make and model _____; heating capacity _____

_____ gph. 100° rise. Storage tank: material _____; capacity _____ gallons.

Gas service: ☐ utility company; ☐ liq. pet. gas; ☐ other _____ Gas piping: ☐ cooking; ☐ house heating.

Footing drains connected to: ☐ storm sewer; ☐ sanitary sewer; ☐ dry well. Sump pump; make and model _____

_____; capacity _____; discharges into _____

23. HEATING:

☐ Hot water. ☐ Steam. ☐ Vapor. ☐ One-pipe system. ☐ Two-pipe system.

☐ Radiators. ☐ Convectors. ☐ Baseboard radiation. Make and model _____

Radiant panel: ☐ floor; ☐ wall; ☐ ceiling. Panel coil: material _____

☐ Circulator. ☐ Return pump. Make and model _____; capacity _____ gpm.

Boiler: make and model _____ Output _____ Btuh.; net rating _____ Btuh.

Additional information: _____

Warm air: ☐ Gravity. ☐ Forced. Type of system _____

Duct material: supply _____; return _____ Insulation _____, thickness _____ ☐ Outside air intake.

Furnace: make and model _____ Input _____ Btuh.; output _____ Btuh.

Additional information: _____

☐ Space heater; ☐ floor furnace; ☐ wall heater. Input _____ Btuh.; output _____ Btuh.; number units _____

Make, model _____ Additional information: _____

Controls: make and types _____

Additional information: _____

Fuel: ☐ Coal; ☐ oil; ☐ gas; ☐ liq. pet. gas; ☐ electric; ☐ other _____; storage capacity _____

Additional information: _____

Firing equipment furnished separately: ☐ Gas burner, conversion type. ☐ Stoker: hopper feed ☐; bin feed ☐

Oil burner: ☐ pressure atomizing; ☐ vaporizing _____

Make and model _____ Control _____

Additional information: _____

Electric heating system: type _____ Input _____ watts; @ _____ volts; output _____ Btuh.

Additional information: _____

Ventilating equipment: attic fan, make and model _____; capacity _____ cfm.

kitchen exhaust fan, make and model _____

Other heating, ventilating. or cooling equipment _____

24. ELECTRIC WIRING:

Service: ☐ overhead; ☐ underground. Panel: ☐ fuse box; ☐ circuit-breaker; make _____ AMP's _____ No. circuits _____

Wiring: ☐ conduit; ☐ armored cable; ☐ nonmetallic cable; ☐ knob and tube; ☐ other _____

Special outlets: ☐ range; ☐ water heater; ☐ other _____

☐ Doorbell. ☐ Chimes. Push-button locations _____ Additional information: _____

25. LIGHTING FIXTURES:

Total number of fixtures _____ Total allowance for fixtures, typical installation, $ _____

Nontypical installation _____

Additional information: _____

26. INSULATION:

Location	Thickness	Material, Type, and Method of Installation	Vapor Barrier
Roof			
Ceiling			
Wall			
Floor			

27. MISCELLANEOUS: (Describe any main dwelling materials, equipment, or construction items not shown elsewhere; or use to provide additional information where the space provided was inadequate. Always reference by item number to correspond to numbering used on this form.) _____

_____

_____

_____

_____

_____

Fig. 3-1 Brief specification form. (continued)

_____
_____
_____
_____
_____
_____

HARDWARE: *(make, material, and finish.)* _____
_____
_____

SPECIAL EQUIPMENT: *(State material or make, model and quantity.   Include only equipment and appliances which are acceptable by local law, custom and applicable FHA standards.   Do not include items which, by established custom, are supplied by occupant and removed when he vacates premises or chattles prohibited by law from becoming realty.)*_____
_____
_____
_____
_____
_____
_____
_____
_____
_____

PORCHES:
_____
_____
_____

TERRACES:
_____
_____
_____

GARAGES:
_____
_____
_____

WALKS AND DRIVEWAYS:
Driveway: width _____ ; base material _____ ; thickness _____ "; surfacing material _____ ; thickness _____ "
Front walk: width _____ ; material _____ ; thickness _____ ". Service walk: width _____ ; material _____ ; thickness _____ "
Steps: material _____ ; treads _____ "; risers _____ ". Cheek walls _____

OTHER ONSITE IMPROVEMENTS:
(Specify all exterior onsite improvements not described elsewhere, including items such as unusual grading, drainage structures, retaining walls, fence, railings, and accessory structures.)
_____
_____
_____

LANDSCAPING, PLANTING, AND FINISH GRADING:
Topsoil _____ " thick: ☐ front yard; ☐ side yards; ☐ rear yard to _____ feet behind main building.
Lawns *(seeded, sodded, or sprigged)*: ☐ front yard _____ ; ☐ side yards _____ ; ☐ rear yard_____
Planting: ☐ as specified and shown on drawings; ☐ as follows:

_____ Shade trees, deciduous, _____ " caliper.	_____ Evergreen trees. _____ ' to _____ ', B & B.
_____ Low flowering trees, deciduous, _____ ' to _____ '	_____ Evergreen shrubs. _____ ' to _____ ', B & B.
_____ High-growing shrubs, deciduous, _____ ' to _____ '	_____ Vines, 2-year _____
_____ Medium-growing shrubs, deciduous, _____ ' to _____ '	_____
_____ Low-growing shrubs, deciduous, _____ ' to _____ '	_____

IDENTIFICATION.—This exhibit shall be identified by the signature of the builder, or sponsor, and/or the proposed mortgagor if the latter is known at the time of application.

Date_____   Signature _____

Signature _____

FHA Form 2005
VA Form 26-1852

Fig. 3-1 Brief specification form (continued)

DIVISION 1—GENERAL REQUIREMENTS

01010 SUMMARY OF WORK
01100 ALTERNATIVES
01150 MEASUREMENT & PAYMENT
01200 PROJECT MEETINGS
01300 SUBMITTALS
01400 QUALITY CONTROL
01500 TEMPORARY FACILITIES &
      CONTROLS
01600 MATERIAL & EQUIPMENT
01700 PROJECT CLOSEOUT

DIVISION 2—SITE WORK

02010 SUBSURFACE EXPLORATION
02100 CLEARING
02110 DEMOLITION
02200 EARTHWORK
02250 SOIL TREATMENT
02300 PILE FOUNDATIONS
02350 CAISSONS
02400 SHORING
02500 SITE DRAINAGE
02550 SITE UTILITIES
02600 PAVING & SURFACING
02700 SITE IMPROVEMENTS
02800 LANDSCAPING
02850 RAILROAD WORK
02900 MARINE WORK
02950 TUNNELING

DIVISION 3—CONCRETE

03100 CONCRETE FORMWORK
03150 FORMS
03200 CONCRETE REINFORCEMENT
03250 CONCRETE ACCESSORIES
03300 CAST-IN-PLACE CONCRETE
03350 SPECIALLY FINISHED
      (ARCHITECTURAL) CONCRETE
03360 SPECIALLY PLACED CONCRETE
03400 PRECAST CONCRETE
03500 CEMENTITIOUS DECKS
03600 GROUT

DIVISION 4—MASONRY

04100 MORTAR
04150 MASONRY ACCESSORIES
04200 UNIT MASONRY
04400 STONE
04500 MASONRY RESTORATION &
      CLEANING
04550 REFRACTORIES

DIVISION 5—METALS

05100 STRUCTURAL METAL FRAMING
05200 METAL JOISTS
05300 METAL DECKING
05400 LIGHTGAGE METAL FRAMING
05500 METAL FABRICATIONS
05700 ORNAMENTAL METAL
05800 EXPANSION CONTROL

DIVISION 6—WOOD & PLASTICS

06100 ROUGH CARPENTRY
06130 HEAVY TIMBER CONSTRUCTION
06150 TRESTLES
06170 PREFABRICATED STRUCTURAL
      WOOD
06200 FINISH CARPENTRY
06300 WOOD TREATMENT
06400 ARCHITECTURAL WOODWORK
06500 PREFABRICATED STRUCTURAL
      PLASTICS
06600 PLASTIC FABRICATIONS

DIVISION 7—THERMAL & MOISTURE PROTECTION

07100 WATERPROOFING

07150 DAMPPROOFING
07200 INSULATION
07300 SHINGLES & ROOFING TILES
07400 PREFORMED ROOFING & SIDING
07500 MEMBRANE ROOFING
07570 TRAFFIC TOPPING
07600 FLASHING & SHEET METAL
07800 ROOF ACCESSORIES
07900 SEALANTS

DIVISION 8—DOORS & WINDOWS

08100 METAL DOORS & FRAMES
08200 WOOD & PLASTIC DOORS
08300 SPECIAL DOORS
08400 ENTRANCES & STOREFRONTS
08500 METAL WINDOWS
08600 WOOD & PLASTIC WINDOWS
08650 SPECIAL WINDOWS
08700 HARDWARE & SPECIALTIES
08800 GLAZING
08900 WINDOW WALLS/CURTAIN WALLS

DIVISION 9—FINISHES

09100 LATH & PLASTER
09250 GYPSUM WALLBOARD
09300 TILE
09400 TERRAZZO
09500 ACOUSTICAL TREATMENT
09540 CEILING SUSPENSION SYSTEMS
09550 WOOD FLOORING
09650 RESILIENT FLOORING
09680 CARPETING
09700 SPECIAL FLOORING
09760 FLOOR TREATMENT
09800 SPECIAL COATINGS
09900 PAINTING
09950 WALL COVERING

DIVISION 10—SPECIALTIES

10100 CHALKBOARDS & TACKBOARDS
10150 COMPARTMENTS & CUBICLES
10200 LOUVERS & VENTS
10240 GRILLES & SCREENS
10260 WALL & CORNER GUARDS
10270 ACCESS FLOORING
10280 SPECIALTY MODULES
10290 PEST CONTROL
10300 FIREPLACES
10350 FLAGPOLES
10400 IDENTIFYING DEVICES
10450 PEDESTRIAN CONTROL DEVICES
10500 LOCKERS
10530 PROTECTIVE COVERS
10550 POSTAL SPECIALTIES
10600 PARTITIONS
10650 SCALES
10670 PROTECTIVE SHELVING
10700 SUNCONTROLDEVICES(EXTERIOR)
10750 TELEPHONE ENCLOSURES
10800 TOILET & BATH ACCESSORIES
10900 WARDROBE SPECIALTIES

DIVISION 11—EQUIPMENT

11050 BUILT-IN MAINTENANCE
      EQUIPMENT
11100 BANK & VAULT EQUIPMENT
11150 COMMERCIAL EQUIPMENT
11170 CHECKROOM EQUIPMENT
11180 DARKROOM EQUIPMENT
11200 ECCLESIASTICAL EQUIPMENT
11300 EDUCATIONAL EQUIPMENT
11400 FOOD SERVICE EQUIPMENT
11480 VENDING EQUIPMENT
11500 ATHLETIC EQUIPMENT
11550 INDUSTRIAL EQUIPMENT
11600 LABORATORY EQUIPMENT
11630 LAUNDRY EQUIPMENT
11650 LIBRARY EQUIPMENT

11700 MEDICAL EQUIPMENT
11800 MORTUARY EQUIPMENT
11830 MUSICAL EQUIPMENT
11850 PARKING EQUIPMENT
11860 WASTE HANDLING EQUIPMENT
11870 LOADING DOCK EQUIPMENT
11880 DETENTION EQUIPMENT
11900 RESIDENTIAL EQUIPMENT
11970 THEATER & STAGE EQUIPMENT
11990 REGISTRATION EQUIPMENT

DIVISION 12—FURNISHINGS

12100 ARTWORK
12300 CABINETS & STORAGE
12500 WINDOW TREATMENT
12550 FABRICS
12600 FURNITURE
12670 RUGS & MATS
12700 SEATING
12800 FURNISHING ACCESSORIES

DIVISION 13—SPECIAL CONSTRUCTION

13010 AIR SUPPORTED STRUCTURES
13050 INTEGRATED ASSEMBLIES
13100 AUDIOMETRIC ROOM
13250 CLEAN ROOM
13350 HYPERBARIC ROOM
13400 INCINERATORS
13440 INSTRUMENTATION
13450 INSULATED ROOM
13500 INTEGRATED CEILING
13540 NUCLEAR REACTORS
13550 OBSERVATORY
13600 PREFABRICATED STRUCTURES
13700 SPECIAL PURPOSE ROOMS &
      BUILDINGS
13750 RADIATION PROTECTION
13770 SOUND & VIBRATION CONTROL
13800 VAULTS
13850 SWIMMING POOLS

DIVISION 14—CONVEYING SYSTEMS

14100 DUMBWAITERS
14200 ELEVATORS
14300 HOISTS & CRANES
14400 LIFTS
14500 MATERIAL HANDLING SYSTEMS
14570 TURNTABLES
14600 MOVING STAIRS & WALKS
14700 TUBE SYSTEMS
14800 POWERED SCAFFOLDING

DIVISION 15—MECHANICAL

15010 GENERAL PROVISIONS
15050 BASIC MATERIALS & METHODS
15180 INSULATION
15200 WATER SUPPLY & TREATMENT
15300 WASTE WATER DISPOSAL &
      TREATMENT
15400 PLUMBING
15500 FIRE PROTECTION
15600 POWER OR HEAT GENERATION
15650 REFRIGERATION
15700 LIQUID HEAT TRANSFER
15800 AIR DISTRIBUTION
15900 CONTROLS & INSTRUMENTATION

DIVISION 16—ELECTRICAL

16010 GENERAL PROVISIONS
16100 BASIC MATERIALS & METHODS
16200 POWER GENERATION
16300 POWER TRANSMISSION
16400 SERVICE & DISTRIBUTION
16500 LIGHTING
16600 SPECIAL SYSTEMS
16700 COMMUNICATIONS
16850 HEATING & COOLING
16900 CONTROLS & INSTRUMENTATION

Fig. 3-2 CSI format for specifications

DIVISION 6 – WOOD AND PLASTICS

Section 06200 – FINISH CARPENTRY

General: This section covers all finish woodwork and related items not covered elsewhere in these specifications. The contractor shall furnish all materials, labor, and equipment necessary to complete the work, including rough hardware, finish hardware, and specialty items.

Protection of Materials: All millwork (finish woodwork*) and trim is to be delivered in a clean and dry condition and shall be stored to insure proper ventilation and protection from dampness. Do not install finish woodwork until concrete, masonry, plaster, and related work is dry.

Materials: All materials are to be the best of their respective kind. Lumber shall bear the mark and grade of the association under whose rules it is produced. All millwork shall be kiln dried to a maximum moisture content of 12%.

   1. Exterior trim shall be select grade white pine, S4S.
   2. Interior trim and millwork shall be select grade white pine, thoroughly sanded at the time of installation.

Installation: All millwork and trim shall be installed with tight fitting joints and formed to conceal future shrinkage due to drying. Interior woodwork shall be mitered or coped at corners (cut in a special way to form neat joints*). All nails are to be set below the surface of the wood and concealed with an approved putty or filler.

*(explanations in parentheses have been added to aid the student.)

Fig. 3-3 Specifications following CSI format.

division-section organization. All specifications are divided into sixteen divisions, figure 3-2, page 35.

Divisions 2 through 16 deal with the actual construction of the project and are arranged as nearly as possible in the order of work. This makes it easy for estimators and other construction personnel to follow the specifications in the order that the work is to be done. "Division 1 – General Requirements" is an overall division describing such things as contracts; relationships between the owner, architect, and contractor; scheduling of work; temporary utilities; and project closeout.

Within these divisions, individual units of work are treated as *sections*. For example, one section of "Division 8 – Doors and Windows" is Metal Windows. This section contains all of the detailed specifications for the metal windows to be installed in the project. Figure 3-3 is an

example of one section of specifications following this format.

Each section is identified by a 5-digit number that allows modern data processing techniques to be used for recordkeeping. When sections are not required for a particular set of specifications, they are omitted. The next required section is then used without changing its number.

BIDDING

Once the owner and architect have finalized plans, working drawings, and specifications for a project, they must select a contractor to construct it. A *contractor* coordinates the building of a project according to a written agreement for a specified sum of money. On small jobs, selecting a contractor may simply mean discussing the job with a contractor known to either the owner or architect. On large construction projects, contractors normally bid on the job.

A *bid* estimates the cost and the time it will take to complete a construction project according to the required specifications. The bidding process requires a substantial investment of time and money itself. The planned project is listed in newspapers or construction periodicals, figure 3-4. Contractors normally subscribe to these publications so they are aware of what projects are available for bid.

A contractor who intends to bid on a project receives working drawings and specifications from the architect or owner. It is important for the contractor to consider the size of the project. Large firms that specialize in heavy construction do not normally bid on small, single buildings. Likewise, a small construction company would not bid on a project that is too large.

The next step is for the contractor's *estimator* to determine how much labor and material it will take to complete the project. The money paid for this labor and material is called *direct cost*. The estimator must be able to read drawings and specifications and understand construction practices in order to list the materials required for each phase of construction, figure 3-5, page 38. By knowing how long it takes to install each material under all conditions, the estimator can predict the time required for each part of the project.

In preparing the estimate, a percentage of the direct cost is added for operating expenses that are not linked directly to that project. These costs, called *overhead*, include office costs, insurance, and maintenance of equipment. In addition to direct costs and overhead, a percentage is also added for profit, figure 3-6, page 39.

Sometimes, in order to make rough estimates in a minimum of time, square-foot and cubic-foot estimates are used. For a *square-foot estimate*, the square-foot area of all floor space is multiplied by an average price for that type of construction. The following example might be

---

Bids: April 1, 1977

Michoud Assembly Facility
Martin Marietta Corporation
Vertical Assembly Building—Cell"D"—
T.P.S. Application Facility

Scope of Work:

Provide labor and material to construct a steel and gypsum board silo approximately 40 feet in diameter and approximately 120 feet tall. The work includes: piling, foundations, structural steel, interior and exterior platforms, access doors, and roof cover, industrial air conditioning, exhaust, piping, fire protection and detection, power and lighting and interface with existing utilities.

Estimated Value: $1,000,000 to $2,000,000

Plans and specifications regarding this project will be available on March 1, 1977. No plans and specifications will be distributed after March 15, 1977.

The Site Inspection for prospective bidders will be held on March 16, 1977 at 2:00 P.M. local time. Contact L.D. Tretbar for arrangements at 255-4502.

Sealed bids will be received at the location indicated below until 2:00 P.M. C.S.T. on April 1, 1977.

Mr. L.D. Tretbar
Martin Marietta Corporation
Michoud Operations
Post Office Box 29304
New Orleans, Louisiana 70189

Fig. 3-4 An invitation to bid on a project. *(Martin Marietta Corp.)*

---

used to do a square-foot estimate of a store with one floor measuring 75 feet by 140 feet.

1. Find the area of the floor: 75 ft. x 140 ft = 10,500 sq. ft.

2. Multiply the area by the cost per square foot for this type of construction: 10,500 sq. ft. x $24.00 = $252,000.00

Cubic-foot estimates are found the same way, except the area of the floor is multiplied by the height of the ceiling. This gives the total volume of the building. The volume is then multiplied by the average cost per cubic foot for that type of construction. Square-foot and cubic-foot estimates are not accurate enough to be used for finding a bidding price.

When the contractor has determined what the price will be for the project, it is submitted

estimating data sheet

JOB TITLE 1460 East Ave.   NAME A. Hahn

Grade

INTERIOR TRIM								
	Bedroom #2 — All Select Pine Trim							
2	Window Stools	3/4 x 2½ x 3'-4"						
	Total Stools	6'-8"	Lin. Ft.					
2	Window Aprons	3/4 x 2¾ x 3'-4"						
	Total Aprons	6'-8"	Lin. Ft.					
2	Casings	11/16 x 2¼ x 3'-4"						
4	Casings	11/16 x 2¼ x 4'-0"						
	Total Window Csg.	22'-8"	Lin. Ft.					
1	Door Jamb	4 5/8 x 2'-6" x 6'-8"						
1	Door Jamb	4 5/8 x 6'-0" x 6'-8"						
2	Casings	11/16 x 2¼ x 2'-6"						
2	Casings	11/16 x 2¼ x 6'-6"						
8	Casings	11/16 x 2¼ x 7'-0"						
	Total Door Csg.	74'-0"	Lin. Ft.					
	Baseboard	11/16 x 3¼ x 58'-0"						
	Closet Rod - chrome	8'-0"						
	Closet Shelf #2 Com. Pine 3/4 x 12 x 8'-0"							

Fig. 3-5 Estimator's worksheet

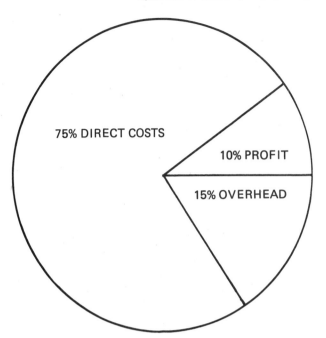

Fig. 3-6 On one construction project: 75% of the cost was for direct expenses to the contractor; 15% was for overhead, such as office expenses and equipment maintenance; and 10% was for profit.

to the architect or owner as a bid. All bids remain sealed until a predetermined date. On that day, all bids are opened and the contractor submitting the lowest bid for completing the project, according to the plans and specifications, is awarded the job.

CONTRACTS

When the job is awarded, a legal agreement is signed that states the contractor will perform the work and the owner will pay for the work. This agreement is a *contract*. A verbal agreement between two people is a legal contract, but construction contracts are almost always in the form of written documents signed by all parties involved, figure 3-7, pages 40 thru 47. These contracts include provisions for:

- *Completion schedule.* It is customary to specify the date by which the project is to be completed. On some large projects, dates for completion of the various stages of construction are specified.

- *Schedule of payments.* Sometimes the contractor receives a percentage of the contract price after the completion of each stage of construction. A typical schedule of payments for a house is 20

percent when the foundation is complete; 30 percent when the structure is enclosed; 30 percent when the rough wiring, rough plumbing, and rough heating and air conditioning is installed; and the remaining 20 percent when the house is completed. Another method is for the contractor to receive partial payment for the work done each month.

- *Responsibilities of all parties involved.* The owner is usually responsible for having the property surveyed. The architect may be responsible for administering the contract. The contractor is responsible for the construction and security of the site during the construction period.

- *Insurance.* Certain kinds of insurance are required during the construction. The contractor is required to have liability insurance. This protects the contractor against being sued for accidents occurring on the site. The owner is required to have property insurance.

- *Workmen's compensation.* This is another form of insurance that provides income for the contractor's employees if they are injured at work.

THE AMERICAN INSTITUTE OF ARCHITECTS

AIA Document A107

Standard Form of Agreement Between
Owner and Contractor

Short Form Agreement for **Small Construction Contracts**

Where the Basis of Payment is a

STIPULATED SUM

*THIS DOCUMENT HAS IMPORTANT LEGAL CONSEQUENCES; CONSULTATION WITH
AN ATTORNEY IS ENCOURAGED WITH RESPECT TO ITS COMPLETION OR MODIFICATION*

*For other contracts the AIA issues Standard Forms of Owner-Contractor Agreements and Standard General Conditions
of the Contract for Construction for use in connection therewith.*

This document has been approved and endorsed by The Associated General Contractors of America.

AGREEMENT

made this   day of   in the year Nineteen
Hundred and

BETWEEN the Owner:

and the Contractor:

the Project:

the Architect:

The Owner and Contractor agree as set forth below.

AIA DOCUMENT A107 • SMALL CONSTRUCTION CONTRACT • JANUARY 1974 EDITION • AIA® • ©1974
THE AMERICAN INSTITUTE OF ARCHITECTS, 1735 NEW YORK AVE., N.W., WASHINGTON, D. C. 20006

Fig. 3-7 Construction contract   *(This document has been reproduced with the permission of the American Institute
of Architects. Further reproduction is not authorized.)*

ARTICLE 1
THE WORK

The Contractor shall perform all the Work required by the Contract Documents for
(Here insert the caption descriptive of the Work as used on other Contract Documents.)

ARTICLE 2
TIME OF COMMENCEMENT AND COMPLETION

The Work to be performed under this Contract shall be commenced

and completed

ARTICLE 3
CONTRACT SUM

The Owner shall pay the Contractor for the performance of the Work, subject to additions and deductions by Change Order as provided in the General Conditions, in current funds, the Contract Sum of
(State here the lump sum amount, unit prices, or both, as desired.)

Fig. 3-7 Construction contract (continued) *(This document has been reproduced with the permission of the American Institute of Architects. Further reproduction is not authorized.)*

ARTICLE 4
PROGRESS PAYMENTS

Based upon Applications for Payment submitted to the Architect by the Contractor and Certificates for Payment issued by the Architect, the Owner shall make progress payments on account of the Contract Sum to the Contractor as follows:

ARTICLE 5
FINAL PAYMENT

The Owner shall make final payment   days after completion of the Work, provided the Contract be then fully performed, subject to the provisions of Article 16 of the General Conditions.

ARTICLE 6
ENUMERATION OF CONTRACT DOCUMENTS

The Contract Documents are as noted in Paragraph 7.1 of the General Conditions and are enumerated as follows:
(List below the Agreement, Conditions of the Contract (General, Supplementary, and other Conditions), Drawings, Specifications, Addenda and accepted Alternates, showing page or sheet numbers in all cases and dates where applicable.)

Fig. 3-7 Construction contract (continued) *(This document has been reproduced with the permission of the American Institute of Architects. Further reproduction is not authorized.)*

GENERAL CONDITIONS

ARTICLE 7
CONTRACT DOCUMENTS

7.1 The Contract Documents consist of this Agreement (which includes the General Conditions), Supplementary and other Conditions, the Drawings, the Specifications, all Addenda issued prior to the execution of this Agreement, all modifications, Change Orders, and written interpretations of the Contract Documents issued by the Architect. These form the Contract and what is required by any one shall be as binding as if required by all. The intention of the Contract Documents is to include all labor, materials, equipment and other items as provided in Paragraph 10.2 necessary for the proper execution and completion of the Work and the terms and conditions of payment therefor, and also to include all Work which may be reasonably inferable from the Contract Documents as being necessary to produce the intended results.

7.2 The Contract Documents shall be signed in not less than triplicate by the Owner and the Contractor. If either the Owner or the Contractor do not sign the Drawings, Specifications, or any of the other Contract Documents, the Architect shall identify them. By executing the Contract, the Contractor represents that he has visited the site and familiarized himself with the local conditions under which the Work is to be performed.

7.3 The term Work as used in the Contract Documents includes all labor necessary to produce the construction required by the Contract Documents, and all materials and equipment incorporated or to be incorporated in such construction.

ARTICLE 8
ARCHITECT

8.1 The Architect will provide general administration of the Contract and will be the Owner's representative during construction and until issuance of the final Certificate for Payment.

8.2 The Architect shall at all times have access to the Work wherever it is in preparation and progress.

8.3 The Architect will make periodic visits to the site to familiarize himself generally with the progress and quality of the Work and to determine in general if the Work is proceeding in accordance with the Contract Documents. On the basis of his on-site observations as an architect, he will keep the Owner informed of the progress of the Work, and will endeavor to guard the Owner against defects and deficiencies in the Work of the Contractor. The Architect will not be required to make exhaustive or continuous on-site inspections to check the quality or quantity of the Work. The Architect will not be responsible for construction means, methods, techniques, sequences or procedures, or for safety precautions and programs in connection with the Work, and he will not be responsible for the Contractor's failure to carry out the Work in accordance with the Contract Documents.

8.4 Based on such observations and the Contractor's Applications for Payment, the Architect will determine the amounts owing to the Contractor and will issue Certificates for Payment in accordance with Article 16.

8.5 The Architect will be, in the first instance, the interpreter of the requirements of the Contract Documents. He will make decisions on all claims and disputes between the Owner and the Contractor. All his decisions are subject to arbitration.

8.6 The Architect will have authority to reject Work which does not conform to the Contract Documents.

ARTICLE 9
OWNER

9.1 The Owner shall furnish all surveys.

9.2 The Owner shall secure and pay for easements for permanent structures or permanent changes in existing facilities.

9.3 The Owner shall issue all instructions to the Contractor through the Architect.

ARTICLE 10
CONTRACTOR

10.1 The Contractor shall supervise and direct the work, using his best skill and attention. The Contractor shall be solely responsible for all construction means, methods, techniques, sequences and procedures and for coordinating all portions of the Work under the Contract.

10.2 Unless otherwise specifically noted, the Contractor shall provide and pay for all labor, materials, equipment, tools, construction equipment and machinery, water, heat, utilities, transportation, and other facilities and services necessary for the proper execution and completion of the Work.

10.3 The Contractor shall at all times enforce strict discipline and good order among his employees, and shall not employ on the Work any unfit person or anyone not skilled in the task assigned to him.

10.4 The Contractor warrants to the Owner and the Architect that all materials and equipment incorporated in the Work will be new unless otherwise specified, and that all Work will be of good quality, free from faults and defects and in conformance with the Contract Documents. All Work not so conforming to these standards may be considered defective.

10.5 The Contractor shall pay all sales, consumer, use and other similar taxes required by law and shall secure all permits, fees and licenses necessary for the execution of the Work.

10.6 The Contractor shall give all notices and comply with all laws, ordinances, rules, regulations, and orders of any public authority bearing on the performance of

---

Fig. 3-7 Construction contract (continued) *(This document has been reproduced with the permission of the American Institute of Architects. Further reproduction is not authorized.)*

the Work, and shall notify the Architect if the Drawings and Specifications are at variance therewith.

10.7 The Contractor shall be responsible for the acts and omissions of all his employees and all Subcontractors, their agents and employees and all other persons performing any of the Work under a contract with the Contractor.

10.8 The Contractor shall review, stamp with his approval and submit all samples and shop drawings as directed for approval of the Architect for conformance with the design concept and with the information given in the Contract Documents. The Work shall be in accordance with approved samples and shop drawings.

10.9 The Contractor at all times shall keep the premises free from accumulation of waste materials or rubbish caused by his operations. At the completion of the Work he shall remove all his waste materials and rubbish from and about the Project as well as his tools, construction equipment, machinery and surplus materials, and shall clean all glass surfaces and shall leave the Work "broom clean" or its equivalent, except as otherwise specified.

10.10 The Contractor shall indemnify and hold harmless the Owner and the Architect and their agents and employees from and against all claims, damages, losses and expenses including attorneys' fees arising out of or resulting from the performance of the Work, provided that any such claim, damage, loss or expense (1) is attributable to bodily injury, sickness, disease or death, or to injury to or destruction of tangible property (other than the Work itself) including the loss of use resulting therefrom, and (2) is caused in whole or in part by any negligent act or omission of the Contractor, any Subcontractor, anyone directly or indirectly employed by any of them or anyone for whose acts any of them may be liable, regardless of whether or not it is caused in part by a party indemnified hereunder. In any and all claims against the Owner or the Architect or any of their agents or employees by any employee of the Contractor, any Subcontractor, anyone directly or indirectly employed by any of them or anyone for whose acts any of them may be liable, the indemnification obligation under this Paragraph 10.10 shall not be limited in any way by any limitation on the amount or type of damages, compensation or benefits payable by or for the Contractor or any Subcontractor under workmen's compensation acts, disability benefit acts or other employee benefit acts. The obligations of the Contractor under this Paragraph 10.10 shall not extend to the liability of the Architect, his agents or employees arising out of (1) the preparation or approval of maps, drawings, opinions, reports, surveys, Change Orders, designs or specifications, or (2) the giving of or the failure to give directions or instructions by the Architect, his agents or employees provided such giving or failure to give is the primary cause of the injury or damage.

ARTICLE 11
SUBCONTRACTS

11.1 A Subcontractor is a person who has a direct contract with the Contractor to perform any of the Work at the site.

11.2 Unless otherwise specified in the Contract Documents or in the Instructions to Bidders, the Contractor, as soon as practicable after the award of the Contract, shall furnish to the Architect in writing a list of the names of Subcontractors proposed for the principal portions of the Work. The Contractor shall not employ any Subcontractor to whom the Architect or the Owner may have a reasonable objection. The Contractor shall not be required to employ any Subcontractor to whom he has a reasonable objection. Contracts between the Contractor and the Subcontractor shall be in accordance with the terms of this Agreement and shall include the General Conditions of this Agreement insofar as applicable.

ARTICLE 12
SEPARATE CONTRACTS

12.1 The Owner reserves the right to award other contracts in connection with other portions of the Project or other work on the site under these or similar Conditions of the Contract.

12.2 The Contractor shall afford other contractors reasonable opportunity for the introduction and storage of their materials and equipment and the execution of their work, and shall properly connect and coordinate his Work with theirs.

12.3 Any costs caused by defective or ill-timed work shall be borne by the party responsible therefor.

ARTICLE 13
ROYALTIES AND PATENTS

The Contractor shall pay all royalties and license fees. The Contractor shall defend all suits or claims for infringement of any patent rights and shall save the Owner harmless from loss on account thereof.

ARTICLE 14
ARBITRATION

All claims or disputes arising out of this Contract or the breach thereof shall be decided by arbitration in accordance with the Construction Industry Arbitration Rules of the American Arbitration Association then obtaining unless the parties mutually agree otherwise. Notice of the demand for arbitration shall be filed in writing with the other party to the Contract and with the American Arbitration Association and shall be made within a reasonable time after the dispute has arisen.

ARTICLE 15
TIME

15.1 All time limits stated in the Contract Documents are of the essence of the Contract.

15.2 If the Contractor is delayed at any time in the progress of the Work by changes ordered in the Work, by labor disputes, fire, unusual delay in transportation, unavoidable casualties, causes beyond the Contractor's control, or by any cause which the Architect may determine justifies the delay, then the Contract Time shall be extended by Change Order for such reasonable time as the Architect may determine.

AIA DOCUMENT A107 • SMALL CONSTRUCTION CONTRACT • JANUARY 1974 EDITION • AIA® • ©1974
THE AMERICAN INSTITUTE OF ARCHITECTS, 1735 NEW YORK AVE., N.W., WASHINGTON, D. C. 20006

Fig. 3-7 Construction contract (continued) *(This document has been reproduced with the permission of the American Institute of Architects. Further reproduction is not authorized.)*

ARTICLE 16
PAYMENTS

16.1 Payments shall be made as provided in Article 4 of this Agreement.

16.2 Payments may be withheld on account of (1) defective Work not remedied, (2) claims filed, (3) failure of the Contractor to make payments properly to Subcontractors or for labor, materials, or equipment, (4) damage to another contractor, or (5) unsatisfactory prosecution of the Work by the Contractor.

16.3 Final payment shall not be due until the Contractor has delivered to the Owner a complete release of all liens arising out of this Contract or receipts in full covering all labor, materials and equipment for which a lien could be filed, or a bond satisfactory to the Owner indemnifying him against any lien.

16.4 The making of final payment shall constitute a waiver of all claims by the Owner except those arising from (1) unsettled liens, (2) faulty or defective Work appearing after Substantial Completion, (3) failure of the Work to comply with the requirements of the Contract Documents, or (4) terms of any special guarantees required by the Contract Documents. The acceptance of final payment shall constitute a waiver of all claims by the Contractor except those previously made in writing and still unsettled.

ARTICLE 17
PROTECTION OF PERSONS AND PROPERTY

The Contractor shall be responsible for initiating, maintaining, and supervising all safety precautions and programs in connection with the Work. He shall take all reasonable precautions for the safety of, and shall provide all reasonable protection to prevent damage, injury or loss to (1) all employees on the Work and other persons who may be affected thereby, (2) all the Work and all materials and equipment to be incorporated therein, and (3) other property at the site or adjacent thereto. He shall comply with all applicable laws, ordinances, rules, regulations and orders of any public authority having jurisdiction for the safety of persons or property or to protect them from damage, injury or loss. All damage or loss to any property caused in whole or in part by the Contractor, any Subcontractor, any Subsubcontractor or anyone directly or indirectly employed by any of them, or by anyone for whose acts any of them may be liable, shall be remedied by the Contractor, except damage or loss attributable to faulty Drawings or Specifications or to the acts or omissions of the Owner or Architect or anyone employed by either of them or for whose acts either of them may be liable but which are not attributable to the fault or negligence of the Contractor.

ARTICLE 18
CONTRACTOR'S LIABILITY INSURANCE

The Contractor and each separate Contractor shall purchase and maintain such insurance as will protect him from claims under workmen's compensation acts and other employee benefit acts, from claims for damages because of bodily injury, including death, and from claims for damages to property which may arise out of or result from the Contractor's operations under this Contract, whether such operations be by himself or by any Subcontractor or anyone directly or indirectly employed by any of them. This insurance shall be written for not less than any limits of liability specified as part of this Contract, or required by law, whichever is the greater, and shall include contractual liability insurance as applicable to the Contractor's obligations under Paragraph 10.10. Certificates of such insurance shall be filed with the Owner and each separate Contractor.

ARTICLE 19
OWNER'S LIABILITY INSURANCE

The Owner shall be responsible for purchasing and maintaining his own liability insurance and, at his option, may maintain such insurance as will protect him against claims which may arise from operations under the Contract.

ARTICLE 20
PROPERTY INSURANCE

20.1 Unless otherwise provided, the Owner shall purchase and maintain property insurance upon the entire Work at the site to the full insurable value thereof. This insurance shall include the interests of the Owner, the Contractor, Subcontractors and Sub-subcontractors in the Work and shall insure against the perils of Fire, Extended Coverage, Vandalism and Malicious Mischief.

20.2 Any insured loss is to be adjusted with the Owner and made payable to the Owner as trustee for the insureds, as their interests may appear, subject to the requirements of any mortgagee clause.

20.3 The Owner shall file a copy of all policies with the Contractor prior to the commencement of the Work.

20.4 The Owner and Contractor waive all rights against each other for damages caused by fire or other perils to the extent covered by insurance provided under this paragraph. The Contractor shall require similar waivers by Subcontractors and Sub-subcontractors.

ARTICLE 21
CHANGES IN THE WORK

21.1 The Owner without invalidating the Contract may order Changes in the Work consisting of additions, deletions, or modifications, the Contract Sum and the Contract Time being adjusted accordingly. All such Changes in the Work shall be authorized by written Change Order signed by the Owner or the Architect as his duly authorized agent.

21.2 The Contract Sum and the Contract Time may be changed only by Change Order.

21.3 The cost or credit to the Owner from a Change in the Work shall be determined by mutual agreement.

Fig. 3-7 Construction contract   (continued) *(This document has been reproduced with the permission of the American Institute of Architects. Further reproduction is not authorized.)*

ARTICLE 22
CORRECTION OF WORK

The Contractor shall correct any Work that fails to conform to the requirements of the Contract Documents where such failure to conform appears during the progress of the Work, and shall remedy any defects due to faulty materials, equipment or workmanship which appear within a period of one year from the Date of Substantial Completion of the Contract or within such longer period of time as may be prescribed by law or by the terms of any applicable special guarantee required by the Contract Documents. The provisions of this Article 22 apply to Work done by Subcontractors as well as to Work done by direct employees of the Contractor.

ARTICLE 23
TERMINATION BY THE CONTRACTOR

If the Architect fails to issue a Certificate of Payment for a period of thirty days through no fault of the Contractor, or if the Owner fails to make payment thereon for a period of thirty days, the Contractor may, upon seven days written notice to the Owner and the Architect, terminate the Contract and recover from the Owner payment for all Work executed and for any proven loss sustained upon any materials, equipment, tools, and construction equipment and machinery, including reasonable profit and damages.

ARTICLE 24
TERMINATION BY THE OWNER

If the Contractor defaults or neglects to carry out the Work in accordance with the Contract Documents or fails to perform any provision of the Contract, the Owner may, after seven days' written notice to the Contractor and without prejudice to any other remedy he may have, make good such deficiencies and may deduct the cost thereof from the payment then or thereafter due the Contractor or, at his option, may terminate the Contract and take possession of the site and of all materials, equipment, tools, and construction equipment and machinery thereon owned by the Contractor and may finish the Work by whatever method he may deem expedient, and if the unpaid balance of the Contract Sum exceeds the expense of finishing the Work, such excess shall be paid to the Contractor, but if such expense exceeds such unpaid balance, the Contractor shall pay the difference to the Owner.

ARTICLE 25
MISCELLANEOUS PROVISIONS

Fig. 3-7 Construction contract (continued) *(This document has been reproduced with the permission of the American Institute of Architects. Further reproduction is not authorized.)*

This Agreement executed the day and year first written above.

OWNER _____   CONTRACTOR _____

_____   _____

Fig. 3-7 Construction contract   (continued) *(This document has been reproduced with the permission of the American Institute of Architects. Further reproduction is not authorized.)*

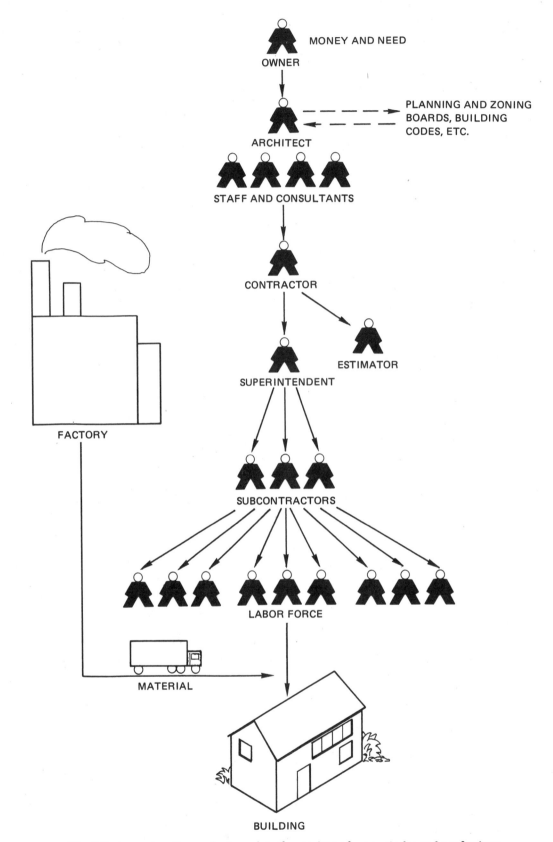

Fig. 3-8 A construction project requires the services of many trades and professions.

- *Termination of the contract.* The contract describes conditions under which the contract may be ended. Contracts may be terminated if one party fails to comply with the contract; when one of the parties is disabled or dies; and for several other reasons.

There are two kinds of contracts in use for most construction. Each of these offers certain advantages and disadvantages.

Fixed-sum (sometimes called lump-sum) contracts are most often used. With a *fixed-sum contract*, the contractor agrees to complete the project for a certain amount of money. The greatest advantage of this kind of contract is that the owner knows in advance exactly what the cost will be. However, the contractor does not know what hidden problems may be encountered. Therefore the contractor's price must be high enough to cover unforseen circumstances, such as excessive rock in the excavation or sudden increases in the cost of materials.

A *cost-plus contract* is one in which the contractor agrees to complete the work for the actual cost, plus a percentage for overhead and profit. The advantage of this type of contract is that the contractor does not have to allow for unforeseen problems, so the final price is apt to be less. A cost-plus contract is also useful when changes are apt to be made during the course of construction. The main disadvantage of this kind of contract is that the owner does not know exactly what the cost will be until the project is completed.

CONTRACTORS

According to the agreement signed, a general contractor is responsible for directing the entire construction operation from start to finish. The contractor supplies the workers, equipment, and materials for the project and guarantees to complete the work in the time specified in the contract, figure 3-8.

It is not always practical for a contractor's construction company to employ all of the

Fig. 3-9 Plasterers usually subcontract to do the work on a project. *(Gypsum Assoc.)*

specialists required for every project. Instead, the contractor may hire *subcontractors* to perform certain parts of the work. Subcontractors specialize in electrical work, plumbing, heating and air-conditioning, or other trades, figure 3-9. The bidding process is used to select a subcontractor. The cost for each subcontractor is included in the contractor's bid to the owner.

Contractors must have a thorough knowledge of the kind of work they are doing. General construction contractors must be familiar with all areas of construction as well as understand good business practices. Subcontractors must also have the ability to manage their businesses, but their skills are geared for their particular trade.

Most contractors begin their careers in construction by working for other contractors. The knowledge necessary to work in construction can be acquired in vocational schools, technical schools, apprentice programs, or through on-the-job training.

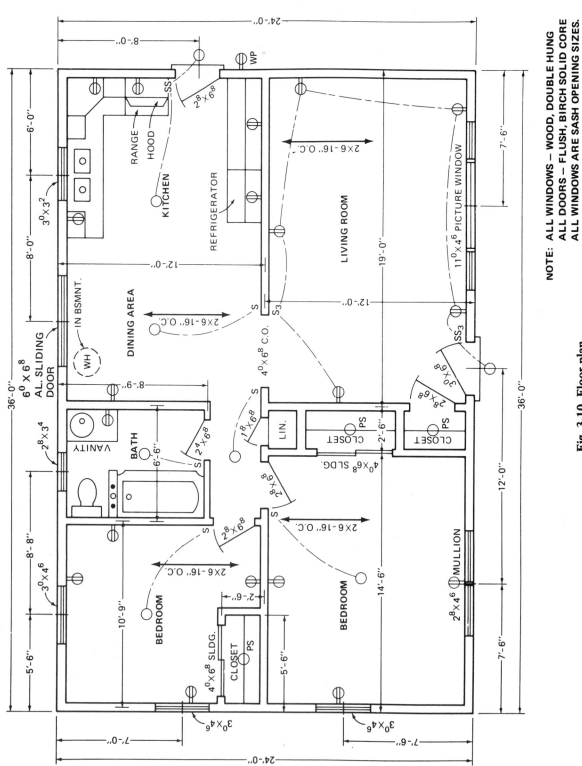

NOTE: ALL WINDOWS – WOOD, DOUBLE HUNG
ALL DOORS – FLUSH, BIRCH SOLID CORE
ALL WINDOWS ARE SASH OPENING SIZES.

Fig. 3-10 Floor plan.

─── ACTIVITIES ───

A. ESTIMATING

Estimators use a variety of forms to record data about materials. These forms clearly list the material description, quantity, size, and price.

Refer to the floor plan in figure 3-10 and complete an estimating data sheet for the windows and doors. Record the catalog numbers, descriptions, and prices from suppliers' catalogs. Your instructor will provide blank data sheets and suppliers' catalogs.

B. FLOW CHARTS

Draw a flow chart showing the steps a construction project goes through from the time the architect completes the design until the general contractor signs the contract. Wherever possible, name the construction career involved. A suggested design for this chart is shown in figure 3-11. Charts similar to this, called critical-path networks are often used by contractors to schedule work on a construction project.

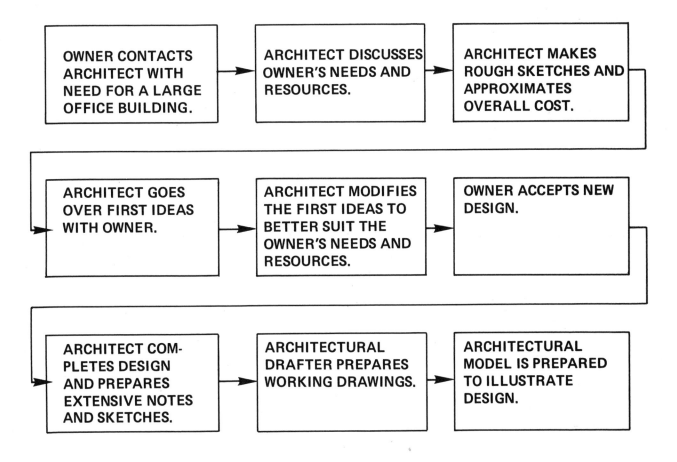

Fig. 3-11 Flow chart showing steps in design process

REVIEW

Multiple Choice

Select the best answer for each of the following questions.

1. On which construction document is a summary of the work to be performed likely to be found?

   a. Specifications   c. Contract
   b. Working drawings   d. Estimate

2. Which of the following personnel has the primary responsibility for predicting the amount of time required to do the finished carpentry work on a construction project.

   a. Carpenter   c. Architect
   b. Specification writer   d. Estimator

3. According to the CSI format, what is the number of the division for sound control if there is no equipment or conveying system to be included?

   a. 11   c. 13
   b. 12   d. 14

4. Which of the following is considered an advantage to the owner in a cost-plus contract?

   a. The exact price of the contract is known before construction begins.
   b. If unforeseen problems arise, the contractor receives extra pay.
   c. The contractor does not need to allow extra to cover unforeseen problems.
   d. The owner is assured of better quality work.

5. Which of the following is considered an advantage to the owner in a fixed-sum contract?

   a. The contractor allows enough extra to cover any unforeseen problems.
   b. It is possible to make changes on the working drawings after work has begun.
   c. The owner is assured of better quality work.
   d. The exact price of the contract is known before construction begins.

6. If the average cost per square foot for a certain type of construction is $37.00, what is the cost for a building measuring 140 feet by 270 feet?

   a. $37,800.00   c. $113,400.00
   b. $1,398,600.00   d. $11,986,000.00

7. Which of the following is an example of overhead cost?

   a. Heating the contractor's office
   b. Cost of materials for a construction project
   c. Profit
   d. Subcontractor's fees

8. What is a schedule of payments?

    a. A method for determining how much the general contractor is to receive
    b. A method for determining how much each subcontractor is to receive
    c. A breakdown of when the contractor is to receive payments
    d. A method of keeping payroll records

9. How does the general contractor usually estimate the cost of the subcontractor's work?

    a. From the subcontractor's bids
    b. The general contractor figures these costs
    c. The general contractor's estimator figures these costs
    d. The architect figures these costs into the design

10. What construction document describes the quality of materials to be used?

    a. Contract   c. Bid
    b. Working drawings   d. Specifications

SECTION 2
SECTION 2
SECTION 2
SECTION 2

CONSTRUCTION MATERIALS

UNIT 4.
CONCRETE AND MASONRY

OBJECTIVES

After completing this unit, the student will be able to:

- outline the process for converting natural resources into concrete.

- describe the most important physical properties of concrete and masonry materials.

During the planning stages of any construction project, designers must determine what material to use for every part of a structure. Practically every material available to industry can be used to some advantage in construction, figure 4-1. However, relatively few of these materials are used in the structural parts (giving basic strength) of most construction. Concrete, for instance, is an important structural material in construction. Architects, engineers, and specification writers must rely on their knowledge of these materials to select those with the most desirable properties for each use.

CONCRETE

Concrete has been used for centuries as a basic building material. Concrete consists of hard particles, called *aggregates*, held together by cement. Modern concrete can be designed to provide great strength and an attractive appearance, figure 4-2, page 58.

Portland Cement

Most modern concrete is made with *portland cement*, so named because of its resemblence to a rock found on the Isle of Portland. To

Fig. 4-1 Hundreds of products were used in the construction of these buildings.

Fig. 4-2 Concrete provides strength and can be cast into any shape.

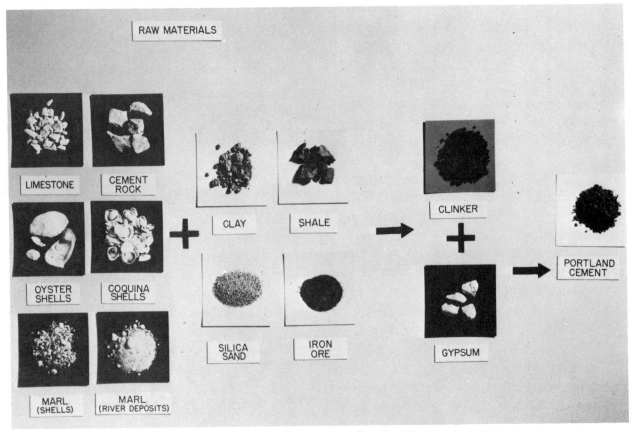

Fig. 4-3 Ingredients of portland cement   *(Portland Cement Assoc.)*

Proportions for various mixes of concrete	Cement (cu. ft.)	Coarse Aggregate (cu. ft.)	Fine Aggregate (cu. ft.)	Gal. Water	
				wet sand	dry sand
3/4″ max. aggregate	1	2 1/4	2	5	6
1″ max. aggregate	1	3	2 1/4	5	6
1 1/2″ max. aggregate	1	3 1/2	2 1/2	5	6

Fig. 4-4 Typical concrete mixes

manufacture portland cement, limestone is quarried (dug out), crushed, and mixed with silica, iron oxide, and alumina, figure 4-3. If the limestone does not contain enough alumina and silica, sand is added. These materials are heated to a temperature of 2600° to 3000°F (1400° to 1650°C) in a rotary kiln. The material produced by this heating is called *clinker*. The clinker is ground to a fine powder. Gypsum is then added to control the amount of time required for the cement to *set* (harden). The finished portland cement is shipped in bulk or bagged.

A special type of portland cement, called *air-entraining* portland cement, is used where freezing and thawing is a problem. Small amounts of special materials are added to the cement resulting in millions of tiny air bubbles in the cured concrete. This reduces the effects of freezing and thawing.

Aggregates

All concrete contains fine and coarse aggregates. The fine aggregate is normally sand. Coarse aggregates are crushed stone and gravel over 1/4 inch in diameter. For special purposes, lightweight aggregate may be used to develop concretes weighing less than one-fourth of normal concrete. Some common lightweight aggregates are expanded *shale, vermiculite,* and *perlite*. These are made from natural rocks which expand, like popcorn, when they are heated. They are not normally used in concrete where weight is not an important factor.

Mixing Concrete

Several variables affect the proportions of materials required for a good concrete mixture. The maximum size of the coarse aggregates is determined by the size of concrete member (part). It is generally best to use the largest coarse aggregates that result in a finished product with no *voids* (air pockets). The amount of fine aggregate required varies with the size of coarse aggregate used, figure 4-4. The aggregates should be carefully measured and thoroughly mixed with the cement before the water is added.

The amount of water used in concrete is very important. If too little water is used, the concrete does not develop to its full strength. If too much water is used, the fine and coarse aggregates separate and weak concrete results. The exact amount of water needed varies depending on the water contained in the aggregate. Only water that is clean enough to drink should be used, since dirt or oil interferes with the reaction between the cement and water.

Slump tests measure the stiffness of concrete mixtures. Freshly mixed concrete is placed in a slump cone. The cone is then carefully emptied onto a flat surface. The number of inches that the concrete settles is the *slump* of that mix, figure 4-5. Water should not be added to increase the slump. A cement mason, construction crew supervisor, or construction inspector usually conducts a slump test.

Fig. 4-5 In a concrete slump test, the slump is the number of inches the concrete sags after being released from the cone. *(Portland Cement Assoc.)*

Reinforced Concrete

Concrete is a valuable building material because of its permanence and high *compressive strength* (resistance to crushing). However, concrete has low *tensile strength* (resistance to pulling apart). To increase the tensile strength of concrete members, they are reinforced with steel rods or mesh, figures 4-6 and 4-7.

Bars used for concrete reinforcement are usually *deformed*. This means they have raised projections on the surface so they will not move in the cured concrete. These bars are commonly referred to as *rebar*. Rebar is available in sizes from #2 to #18. The number size indicates the diameter in eighths of an inch. Thus, a #5 rebar has a diameter of 5/8 inch. Wire mesh is specified by the gauge diameter of the wire and the spacing of the wires. Mesh

Fig. 4-6 Steel rods are used to reinforce concrete. *(Portland Cement Assoc.)*

Fig. 4-7 Ironworkers lay wire mesh to reinforce concrete. *(Cem-Fill Corp.)*

made with 10-gauge wire in both directions forming 6-inch squares is designated as 6 x 6-10/10 mesh.

In applications where bending loads are placed on concrete members, part of the member is subjected to tensile forces, figure 4-8. It is important that the steel reinforcement be positioned correctly to withstand that force. Usually the size and placement of reinforcement is specified by an engineer. Ironworkers, or rodsetters, place the reinforcing steel in position in the concrete form.

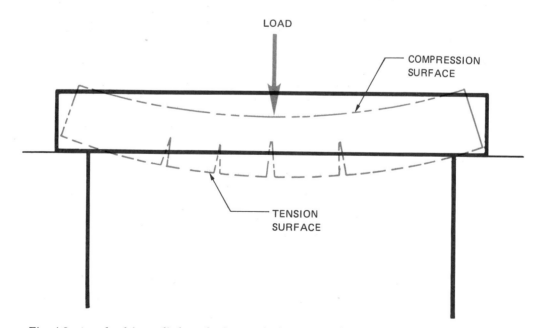

Fig. 4-8 As a load is applied to the beam, the bottom surface attempts to stretch and the top surface attempts to become shorter.

MASONRY

Masonry construction involves joining units of stone, concrete, clay, and similar materials with mortar. Several kinds of stone, including limestone, marble, and granite, are used in masonry construction. All masonry units, except stone, are manufactured or made at another site and transported to the construction area.

Mortar

Mortar for masonry construction consists of portland cement, hydrated lime, and sand mixed with water. The proportions of the mortar mix are stated in that order and by volume. For example, 1:1 1/2:4 mortar consists of 1 part portland cement, 1 1/2 parts lime, and 4 parts sand. On some jobs masonry cement is used instead of portland cement and lime. *Masonry cement* is a preblended mix of portland cement and hydrated lime.

The amount of water varies depending on the condition of the materials being used. Mortar mixed with dry sand requires more water than mortar mixed with wet sand. Also, some masonry units absorb water from the mortar more rapidly than others. The best way to determine the proper amount of water is through

Fig. 4-9 Concrete blocks are frequently used to build foundations because of their high compressive strength. *(Richard T. Kreh, Sr.)*

trial and error. Just enough water should be used so the mortar sticks to the trowel after a vertical snap of the wrist.

Block

Blocks for masonry construction may be made of several materials, but the most common is concrete. Concrete block is especially popular where heavy loads must be borne. This is because of the high compressive strength of concrete and the ease of handling individual blocks, figure 4-9.

Concrete blocks come in assorted sizes and shapes, figure 4-10. The size of a concrete block

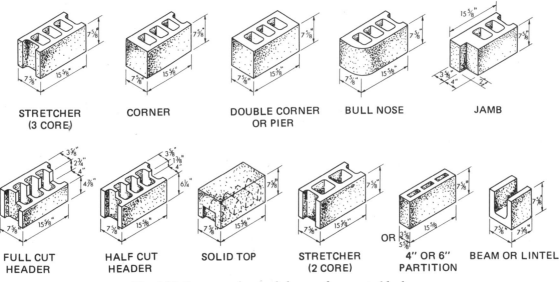

STRETCHER (3 CORE) CORNER DOUBLE CORNER OR PIER BULL NOSE JAMB

FULL CUT HEADER HALF CUT HEADER SOLID TOP STRETCHER (2 CORE) 4" OR 6" PARTITION BEAM OR LINTEL

Fig. 4-10 Common sizes and shapes of concrete blocks

is specified by nominal dimensions. Nominal dimensions are not actually the size specified. They are either smaller or larger depending upon the material. An 8″ x 8″ x 16″-inch nominal size block, for instance, is actually 3/8 inch smaller in all dimensions. This allows for a 3/8-inch mortar joint.

Different types of block are available to give a pleasing appearance or for special use, figure 4-11. Some blocks are made with light-weight aggregates. These lightweight blocks are used for walls where there is inadequate support from beneath for heavier materials. Scored blocks are also available to give a special appearance.

Fig. 4-11(A) Concrete blocks are sometimes arranged to create a special effect.

Fig. 4-11(B) Concrete blocks are also split to look like natural stone.

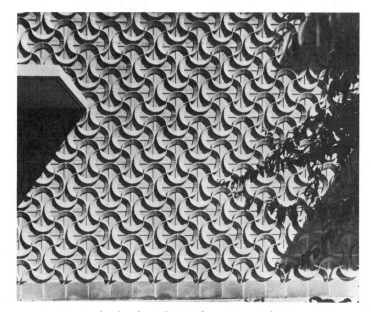

Fig. 4-11(C) Concrete blocks can also be shaped to make patterns. *(National Concrete Masonry Assoc.)*

Fig. 4-12(A)   The raw materials for brick include shale and clay.
(Powell & Minnock Brick Works, Inc.)

Fig. 4-12(B)   The shale or clay is finely ground, mixed with water, and forced into a mold.
(Powell & Minnock Brick Works, Inc.)

Fig. 4-12(C)   The *green* (not fired) bricks are then released from the mold and cut to size by a wire cutter.

Fig. 4-12(D)   The cut bricks are slowly passed through a kiln where they are fired.   *(Powell & Minnock Brick Works, Inc.)*

Brick

Bricks are small rectangular units made of fired (baked in a kiln) inorganic materials such as clay or shale. This manufacturing process is illustrated in figure 4-12.

There are several kinds of bricks, but most can be classified as either common brick, face brick, fire brick, or special brick. *Common bricks* are the frequently seen red bricks used where special shapes and colors are not required, figure 4-13. *Face bricks* are similar to common bricks but have a finer surface finish. *Fire brick* is similar in size and shape to common brick but is used in areas that come in contact with fire or

Fig. 4-13 Brick is frequently used to create a pleasing appearance. *(Bethlehem Steel Corp.)*

SIZES OF MODULAR BRICK								
Unit Designation	Nominal Dimensions, in.			Joint Thickness, in.	Manufactured Dimensions, in.			Modular Coursing, in.
	T	H	L		T	H	L	
Standard Modular	4	2 2/3	8	3/8	3 5/8	2 1/4	7 5/8	3C = 8
				1/2	3 1/2	2 1/4	7 1/2	
Engineer	4	3 1/5	8	3/8	3 5/8	2 13/16	7 5/8	5C = 16
				1/2	3 1/2	2 11/16	7 1/2	
Economy 8 or Jumbo Closure	4	4	8	3/8	3 5/8	3 5/8	7 5/8	1C = 4
				1/2	3 1/2	3 1/2	7 1/2	
Double	4	5 1/3	8	3/8	3 5/8	4 15/16	7 5/8	3C = 16
				1/2	3 1/2	4 13/16	7 1/2	
Roman	4	2	12	3/8	3 5/8	1 5/8	11 5/8	2C = 4
				1/2	3 1/2	2 1/4	11 1/2	
Norman	4	2 2/3	12	3/8	3 5/8	2 1/4	11 5/8	3C = 8
				1/2	3 1/2	2 1/4	11 1/2	
Norwegian	4	3 1/5	12	3/8	3 5/8	2 13/16	11 5/8	5C = 16
				1/2	3 1/2	2 11/16	11 1/2	
Economy 12 or Jumbo Utility	4	4	12	3/8	3 5/8	3 5/8	11 5/8	1C = 4
				1/2	3 1/2	3 1/2	11 1/2	
Triple	4	5 1/3	12	3/8	3 5/8	4 15/16	11 5/8	3C = 16
				1/2	3 1/2	4 13/16	11 1/2	
SCR brick	6	2 2/3	12	3/8	5 5/8	2 1/4	11 5/8	3C = 8
				1/2	5 1/2	2 1/4	11 1/2	
6-in. Norwegian	6	3 1/5	12	3/8	5 5/8	2 13/16	11 5/8	5C = 16
				1/2	5 1/2	2 11/16	11 1/2	
6-in. Jumbo	6	4	12	3/8	5 5/8	3 5/8	11 5/8	1C = 4
				1/2	5 1/2	3 1/2	11 1/2	
8-in. Jumbo	8	4	12	3/8	7 5/8	3 5/8	11 5/8	1C = 4
				1/2	7 1/2	3 1/2	11 1/2	

Fig. 4-14 Actual and nominal sizes of several types of modular bricks

extreme heat. *Special bricks* include such types as paving bricks and odd shapes. Several brick sizes are shown in figure 4-14.

Masons

Masons are skilled in building with masonry units and mortar and finishing concrete surfaces. *Stonemasons* build the stone exterior of structures. They work with two types of stone – natural cut, such as marble, granite, and limestone; and artificial stone made from cement, marble chips, or other masonry materials.

Bricklayers build walls, partitions, fireplaces, and other structures with brick, concrete blocks, and other masonry units. They also install firebrick linings in industrial furnaces.

Cement masons finish concrete surfaces, such as patios and floors. They know which chemical additives speed or slow the setting time and understanding the effects of heat, cold, and wind on the curing process. Cement masons also recognize by sight and touch what is happening in the cement mixture so they can prevent structural defects.

Masons and bricklayers are assisted by *tenders* or helpers. To name just a few of their duties, these laborers supply the masons with masonry units and other materials, mix mortar, and set up and move scaffolding.

—————— ACTIVITIES ——————

A. SLUMP TEST

A cement mason on a construction site often performs a slump test on a concrete mixture to test its stiffness. Prepare a concrete mixture from the proportions given, then perform a slump test to determine the mixture's stiffness. If the slump is between one and four inches, use the batch to complete Activity B.

Equipment and Materials

1/4-cubic foot portland cement
1/2-cubic foot clean sand
3/4 cubic foot of 3/4-inch aggregate
Slump cone
Folding rule or tape measure

Procedure

CAUTION: Safety glasses should be worn whenever you work with mortar or concrete. This is to prevent it from splashing in your eyes.

1. Thoroughly mix the sand and the coarse aggregate with the portland cement.

2. Mix in five quarts of clean water. If the sand is very dry, it may be necessary to mix in an additional 1/2 quart of water.

3. Fill the slump cone with freshly mixed concrete and *consolidate* (work out the air bubbles) with a rod.

4. Carefully empty the cone onto a flat surface.

5. Measure the vertical distance from a rod laid across the top of the empty cone to the top of the concrete sample, figure 4-15. This is the slump of the batch. If the slump is between 1 and 4 inches, use this batch for Activity B.

Fig. 4-15 Measure the distance from the straightedge laying on top of the slump cone to the top of the concrete. *(Portland Cement Assoc.)*

B.   REINFORCING CONCRETE

(This activity requires seven (7) days for the concrete to cure.)

Assume you are an ironworker.   Following the procedure outlined, add reinforcement to the forms provided.   This reinforced steel will increase the tensile strength of the concrete beam.

Equipment and Materials

2 forms, approximately 1 1/2″ W x 3″ D x 23″ L, figure 4-16.
Waxed paper or plastic wrap
2 pieces of #2 rebar, 24 inches long
2 chairs to support 2 bars at a height of 3/4 inch
Concrete to fill forms
4-pound hammer

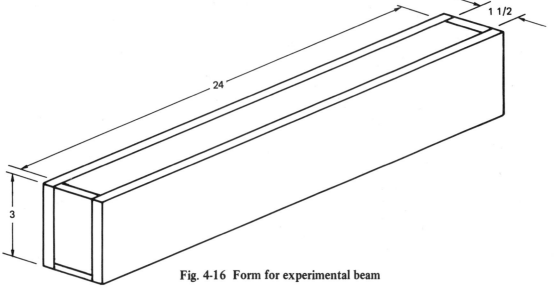

Fig. 4-16 Form for experimental beam

Procedure

CAUTION: Safety glasses must be worn for this activity.

1. Line forms with waxed paper or plastic wrap to prevent cured concrete from sticking to forms.

2. Place two pieces of rebar in one of the forms. The rebar should be positioned 3/4 inch from the bottom of the form on chairs made of stiff wire, figure 4-17.

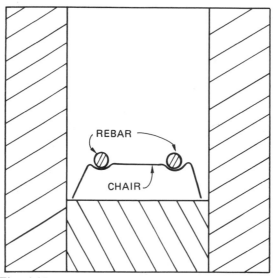

Fig. 4-17 Cross-sectional view of form for experimental beam, with reinforcement in place. Chairs may be made of any stiff wire.

3. Fill both forms with concrete and consolidate, being careful not to displace the rebar.

4. Write your name in the top of the fresh concrete to help locate the top surface after the concrete is removed from the form.

5. Allow seven (7) days for the concrete to cure.

6. After 7 days, position each concrete beam between two supports. The reinforced beam should be positioned with the rebar on the bottom.

7. Strike each beam at the midpoint with a 4-pound hammer. Notice the difference between the beams as they are broken.

C. MASONRY

Bricklayers use mortar and trowel to lay bricks. They must work carefully to ensure all joints are a uniform thickness and each *course* (row) is straight. In this activity you will mix mortar and lay three courses of bricks.

Equipment and Materials

9 common bricks
1/4 cubic foot hydrated lime
1 cubic foot clean sand

2″ x 4″ x 4′ piece of lumber
Brick mason's trowel

Procedure

CAUTION: Wear safety glasses when working with mortar. Lime is an irritant.

1. Mix lime and sand thoroughly. When dry ingredients are well blended, mix in only enough water so that mortar adheres to the brick.

2. Pick up a trowel load of mortar and snap the wrist to set the mortar and remove the excess, figure 4-18. Spread approximately a 1/2-inch bed of mortar on a 36-inch length of the 2″ x 4″ x 4′ piece of lumber.

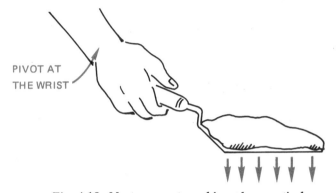

PIVOT AT THE WRIST

Fig. 4-18 Mortar on a trowel is *set* by a vertical snap of the wrist.

3. Place one brick in the mortar at one end and tap it with the trowel handle to obtain a 3/8-inch mortar joint.

4. Butter (spread) mortar onto one end of another brick and place this end against the end of the first brick. Tap this brick down to obtain a 3/8-inch joint.

5. Continue this process until four bricks are laid out in a straight line on the 2″ x 4″ x 4′ lumber with 3/8-inch joints.

6. After each brick is laid, use a slicing motion of the trowel to clean off the excess mortar. This can be reused on the next brick.

7. Repeat the process for a second course. The ends of the bricks in the second course should fall at the middle of the bricks in the first course, figure 4-19.

8. Lay a third course with the end joints in line with those of the first course. Masons use levels and mason's lines to ensure a straight line. This will be covered in a later unit.

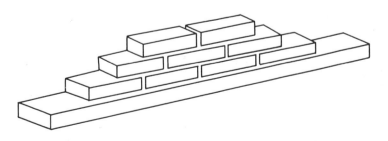

Fig. 4-19 The joints in each course of bricks should line up with the center of the bricks on the preceding course.

REVIEW

Multiple Choice

Select the best answer for each of the following questions.

1. Which of the following is an ingredient in portland cement?

   a. Coarse aggregate
   b. Hydrated lime
   c. Water
   d. Gypsum

2. Which of the following is included in a typical concrete mix?

   a. Alumina
   b. Hydrated lime
   c. Gypsum
   d. Fine aggregate

3. What is the diameter of #4 rebar?

   a. 1/4 inch
   b. 1/2 inch
   c. 1 inch
   d. 1 1/4 inch

4. Which type of portland cement would probably be used where it will be exposed to frequent freezing and thawing?

   a. Air-entrained
   b. High-density
   c. Low-density
   d. Sulphate

5. Where should rebar be placed in a beam?

   a. Near the top
   b. Near the bottom
   c. In the center
   d. Rebar is not used in beams

6. Which of the following terms is associated with concrete?

   a. Clay
   b. Mortar
   c. Course
   d. Aggregate

7. Which of the following terms is associated with masonry?

   a. Clay
   b. Rebar
   c. Crusher operator
   d. Clinker

8. Which of the following is a characteristic of concrete and masonry material?

   a. High tensile strength
   b. High compressive strength
   c. High bending strength
   d. Changes dimensions on contact with moisture

UNIT 5.
STEEL AND FOREST PRODUCTS

OBJECTIVES

After completing this unit, the student will be able to:

- outline the process of converting natural resources into steel, wood, and wood products.

- describe the most important physical properties of steel, wood, and wood products.

Steel and forest products are two other important structural materials used in the construction industry. These materials can be manufactured into a variety of shapes and forms with almost limitless properties.

STEEL

Metal is either ferrous or nonferrous. Metal containing a large percentage of iron is called *ferrous* metal. Metal with little or no iron is *nonferrous*. Ferrous metal is used as a structural building material because of its high strength, figure 5-1. *Steel* is an alloy (mixture) of iron and a small amount (not over 2 percent) of carbon and other materials.

Steelmaking

Iron ore is mined from open pits and transported to a blast furnace. The blast furnace is layered with iron ore, limestone, and coke (a material made from coal). Hot air is forced through the layers. This causes the coke to burn. As the by-products of the burning coke pass through the iron ore and limestone, the impurities in the ore float to the top forming

Fig. 5-1 More than 1,250 tons of structural steel are used in this building. *(Bethlehem Steel Corp.)*

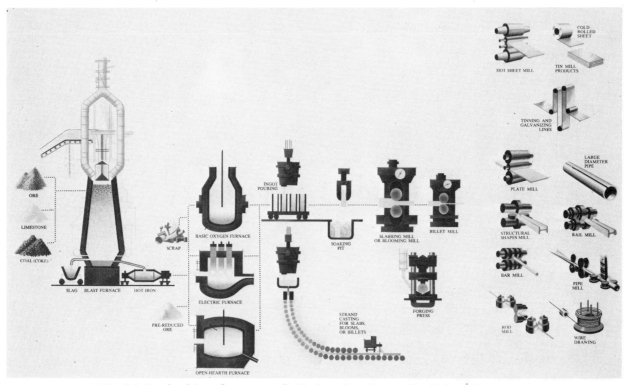

Fig. 5-2 Steelmaking: from ore to finished steel products *(Bethlehem Steel Corp.)*

slag. The molten iron is drawn off at the bottom of the blast furnace, figure 5-2.

To make steel, the iron produced in the blast furnace is *oxidized* (chemically combined with oxygen) and further purified. A common steelmaking process is the open-health process. In this process pig iron, the product of the blast furnace, is put into a pan-shaped furnace with limestone and varying amounts of scrap metal. A gas flame then heats the top surface of the furnace load. After this melting process, the molten metal is drawn off from the bottom and mixed with carbon and other alloying elements. The steel is then poured into molds to cool and solidifies into *ingots* (blocks of a convenient size).

Shaping Steel

Ingots of steel are further processed into a variety of shapes, figure 5-3. The shaping process used and the ingredients of the steel determine the properties of the steel.

Blooming Mill. The steel ingots are heated and rolled in a blooming mill. A *blooming mill* is a set of rollers that rolls the ingots into a large slab called a *bloom*. Rolling in the blooming mill also tends to compress the coarse grain structure of the cast ingot, thereby making the steel tougher.

Fig. 5-3. These 14-inch wide-flange beams weigh 730 pounds per foot. *(Bethlehem Steel Corp.)*

Hot Rolling. The bloom may be reheated or it may go directly from the blooming mill to the rolling mill. In the rolling mill it is passed through a series of rollers to produce the desired shape, figure 5-4. The red-hot steel is passed through the rollers several times, reducing the size on each pass. When the desired size and shape is reached, the piece is cooled and cut to length. Because the red-hot steel contracts as it cools, there may be small variations in the size of hot-rolled parts.

Cold Rolling. To produce steel with closely controlled dimensions and a smooth surface, hot-rolled steel may be cold rolled. The steel is cleaned in a chemical solution, then rolled without heat. As it is cold rolled, it increases in strength, but becomes less ductile. *Ductility* refers to the ability of any material to withstand bending and forming.

Cold Drawing. Wire is formed by pulling cold steel through openings called *dies*, figure 5-5. The wire is reduced in size each time it passes through one of a series of dies. This produces high-strength wire of an accurate size.

Pipe. Pipe may be classified as seamless or welded. Seamless pipe is formed by forcing a steel rod over a pointed device called a *mandrel*. A set of rollers around the outside controls the diameter of the pipe. Welded pipe is formed by rolling flat strips into an O shape, then welding the seam.

Types of Steel

The carbon content of steel determines its hardness and strength. Steel with high carbon content is generally stronger and more brittle. The classifications of steel according to carbon content are shown in figure 5-6.

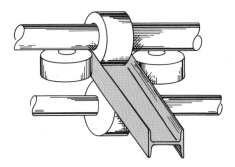

Fig. 5-4 Structural steel shapes are formed by hot rolling. The space between the rollers is tightened up on each successive pass.

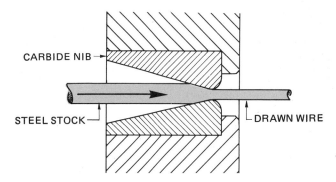

Fig. 5-5 Wire is formed by pulling the steel through a drawing.

TYPE	CHARACTERISTICS
Very Mild	0.05 to 0.15 percent carbon. Soft, tough steel used for sheets, wire, and rivets
Mild Structural	0.15 to 0.25 percent carbon. Ductile, machinable steel used for buildings and bridges
Medium	0.25 to 0.35 percent carbon. Stronger and harder than mild structural, used for machinery and construction.
Medium-hard	0.35 to 0.65 percent carbon. Used where it is subject to wear and abrasion.
Spring	0.85 to 1.05 percent carbon. Used in springs
Tool	1.05 to 1.20 percent carbon. Very hard and strong. Used for making cutting tools.

Fig. 5-6 The classifications of carbon steel.

Fig. 5-7 Hardwood is used mostly for finished woodwork and furniture. *(Western Wood Products Assoc.)*

By alloying other elements with steel, different properties can be developed. Manganese, nickel, copper, chromium, and vanadium are among the most common alloying elements. For example, by alloying chromium with the steel, stainless steel is produced. Stainless steel has great strength and, because of the oxide film that forms on its surface, it does not stain or corrode. *Metallurgists* coordinate and test the quality of steel during its manufacture.

FOREST PRODUCTS

Wood has long been a major building material. Cave dwellers probably used wood in their earliest construction efforts. Sawmills have been in operation for nearly four hundred years. Forest products are especially important to modern industry because the earth's forests are our only renewable source of construction material. Modern industry uses dozens of products from trees, but only major structural materials will be included here.

Classifications of Wood

Wood is classified as either hardwood or softwood. However, these classifications do not indicate the actual hardness of the wood. Many softwoods are as hard as some hardwoods. *Softwoods* are those which come from coniferous (cone-bearing) trees, or those with needle-like leaves. *Hardwoods* come from deciduous trees, or those trees that lose their leaves. Hardwoods are used primarily for furniture, cabinets, paneling, interior trim, and specialty items, figure 5-7. Softwoods are used for general construction and structural purposes, figure 5-8.

SPECIE	PRINCIPAL USES
Douglas Fir	Timbers, pilings, and plywood
Engelman Spruce	Wide range of uses from rough construction to interior finish
Incense Cedar	Closet lining, poles, and siding
Lodgepole Pine	Timbers, poles, and railroad ties. Some general-purpose lumber
Ponderosa Pine	General lumber for residential construction, trim, and furniture
Redwood	Posts, fences, siding, and bridge timbers
Western Hemlock	General construction lumber
Western Larch	Heavy construction lumber
White Pine	Trim, millwork, paneling, and furniture

Fig. 5-8 Common softwoods in construction

Fig. 5-9(A)   Timber fellers use lightweight power saws to cut down trees. *(Weyerhaeuser Co.)*

Fig. 5-9(B)   The logs are loaded into trucks for delivery to the mill. *(Weyerhaeuser Co.)*

Fig. 5-9(C)   There they are sawed into cants. *(Weyerhaeuser Co.)*

Fig. 5-9(D)   The cants are then cut into lumber. *(Weyerhaeuser Co.)*

Fig. 5-9(E)   The lumber is cut into length on trimmer saws. *(Weyerhaeuser Co.)*

Fig. 5-9 (F)   Finally, the lumber is planed to finished size. *(Weyerhaeuser Co.)*

Lumbering

Wood goes through many steps involving a great number of occupations before it is ready for use at the construction site, figure 5-9. Trees are selected for cutting by foresters. Marked trees are then felled, cut up by loggers, and dragged out of the forest. The logs are stacked at a central point where they are loaded into trucks and delivered to the mill. At the mill, the logs are cut into *cants* (large square timbers). The cants are then sawed into lumber by the head *sawyer* or operator of the saw mill. The quantity of lumber obtained from the logs depends on the sawyer's skills and knowledge.

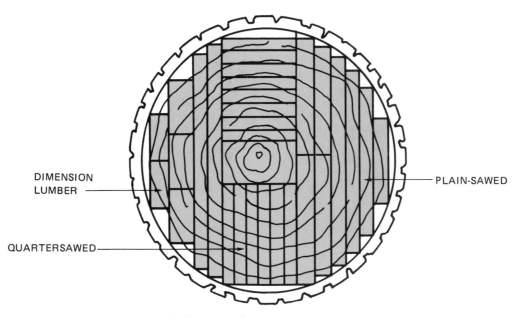

Fig. 5-10 Ways of sawing boards from a log

Most softwoods for general construction are *plain-sawed* or *flat-sawed*, meaning the saw cut is parallel to one side of the log, figure 5-10. Other pieces may be *quartersawed*, so the saw cut is perpendicular to the growth rings of the tree. Plain-sawed lumber generally displays a more attractive grain and is less expensive to produce than quartersawed, figure 5-11. However, it tends to warp and show other defects. Quartersawed lumber is less apt to warp.

Moisture Content of Wood

Wood consists of long tubular cells that contain a large amount of water in a living tree. Considerable drying is required to produce usuable lumber. The moisture content of wood is specified as a percentage of its oven-dry weight. For example, wood at 15 percent moisture content weights 15 percent more than wood which has been thoroughly dried in an oven.

Lumber may be air dried by stacking it in covered piles for several months. Kiln drying is a more common method for modern lumber production. With this method, lumber is stacked in large oven-like rooms, called *kilns*, where it is exposed to warm air and controlled humidity, figure 5-12. Kiln drying requires only a few days and results in better quality lumber.

In either type of drying and in storage after drying, lumber is always stacked with small strips of wood, called *stickers*, between the layers. The stickers allow air to circulate around the lumber, preventing mildew, stains, and other defects.

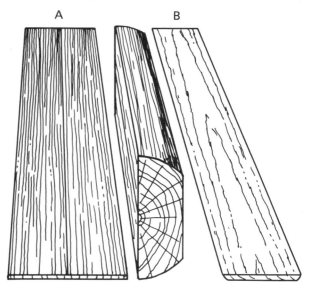

Fig. 5-11 Grain depends on how lumber is cut from the log. Board "A" is quartersawed. Board "B" is plain-sawed. *(U.S. Dept. of Agriculture)*

Fig. 5-12 Lumber is loaded into a kiln for drying. *(U.S. Forest Products Laboratory)*

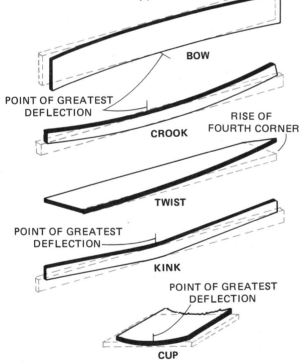

Fig. 5-13 Various types of warp in lumber. *(U.S. Dept of Agriculture)*

Grading

Lumber is graded according to the number and size of various defects that may be present. Most lumber contains some of these defects to a limited extent. As lumber dries it has a tendency to *warp*, that is, become distorted in shape, figure 5-13. *Knots* occur where branches grow from the trunk of a tree. Knots are classified according to their size and whether they are firm or loose in the lumber. *Stains* may be caused by problems in drying. *Decay* may be caused by fungi or insects. All of these defects affect the quality of the lumber.

Surfacing and Milling

Boards and dimension lumber for general use are planed to the proper thickness and width after sawing. This reduces the size to slightly smaller than the nominal dimensions by which it is identified, figure 5-14. Some lumber is further milled to produce molding, siding, and edge-matched boards, figure 5-15.

Thickness		Width	
Nominal	Dressed	Nominal	Dressed
1	3/4	2	1 1/2
1 1/4	1	3	2 1/2
1 1/2	1 1/4	4	3 1/2
2	1 1/2	5	4 1/2
2 1/2	2	6	5 1/2
3	2 1/2	7	6 1/2
3 1/2	3	8	7 1/4
4	3 1/2	9	8 1/4
		10	9 1/4
		11	10 1/4
		12	11 1/4

Note: With nominal sizes, the inch measurement is often assumed. For instance, a 2″ x 4″ piece of lumber is simply called a 2 x 4 (two-by-four).

Fig. 5-14 Nominal and minimum-dressed sizes of lumber.

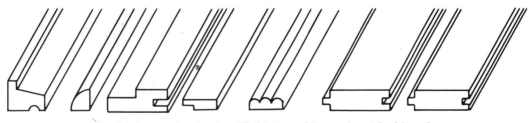

Fig. 5-15 Some lumber is milled into molding and matched boards.

Fig. 5-16 Wood is used as the framing material in many buildings because of its high compressive strength and light weight. *(Richard T. Kreh, Sr.)*

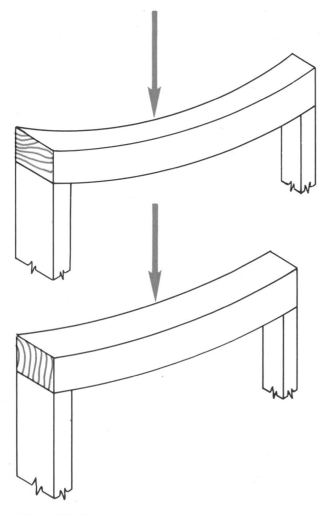

Fig. 5-17 Wood resists transverse forces better when applied parallel to the annular rings than when applied perpendicular to the annular rings.

Properties of Wood

Wood has a few characteristics that should be understood to use it to its greatest advantage. Wood has a high ratio of strength to weight in compression, figure 5-16, but relatively little strength in tension. It also has good transverse strength (resistance to forces applied to its side), but it is better in one direction than the other, figure 5-17.

Wood's ability to retain its size with changes in temperature is useful in some applications. However, it lacks dimensional stability with changes in moisture content. As it loses moisture it shrinks considerably in the direction of the annular rings (growth rings), slightly less across the annular rings and very little in length. These variations in amount of shrinkage are responsible for a major part of the warpage that occurs, figure 5-18. Plain-sawed lumber is affected most by warpage.

Plywood

By gluing thin sheets of wood, called *veneer*, together at right angles to one another, panels can be manufactured that have greater dimensional stability and improved strength. The material assembled in this way is *plywood*, figure 5-19. Plywood has several advantages over solid lumber. It resists splitting, it is dimensionally stable, fewer pieces are required to cover a given area, and it does not warp as easily.

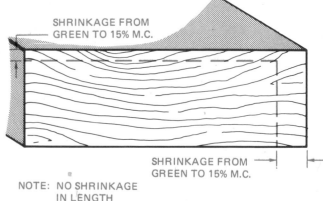

Fig. 5-18 Plain-sawed boards shrink most in width, less in thickness, and almost none in length as they dry.

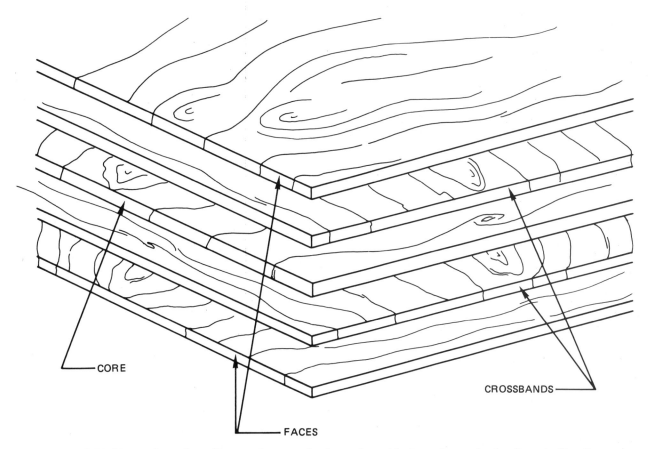

CORE

CROSSBANDS

FACES

Fig. 5-19 Plywood consists of layers of veneer glued together with the grain running in alternate directions.

Veneer for plywood is either rotary cut on a veneer lathe, plain sliced, or quarter slides. The method of cutting determines the appearance. Most plywood for general construction is made of rotary cut softwood because this method is most economical. Plain-sliced and quarter-sliced hardwood, plywood, and premium softwood plywood are used in furniture, cabinets, and paneling. After it is sliced from the log, a veneer clipper cuts the sheets to size. A plywood patcher replaces defected areas with thin plywood patches called *plugs*.

Plywood is available in several types and grades for a variety of uses. It may be bonded with waterproof or nonwaterproof glue. When plywood will be exposed to moisture, such as on building exteriors or concrete forms, it must be made with waterproof glue, figure 5-20. It is further graded according to the quality of its face and core veneers. Special types of plywood

Fig. 5-20 Plywood for concrete formwork is made with waterproof glue.

Table 2: Guide to Appearance Grades of Plywood[1]

For strength properties of appearance grades, see "Plywood Design Specifications," Y510

Interior Type

Use these terms when you specify plywood [2]	Description and Most Common Uses	Typical Grade-trademarks	Face	Back	Inner Plies	Most Common Thicknesses (inch) [3]					
						1/4	5/16	3/8	1/2	5/8	3/4
N-N, N-A, N-B INT-APA	Cabinet quality. For natural finish furniture, cabinet doors, built-ins, etc. Special order items.	N-N G1 INT-APA PS 1-74	N	N.A. or B	C						3/4
N-D INT-APA	For natural finish paneling. Special order item.	N-D G3 INT-APA PS 1-74	N	D	D	1/4					
A-A INT-APA	For applications with both sides on view. Built-ins, cabinets, furniture and partitions. Smooth face; suitable for painting.	A-A G4 INT-APA PS 1-74	A	A	D	1/4		3/8	1/2	5/8	3/4
A-B INT-APA	Use where appearance of one side is less important but two smooth solid surfaces are necessary.	A-B G4 INT-APA PS 1-74	A	B	D	1/4		3/8	1/2	5/8	3/4
A-D INT-APA	Use where appearance of only one side is important. Paneling, built-ins, shelving, partitions, and flow racks.	A-D GROUP 1 INTERIOR PS 1-74 000 (APA)	A	D	D	1/4		3/8	1/2	5/8	3/4
B-B INT-APA	Utility panel with two smooth sides. Permits circular plugs.	BB G3 INT-APA PS 1-74	B	B	D	1/4		3/8	1/2	5/8	3/4
B-D INT-APA	Utility panel with one smooth side. Good for backing, sides of built-ins. Industry: shelving, slip sheets, separator boards and bins.	B-D GROUP 3 INTERIOR PS 1-74 000 (APA)	B	D	D	1/4		3/8	1/2	5/8	3/4
DECORATIVE PANELS INT-APA	Rough sawn, brushed, grooved, or striated faces. For paneling, interior accent walls, built-ins, counter facing, displays, and exhibits.	DECORATIVE GROUP 2 INTERIOR PS 1-74 000 GROUP 1 FACE (APA)	C or btr.	D	D		5/16	3/8	1/2	5/8	
PLYRON INT-APA	Hardboard face on both sides. For counter tops, shelving, cabinet doors, flooring. Faces tempered, untempered, smooth, or screened.	PLYRON INT-APA PS 1-74			C & D				1/2	5/8	3/4

Exterior Type [7]

Use these terms when you specify plywood [2]	Description and Most Common Uses	Typical Grade-trademarks	Face	Back	Inner Plies	Most Common Thicknesses (inch) [3]					
						1/4	5/16	3/8	1/2	5/8	3/4
A-A EXT-APA [4]	Use where appearance of both sides is important. Fences, built-ins, signs, boats, cabinets, commercial refrigerators, shipping containers, tote boxes, tanks, and ducts.	A-A G3 EXT-APA PS 1-74	A	A	C	1/4		3/8	1/2	5/8	3/4
A-B EXT-APA [4]	Use where the appearance of one side is less important.	A-B G1 EXT-APA PS 1-74	A	B	C	1/4		3/8	1/2	5/8	3/4
A-C EXT-APA [4]	Use where the appearance of only one side is important. Soffits, fences, structural uses, boxcar and truck lining, farm buildings. Tanks, trays, commercial refrigerators.	A-C GROUP 4 EXTERIOR PS 1-74 000 (APA)	A	C	C	1/4		3/8	1/2	5/8	3/4
B-B EXT-APA [4]	Utility panel with solid faces.	BB G1 EXT-APA PS 1-74	B	B	C	1/4		3/8	1/2	5/8	3/4
B-C EXT-APA [4]	Utility panel for farm service and work buildings, boxcar and truck lining, containers, tanks, agricultural equipment. Also as base for exterior coatings for walls, roofs.	B-C GROUP 2 EXTERIOR PS 1-74 000 (APA)	B	C	C	1/4		3/8	1/2	5/8	3/4
HDO EXT-APA [4]	High Density Overlay plywood. Has a hard, semi-opaque resin-fiber overlay both faces. Abrasion resistant. For concrete forms, cabinets, counter tops, signs and tanks.	HDO AA G1 EXT-APA PS 1-74	A or B	A or B	C or C plgd		5/16	3/8	1/2	5/8	3/4
MDO EXT-APA [4]	Medium Density Overlay with smooth, opaque, resin-fiber overlay one or both panel faces. Highly recommended for siding and other outdoor applications, built-ins, signs, and displays. Ideal base for paint.	MDO BB G4 EXT-APA PS 1-74	B	B or C	C		5/16	3/8	1/2	5/8	3/4
303 SIDING EXT-APA [6]	Proprietary plywood products for exterior siding, fencing, etc. Special surface treatment such as V groove, channel groove, striated, brushed, rough sawn.	303 SIDING 16 oc GROUP 1 EXTERIOR PS 1-74 000 (APA)	[5]	C	C			3/8	1/2	5/8	
T 1-11 EXT-APA [6]	Special 303 panel having grooves 1/4″ deep, 3/8″ wide, spaced 4″ or 8″ o.c. Other spacing optional. Edges shiplapped. Available unsanded, textured, and MDO.	303 SIDING 16 oc T 1-11 GROUP 1 EXTERIOR PS 1-74 000 (APA)	C or btr.	C	C					5/8	
PLYRON EXT-APA	Hardboard faces both sides, tempered, smooth or screened.	PLYRON EXT-APA PS 1-74			C				1/2	5/8	3/4
MARINE EXT-APA	Ideal for boat hulls. Made only with Douglas fir or western larch. Special solid jointed core construction. Subject to special limitations on core gaps and number of face repairs. Also available with HDO or MDO faces.	MARINE AA EXT-APA PS 1-74	A or B	A or B	B	1/4		3/8	1/2	5/8	3/4

(1) Sanded both sides except where decorative or other surfaces specified.
(2) Available in Group 1, 2, 3, 4 or 5 unless otherwise noted.
(3) Standard 4x8 panel sizes, other sizes available.
(4) Also available in Structural I (all plies limited to Group 1 species) and Structural II (all plies limited to Group 1, 2 or 3 species).
(5) C or better for 5 plies, C Plugged or better for 3 ply panels.
(6) Stud spacing is shown on grade stamp.
(7) For finishing recommendations, see Form V307.

Fig. 5-21 Grade chart for several common types of plywood.

are also available. The American Plywood Association sets standards for most softwood plywood in construction use, figure 5-21.

Hardboard

Hardboard is made by exploding wood chips with high-pressure steam. This separates the individual wood fibers which are then pressed into thin (1/8- to 3/8-inch) sheets. Hardboard made in this manner is called *standard hardboard* and is used extensively for interior purposes. *Tempered hardboard* is treated by heat and chemicals to produce a denser, more durable surface that can be used in exterior applications, figure 5-22. Hardboard is inexpensive, finishes

well, is less apt to warp, and makes use of wood chips and scraps from lumber and plywood production.

Particleboard

Particleboard is another product made from wood chips, figure 5-23. Small chips of wood are coated with synthetic resin glue and pressed into sheets under heat and pressure. Particleboard is manufactured in thicknesses ranging from 1/4 inch to 1 1/2 inches. Particleboard has a smooth surface, uniform thickness, and is dimensionally stable. These qualities make it an excellent backing for surface materials like the plastic laminate used on countertops.

Fig. 5-22 Tempered hardboard sliding *(Weyerhaeuser Co.)*

Fig. 5-23 Particleboard is made of wood chips glued together.

———— ACTIVITIES ————

A. EFFECTS OF MOISTURE ON WOOD

Wood lacks dimensional stability with changes in moisture content. The shrinkage that occurs is responsible for a major part of the warpage in wood. In this activity, you will demonstrate the effects of moisture on wood.

Equipment

2 pieces of softwood, 1″ x 6″ x 6″
Container of water
Drying oven

Procedure

1. Write your name on both pieces of wood.

2. Compare the pieces to be sure they are of equal size in all directions.

3. Place one piece in the drying oven at a low temperature.

4. Soak the other piece in water.

5. After one (1) day remove both pieces and compare their sizes again. Notice the direction in which the greatest change took place.

B. MOISTURE CONTENT OF WOOD

Dry kiln operators season wood by drying it in a kiln or oven. This removes the moisture from the wood so it will not shrink or warp. The moisture content may be measured with electronic instruments or by weighing.

Equipment

Drying oven
Balance or scientific scales
Small wood specimen

Procedure

1. Shave a handful of shavings from a piece of wood.

2. Weigh these and record their exact weight.

3. Place the shavings in a flat container in the oven at a temperature of 200°F for 30 minutes.

4. Weigh the dried wood shavings and record their weight.

5. The weight lost during drying is due to the evaporation of moisture contained in the wood cells. The moisture content is found by subtracting the oven-dried weight from the weight when cut, dividing by the oven-dried weight, then multiplying by 100.

REVIEW QUESTIONS

A. Multiple Choice

Select the best answer for each of the following questions.

1. Which of the following is *not* an ingredient of steel?

   a. Iron   c. Slag
   b. Carbon   d. Alloys

2. In which direction does plain-sawed lumber expand most as it gains moisture?

   a. Length   c. Thickness
   b. Width   d. About the same in all directions

3. Which of the following is most apt to warp?

   a. Plain-sawed lumber   c. Hardboard
   b. Particleboard   d. Plywood

4. Which of the following changes dimensions most with changes in temperature?

   a. Plain-sawed lumber   c. Hardboard
   b. Quartersawed lumber   d. Steel

5. Which of the following changes dimensions most with changes in moisture content?

   a. Plain-sawed lumber   c. Hardboard
   b. Steel   d. Plywood

B. Matching

Choose the material in the right-hand column which is associated with each term in the left-hand column.

   1. Metallurgist   a. Lumber
   2. Drawing die   b. Steel
   3. Veneer lathe   c. Plywood
   4. Kiln
   5. Cants
   6. Blooming mill
   7. Plugging
   8. Quartersaw
   9. Sawyer
  10. Ferrous

UNIT 6.

CONSTRUCTION FINISHING MATERIALS

OBJECTIVES

After completing this unit, the student will be able to:

- describe a variety of construction finishing materials.

- list the important properties of construction finishing materials.

- discuss common applications of each of the materials covered.

As previously stated, nearly all materials are used in some way in the construction industry. The preceding two units discussed the most common structural materials. This unit will discuss a few nonstructural materials. Other materials are discussed in the units dealing with the various stages and types of construction.

GYPSUM PRODUCTS

Gypsum is a natural rock taken from mines throughout the world. To make a usuable product the gypsum rock is crushed, then heated in kilns. The heating drives off the water that was combined with the rock and leaves a fine powder called *plaster of paris*. When plaster of paris is mixed with water, it returns to its former rock state. Plaster of paris is used for patching cracks and small areas on plastered walls.

Plaster

Gypsum plaster is used extensively for finishing interior walls, figure 6-1. It produces a

durable surface and resists the spread of fire. *Gypsum wall plaster* consists of plaster of paris and aggregates such as sand or perlite. *Finish plaster*, which is used for a final coat on plastered walls, is made with plaster and lime.

Fig. 6-1 This plasterer is finishing the interior wall with gypsum plaster. *(United States Gypsum Co.)*

Gypsum Board Products

Two common board products made with gypsum are wallboard and lath. *Gypsum wallboard* is a fireproof wall covering. It consists of a gypsum plaster core, 3/8 inch to 1 inch thick, with a strong paper covering. The sheets are made in a standard width of 4 feet and in lengths from 8 feet to 16 feet. Gypsum wallboard is nailed directly to the wall frame by a lather, who then fills the joints with a special filler.

Gypsum lath is very similar to wallboard. It is made in sheets 16 inches wide by 48 inches long. The pieces of lath are fastened to the wall framing to provide a base over which plaster is applied, figure 6-2.

Gypsum lath and plaster is used to encase structural steel and protect it from fire, figure 6-3. Other shapes are used for special purposes, such as using long planks for roof decking.

GLASS

Glass has been used for windows for hundreds of years. Although the equipment and some of the additives have improved, the basic ingredients are still the same.

Glass is made by combining natural substances, melting them, and shaping the molten glass. Silica, in the form of sand, produces a clear solid when melted and cooled. Soda (sodium carbonate) is added to the sand to lower the melting point and help remove impurities.

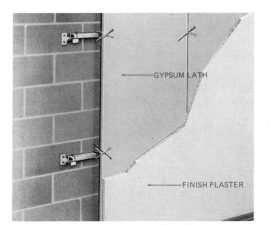

Fig. 6-2 Gypsum lath provides a base for finished plaster. *(Gold Bond Building Products)*

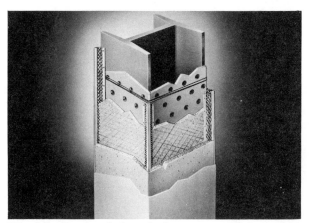

Fig. 6-3 Gypsum lath and plaster are used to protect steel from fire. *(Gold Bond Building Products)*

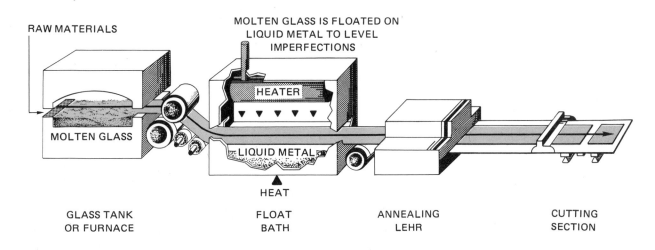

Fig. 6-4 The float bath process is a common method of glassmaking.

Lime is mixed with the other ingredients to make the glass weatherproof.

In modern glassmaking, the ingredients are melted in a furnace, then drawn into thin sheets or plates in a continuous ribbon. Next, the ribbon of glass passes through a long cooling chamber called an *annealing lehr*, figure 6-4, page 85. The cooled glass is finally cut into useful sizes. *Plate glass*, which is thicker than sheet glass, is polished on both sides before it is cut.

Glass can be made with special properties. *Tempered glass* is reheated, then cooled very rapidly. This sets up stresses in the glass and produces glass that is three to five times stronger than regular glass. It is a good safety glass.

Reflective glass is regular glass with a coating of reflective material. Mirrors are an example of reflective glass. Reflective glass is used in buildings to reflect unwanted heat and light. It can also be used to create attractive architectural effects, figure 6-5. *Wired glass* is made with high-strength steel wire embedded in it. Wired glass is used to prevent breakage and for security purposes, figure 6-6.

Insulating glass consists of two sheets of glass sealed around their edges. The air space between the two sheets acts as a barrier to heat and sound, figure 6-7.

PLASTICS

Plastics includes a large group of synthetic materials that can be formed into desired shapes at some point during their processing. Plastics can be made with nearly any property desired. Some are light enough to float on water, some are stronger than steel, some will not burn, and some are as transparent as glass. Because of the limitless properties and shapes available, plastics are an important construction material. Many paints, fabrics, and caulking materials are made with plastics.

Thermosetting and Thermoplastic Materials

There are two categories of plastics, depending on how they react to heat. *Thermosetting plastic* is formed by heat and pressure

Fig. 6-5 Reflective glass is attractive and reduces the cooling load of buildings. *(PPG Industries)*

Fig. 6-6 Wired glass is used for security purposes.

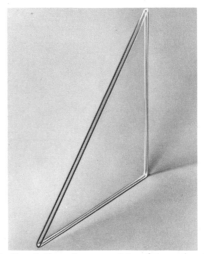

Fig. 6-7 Insulating glass consists of two sheets of glass with air space between them. *(PPG Industries)*

during its manufacture. Once thermosetting materials have been formed and cured, they cannot be reshaped. This can be compared to frying an egg. The raw egg can be molded into any shape, but once it is cooked, further heating will only burn it. *Thermoplastics* can be softened by heating. These materials can be reheated and shaped repeatedly. Thermoplastics can be compared to ice cubes. They can be melted and frozen over and over.

Sheets

Thermoplastic sheets are made by calendering. *Calendering* is the process of heating the raw material, then rolling it between polished rolls.

Transparent plastic sheets are used for unbreakable glazing in place of glass in windows and doors, figure 6-8. Acrylic sheets (Plexiglass® and Lucite®) have up to sixteen times the impact strength of glass. Polycarbonate (Lexan® and Merlon®) has four times the impact strength of acrylics. However, plastic glazing materials are more expensive than glass and scratch easily.

Extrusions

In *extrusion* a soft material, such as hot thermoplastics, is forced through a die to produce a continuous length of material. The extruded material is cooled and cut to length. Any thermoplastic can be extruded. Polyvinyl chloride (PVC) and acrylonitrile butadiene styrene (ABS) are extruded to make plastic pipe, figure 6-9. Plastic pipe is inexpensive, noncorrosive, and lightweight. Vinyl is also extruded to make plastic moldings and trim.

Fig. 6-8 Plastic glazing is used to prevent safety hazards. *(Rohm & Haas Co.)*

Fig. 6-9 Plastic pipe in a sewage treatment plant

Another important material in construction is polyethylene film. Polyethylene, a lightweight and translucent thermoplastic, is extruded into sheets 2 to 6 mils (.002″ to .006″) thick. Polyethylene film is widely used as a vapor barrier, figure 6-10. Where the film will be exposed to direct sunlight, it may be colored black to filter out damaging ultraviolet rays.

Expanded Plastics

Many plastics can be *foamed* by trapping air or gas bubbles in the cured plastic. This results in a very lightweight material with excellent heat insulating properties. Polyethylene, styrene, and urethane are the plastics most often foamed. When plastic is foamed and trimmed into slabs, it is called *foamed boards*, figure 6-11.

Fig. 6-10   Polyethylene is used to prevent moisture from passing through this wall

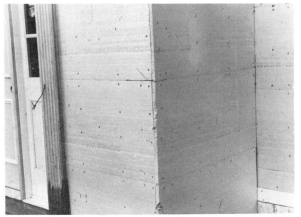

Fig. 6-11   Foamed plastic board is sometimes used for sheathing.

When it is sprayed onto a surface and foamed where it is to be used, it is said to be *foamed in place*. Foamed-in-place polyurethane is used for insulation.

Reinforced Plastics

Plastics can be reinforced with a variety of materials. A material with the desired properties is simply mixed with the raw plastic *resin* (uncured plastic). One of the most familiar reinforced plastics is referred to as fiberglass. Glass fibers with high tensile strength are mixed with polyester, epoxy, or acrylic. Fiberglass-reinforced plastics have high strength and are relatively lightweight, figure 6-12.

SEALANTS

In construction, a *sealant* is any material applied to small openings or flat surfaces to keep water out. Although there are a great number of such materials available, most construction sealants fall into one of the following groups.

Asphalt Coatings

Asphalt is a petroleum product used to make construction sealants. This black substance is either thinned with a solvent or emulsified in water to make it liquid. Asphalt sealant is applied to foundations to prevent ground

Fig. 6-12   Fiberglass reinforced plastic panels provide the only natural light in this stable.

water from seeping into the basement, figure 6-13. It is also used on roofs. In a liquid form, roofers use it to apply roof-covering materials. In a thick, semi-paste form, it is used to seal around chimneys, pipes, and other openings in the roof.

Liquid Sealants

Concrete and masonry materials are porous (have tiny openings) and can be improved by sealing their surfaces. On bridges, runways, and roads, linseed oil can be applied to seal the pores in the concrete. However, linseed oil has a tendency to pick up dirt and become discolored. On buildings where appearance is more important, silicone sealers may be used. Silicone is more expensive than linseed oil sealers, so it is not used for all applications. Both of these sealers are thin liquids which masons apply by spraying, rolling, or brushing.

Caulks

Caulking compounds are used to seal the joints between parts of a building. Commonly caulked joints include the joint between windows or doors and the wall, the joints in metal building panels, and expansion joints in sidewalks and roadways, figure 6-14. In some applications, the caulk serves primarily as a filler and can be relatively hard. However, on tall buildings,

which sway in the wind, and in expansion joints, the caulking compound must be elastic.

The most elastic (stretchable) caulks are silicone and urethane, but they are more expensive than others. Oil-base caulking compound has been used longer than others, but it cures to a hard, nonelastic material and must be replaced after a few years. Butyl caulking compound is fairly elastic, lasts well, and is less expensive than silicone and urethane. The architect generally specifies the type of caulking compound to be used. Workers apply caulking compound with hand- or air-operated guns.

ADHESIVES

Adhesives have been used for thousands of years. The ancient Egyptians used glue to apply decorative veneers to wood objects. Until the twentieth century glues made from animal parts were the only major construction adhesives. More recently, adhesives have been developed with superior strength for almost unlimited applications.

Adhesives have two important properties: adhesion and cohesion. *Adhesion* is the ability of one material to stick to another. *Cohesion* is the attraction that the molecules of a material have for one another. If an adhesive has good adhesion it will stick well to a surface. However, if that adhesive does not have good cohesion, it

Fig. 6-13 Asphalt foundation coating

Fig. 6-14 Joints between construction members are sealed with caulking compound. *(Dow Corning Corp.)*

ADHESIVE	COMMON NAME	PROPERTIES	USES
Animal glues	Hide glue Fish glue	Slow setting No water resistance	General interior woodwork Furniture Largely replaced by synthetics
Casein glue	Casein glue	Powder is mixed with water Can be used down to 35°F Water resistant Powder deteriorates with age	General woodwork where glue must be applied at low temperature Good on oily woods
Polyvinyl	White glue	Sets quickly Not water resistant Transparent when dry	General interior woodwork and furniture
Urea Formaldehyde	Plastic resin glue	Powder is mixed with water Slow setting Water resistant Heat resistant Low bond strength with oily woods	Laminated timbers and general woodworking where moisture resis- tance is desired
Resorcinol Resin	Waterproof glue	2 parts are mixed Dark color Waterproof Expensive	Exterior woodwork and laminated timbers where waterproof glue is required
Contact cement	Contact cement	Type of rubber cement Poor heat resistance Waterproof Low strength Instant bonding	Applying plastic laminates on countertops and cabinets

Fig. 6-15 Common woodworking glues and their most outstanding characteristics

will pull apart when stress is placed on the adhesive joint.

Wood Glues

Animal glue is still used to a limited extent, but other glues have largely replaced it. Most modern glues for woodwork are made with a base of some kind of plastic. These glues have superior strength and other properties. Figure 6-15 lists the most common glues and their outstanding characteristics.

Mastics

Mastics generally rely on cohesion to hold large areas of material in place. Mastics are used to apply floor coverings, roofing materials, and ceramic tiles on walls and floors. Most mastic cements have a latex or synthetic rubber base. They are generally a thick, creamy consistency and are applied with a trowel, figure 6-16. Most mastics are water resistant but do not withstand heat well.

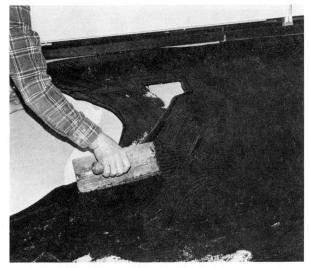

Fig. 6-16 Mastic is usually applied with a trowel.

Fig. 6-17 Epoxy is used for mending cracks in concrete.

Recent Developments in Adhesives

Modern science has developed adhesives for practically every imaginable use. Adhesives are used for assembling parts of automobiles, space vehicles, and buildings. One of these modern adhesives is *epoxy*. Epoxy is used for mending cracks in concrete, figure 6-17. Experiments are being conducted with substituting epoxy for welding on structural steel.

ACTIVITIES

A. GLAZING

When glaziers install windows, they have to cut the glass to size and secure it to the frame, using glazing compound to seal it. Glaze the frame given, following the steps in the procedure.

Equipment and Materials

Frame to be glazed
Glass, larger than frame
Glazing points
Glass cutter
Glazing compound
Steel square
Leather gloves
Putty knife

Procedure

1. Clean the frame to be glazed. Be sure that all old glazing compound and glazing points are removed.

2. Lay a piece of glass on a clean work surface and position the square to cut the glass 1/8 inch shorter than the opening.

3. Hold the glass cutter as shown in figure 6-18 and score the glass in one stroke. Apply firm pressure on the glass cutter and do not go back over the scored line.

CAUTION: Wear gloves when handling glass to protect your hands from cuts.

4. Glass should be broken immediately after it is scored. The scored line will tend to repair itself if left alone. Break the glass by bending down over the straight edge of a workbench, figure 6-19.

CAUTION: Dispose of broken scraps of glass in a safe place. Do not leave broken glass in the work area.

5. Follow the same procedure to cut the glass 1/8 inch narrower than the opening to be glazed.

6. Apply a thin bed of glazing compound to the inside of the frame.

7. Press the glass into the bed of compound and secure the glass with glazing points 3 to 5 inches apart, figure 6-20. Glazing points are pushed into the wood frame with the blade of a putty knife.

8. Seal the glass with glazing compound. Apply a full bead of compound, then smooth and trim it by drawing the putty knife along the edge, figure 6-21.

Fig. 6-18 The glass cutter scores the surface of the glass. (Gloves are removed here to show hand position, but they should be worn when cutting glass.)

Fig. 6-19 The glass is broken along the scored line. (Gloves are removed here to show hand position.)

Fig. 6-20 Glazing points are pushed into the wood frame.

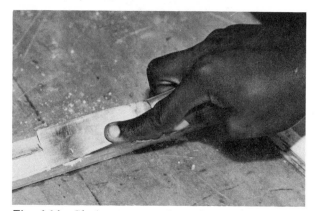

Fig. 6-21 Glazing compound can be smoothed with a putty knife.

B. APPLICATIONS OF MATERIALS

Inspect your school, home, or another structure in your community to find several uses of each of the materials listed below. Draw a cross-section sketch showing how each of the materials is used.

1. Gypsum board
2. Gypsum plaster
3. Wired glass
4. Insulating glass
5. Plastic sheet
6. Plastic film
7. Extruded plastic
8. Asphalt coating
9. Caulking compound
10. Mastic adhesive

REVIEW

Material Descriptions

For each of the materials listed, give (a) one important property, and (b) one application of the material in construction.

1. Polyethylene
2. Gypsum wallboard
3. Mastic
4. Gypsum lath
5. Tempered glass
6. Insulating glass
7. Extruded PVC
8. Foamed plastics
9. Asphalt sealant
10. Silicone sealant
11. Silicone caulking compound
12. Oil-base caulking compound

SECTION 3
SECTION 3
SECTION 3
SECTION 3

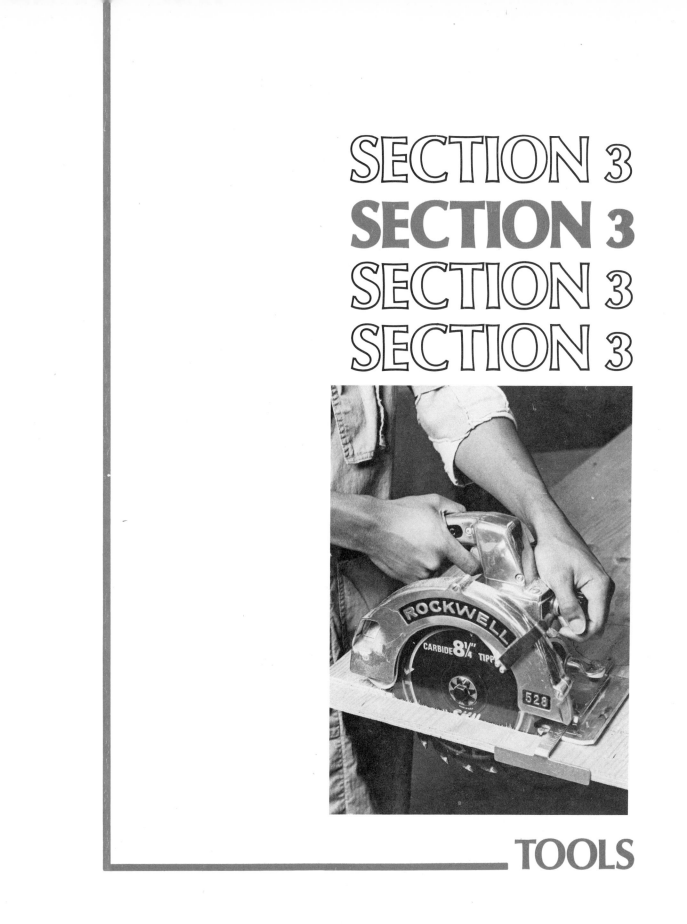

TOOLS

UNIT 7.
MEASUREMENT AND LAYOUT TOOLS

OBJECTIVES

After completing this unit, the student will be able to:

- describe the measurement and layout tools commonly used in the construction industry.

- take accurate measurements to the smallest graduations indicated on the measuring tool being used.

- lay out square corners and angles.

- determine the levelness or plumbness of any line.

A major factor in the quality of any construction project is the degree of accuracy in its layout and measurements. Absolute accuracy can never be achieved, only a relative degree of accuracy. It is always possible to take any measurement more accurately.

Persons in the construction trades should never allow preventable errors in their measurements. Some errors occur naturally due to expansion and contraction during heating and cooling and inaccuracy of equipment. However, with proper equipment, errors can be kept to a minimum.

SYSTEMS OF MEASUREMENT

The *English system of linear measure* is used to measure most distances in building construction. In this system the *yard* is considered the base unit, figure 7-1. The yard is divided into three *feet*; the foot is divided into twelve *inches*: and the inch is divided into fractions of an inch. The inch is divided into two parts (or halves of an inch); the halves may be divided into two parts each, or quarters of an inch; the quarters are divided into two parts each, or eighths of an inch; the eighths are divided into two parts each, or sixteenths; etc.

These are the *fractional parts of an inch*. The fractional parts of an inch are named according to the number of these parts that make up an inch. It is possible to continue dividing these fractional parts until the desired degree of accuracy is reached.

Dimensions for construction are normally specified in feet, inches, and fractional parts of an inch. It is customary to reduce fractions to

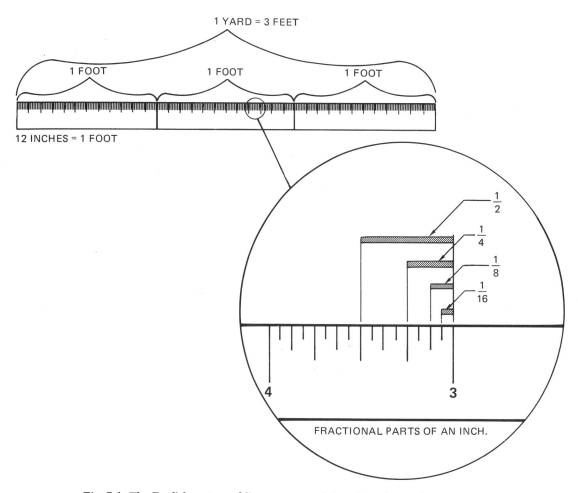

Fig. 7-1 The English system of linear measure is based on the yard. The yard is divided into three feet; each foot into twelve inches; and each inch into fractional parts.

their simplest terms. For example, 26 and 6/16 inches is expressed as 2 feet, 2 3/8 inches. This is commonly written 2'-2 3/8".

The United States is currently adopting a new system of measurement called the *metric system*. This is the system used throughout most of the world. Conversion to the metric system will simplify measurements and calculations. However, this system will probably not be used extensively in construction for several years.

Construction involves the coordination of a large number of materials and parts. The standards for this coordination have been established using the English system. Also, all existing structures are designed and built using the English system. Maintenance and additions to these structures would be more difficult if another system of measurement were used. Tools are available with metric scales and markings for use where necessary.

MEASUREMENT TOOLS

Nearly all of the measuring of distances, called *linear measure*, done in the construction of a building is accomplished with either steel tape measures or folding rules. Measurement of area and volume are only adaptations of linear measure and can also be accomplished with these tools. Area is found by measuring width and length. Volume is found by measuring width, length, and height or depth. All of these involve measuring distances.

Fig. 7-2 Steel tape measures are available in lengths ranging from 6 feet to 100 feet. *(The Stanley Tool Div.)*

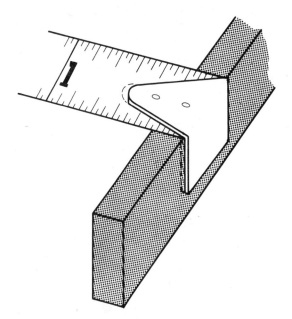

Fig. 7-3 Most 6- to 25-foot tape measures have a sliding hook so they can take both inside and outside measures. As the hook is pushed against a surface for taking inside measurements, it slides back to compensate for its thickness.

FOR INSIDE MEASURE ADD 2"

Fig. 7-4 For inside measurements the width of the case is added to the tape reading.

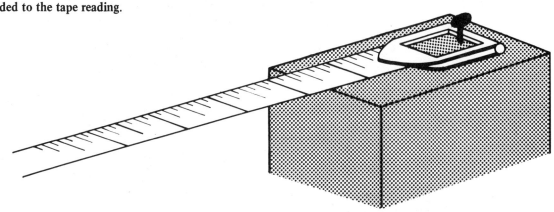

Fig. 7-5 The fitting on a long tape can be hooked on a nail.

Tape measures. Steel tape measures, figure 7-2, are available in several lengths ranging from 6 feet to 100 feet. The 8- to 20-foot lengths are most often used for measuring the sizes and position of building parts. The greater lengths are used to establish building lines and to lay out the building. The shorter sizes usually have a sliding hook on the end so that both inside and outside measurements can be taken, figure 7-3. The size of the case is marked on these tape measures so that inside measurements can be taken, figure 7-4. The longer steel tape measures generally have a fitting that can be hooked over the outside of a corner or slipped over a nail, figure 7-5.

Fig. 7-6 Wood folding rule with metal extension *(The Stanley Tool Div.)*

Fig. 7-7 A folding extension rule can be used for inside measurements.

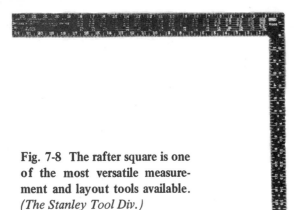

Fig. 7-8 The rafter square is one of the most versatile measurement and layout tools available. *(The Stanley Tool Div.)*

Fig. 7-9 Stair gauges are clamped on the square to lay out repeated angles.

Folding Rule. The folding rule, figure 7-6, is another tool commonly used by construction workers. This tool is especially useful in situations where the flexibility of a tape measure is a disadvantage. Many folding rules are equipped with an extension slide in one end. This brass slide allows the rule to be extended for taking inside measurements, figure 7-7.

LAYOUT TOOLS

Layout tools include all of those that are used for laying out lines and checking angles.

Rafter Square. One of the most commonly used tools for layout work is the rafter square, or framing square, figure 7-8. It includes several tables and scales for laying out octagons, laying out rafters of several types, determining the number of board feet in a piece of lumber (a board foot is 144 cubic inches of lumber), and linear measure scales.

The variety of uses of the rafter square is beyond the scope of this discussion. Although the rafter square is also used as a measurement tool, it is listed here with layout tools because of its great value in layout work. Nearly all building-trade workers rely on it for checking the squareness of corners and laying out parts.

Stair Gauges. Stair gauges are used with the rafter square when several parts must be laid out with the same dimensions. These small fittings are clamped to the square to maintain the desired setting, figure 7-9.

Try Square. The try square is a small square with a 6- to 12-inch blade, figure 7-10. The

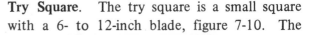

Fig. 7-10 Try square *(The Stanley Tool Div.)*

handle of the try square has a flat surface which allows it to stand up for checking vertical surfaces. The try square is especially useful for checking the flatness of small surfaces or laying out right angles (90-degree angles), figure 7-11.

Combination Square. The combination square, figure 7-12, has a movable head on a 12-inch blade. The head of the combination square has a right-angle surface, a 45-degree angle surface, and a spirit level. The combination square can be substituted for a try square in most cases. In addition, it can be used for laying out 45-degree angles.

Fig. 7-11 Squaring a mark with the try square

Fig. 7-12 The combination square can be used for checking 90- and 45-degree angles. *(The Stanley Tool Div.)*

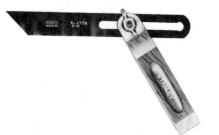

Fig. 7-13 The sliding T bevel can be adjusted for any angle. *(The Stanley Tool Div.)*

Sliding T Bevel. The sliding T bevel, figure 7-13, consists of a handle with movable blade. This blade can be locked in any position, making it useful for laying out various angles. It can be adjusted for 90-degree and 45-degree angles, but rafter squares, try squares, and combination squares are generally preferred for this.

Marking Gauge. The marking gauge is used for marking a line parallel with an edge. Figure 7-14 shows the parts of a marking gauge. In use it is held by the head with the pin pointing slightly toward the user. With the face against the edge of the material, it is pushed away from the user so the pin scribes the desired line, figure 7-15. The scale on the beam of the marking gauge should not be relied upon for accuracy. Adjust the marking gauge with another measuring device.

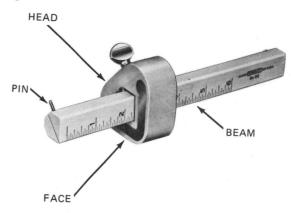

Fig. 7-14 Parts of a marking gauge. *(The Stanley Tool Div.)*

Fig. 7-15 Scribing a line with a marking gauge

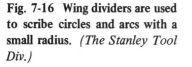

Fig. 7-16 Wing dividers are used to scribe circles and arcs with a small radius. *(The Stanley Tool Div.)*

Fig. 7-17 Trammel points can be attached to a beam of any length to scribe large circles and arcs. *(The Stanley Tool Div.)*

Fig. 7-18 The chalk line reel applies powdered chalk to the line as it is pulled from the case. *(The Stanley Tool Div.)*

Dividers and Trammel Points. Circles and arcs are laid out with dividers, figure 7-16. For a small radius, the dividers are set with a separate measuring device. With the desired radius set, one leg is held on the center of the circle or arc and the other scribes a curved line. For larger radii, trammel points are attached to a bench rule or piece of wood. Once the trammel points are set they can be used in the same manner as dividers. The radius possible with trammel points is limited only by the length of the piece to which they are attached, figure 7-17.

Chalk Line Reel. To mark long straight lines, such as a partition on a floor, a chalk line reel is used, figure 7-18. The reel case contains powdered chalk that coats the line as it is pulled from the reel. The chalk-covered line is then stretched tight while a point near its midpoint is pulled away from the surface to be marked. When the line is released it snaps against the surface to be marked and the chalk is deposited on the surface. This marks a straight line, figure 7-19.

Lines similar to that used in a chalk line reel are also used by masons to indicate the desired height of a *course* (row) of bricks or blocks. The line is stretched along the wall and the masonry units are leveled with this line as they are put in place, figure 7-20. The important characteristics of this line are its ability to be pulled tight without stretching and its strength.

Fig. 7-19 Snapping a chalk line

Fig. 7-20 This mason is laying blocks to a line. *(Richard T. Kreh, Sr.)*

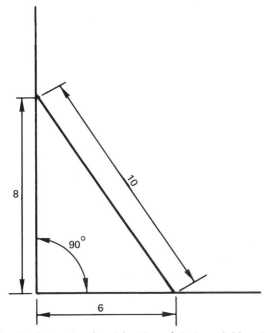

Fig. 7-21 A triangle with sides of 6, 8, and 10 units of length includes a right angle.

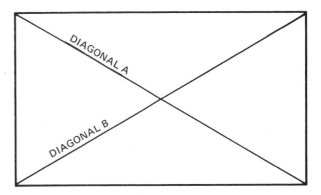

Fig. 7-22 When the length of diagonal A equals the length of diagonal B, the rectangle is square.

6-8-10 Method and Checking Diagonals. Although they are not tools in the usual sense, these are valuable techniques for checking the squareness of large corners and rectangles. It can be proven mathematically that any triangle with sides of 6, 8, and 10 units of length includes a right angle. This principle is used in building construction by measuring 6 feet along one side of a corner, and 8 feet along the other side. If the corner is a 90-degree angle the distance between these points is 10 feet, figure 7-21.

The squareness of a rectangle or square can also be checked by measuring the diagonals. When all of the corners are 90 degrees, the diagonals are of equal length, figure 7-22.

LEVELS

Spirit Level. The spirit level, figure 7-23, makes use of the fact that an air bubble rises to the top of a container filled with liquid. A small, slightly curved glass tube (*vial*) is nearly filled with alcohol (*spirit*). The vial is mounted in an aluminum, magnesium, or wood straightedge.

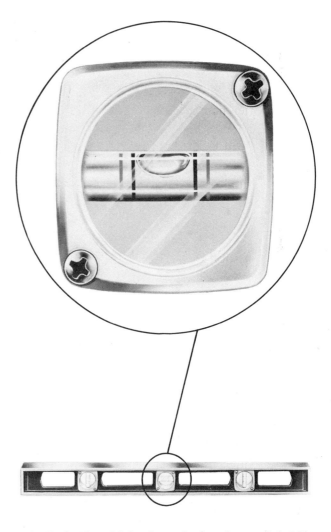

Fig. 7-23 The spirit level uses the fact that an air bubble rises to the top of a container of liquid. *(The Stanley Tool Div.)*

Fig. 7-24 This carpenter uses a 2-foot spirit level to determine if the woodwork is plumb. *(C-E Morgan)*

The level position is marked on the vial. At least one vial is mounted in such a way that it indicates when the straightedge is *plumb*, meaning in a perfectly vertical position, figure 7-24.

Spirit levels are available in sizes ranging from less than one foot to six feet long. Workers in many of the building trades use spirit levels. Carpenters usually use 2-foot levels to install rough and finished woodwork, while masons frequently use longer levels to check their work.

Line Level. The line level, figure 7-25, is a small spirit level with fittings so it can be hung on a tightly stretched line. The line level is used to check the levelness of a line between two points that are too far apart to be checked with a conventional 2- to 6-foot spirit level.

Note: All levels must be treated with great care. A sudden jolt may move the vial within its mounting, making the level inaccurate.

Plumb bob. The plumb bob, figure 7-26, is a pointed weight with some means for attaching a string. When the plumb bob is suspended on its string, the force of gravity causes the string to be perfectly plumb or vertical. In this way a plumb bob can be used to check the plumbness of a line, much the same as a spirit level might be used.

Builder's Level. The builder's level, like a spirit level, is a device for checking the levelness between two or more points. In addition, it can be used for measuring angles on a horizontal plane. Unlike the transit level, it cannot be used for measuring angles on a vertical plane. The basic parts of the builder's level are shown in figure 7-27. The functions of these parts are as follows:

- *Telescope* contains the lens, focusing adjustment, and cross hairs for sighting.
- *Telescope level* is a spirit level used for leveling the instrument prior to use.
- *Clamp screw* locks the instrument in position horizontally.
- *Fine adjusting screw* makes fine adjustments in a horizontal plane.
- *Leveling base* holds four leveling screws for leveling the instrument prior to use.
- *Protractor* is a scale graduated in degrees and minutes (a minute is 1/60 of a degree) for measuring horizontal angles.

Fig. 7-25 The line level is a small spirit level with special fittings so it can be suspended on a tightly stretched line. *(The Stanley Tool Div.)*

Fig. 7-26 The plumb bob causes a line to hang in a perfectly vertical position.

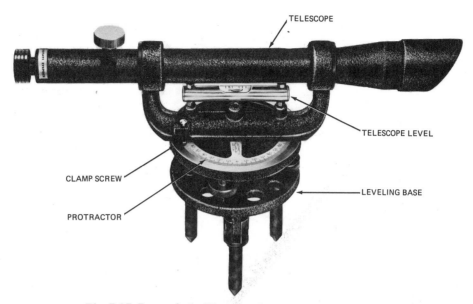

TELESCOPE

TELESCOPE LEVEL

CLAMP SCREW

LEVELING BASE

PROTRACTOR

Fig. 7-27 Parts of a builder's level *(The L.S. Starrett Co.)*

Two accessories are required for most operations performed with the builder's level. The *tripod* is a separate 3-legged stand that provides a stable mounting base for the builder's level. A *target rod* is a separate device with a scale graduated in inches and fractional parts of an inch. This is what one actually focuses on when sighting through the telescope.

The builder's level is used by workers in several of the building trades during many phases of construction. It is used to check the depth and levelness of *excavations* (holes dug or earth moved for foundations or grading), the levelness of footings and foundation walls, the levelness of wood and steel framing, and the positioning of forms for concrete work.

Note: The builder's level is a delicate instrument and must be handled with care. When not in use, the lens should be protected with the lens cap. It should always be stored and transported in a case designed for that purpose. Even when secured in its case, the builder's level should not be subjected to rough handling. Do not rub dust or dirt off the lens. Blow it off or brush it off lightly.

───── **ACTIVITIES** ──────────────────────

A. MARKING STOCK

Accurate measurement and layout are important factors in the construction industry. In this activity you will practice measuring with some of the tools discussed in this unit.

Equipment and Materials

1″ x 12″ x 24″ piece of softwood
Tape measure or folding rule
Combination square or rafter square
Compass or wing dividers

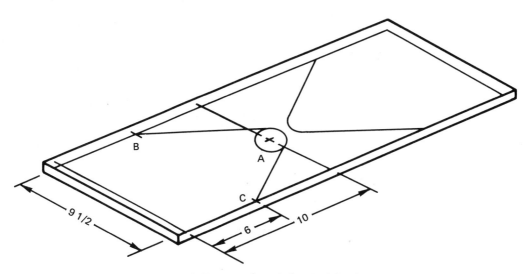

Fig. 7-28 Layout of stock for Activity A.

Procedure

1. Two duplicate pieces of wood stock will be laid out on the ends of a tote carrier that will be constructed in another unit.

2. Using the square, check to see that one end of the lumber is square with one long edge. If not, mark a square line near the end.

3. With the tape measure or folding rule, and using the blade of the square as a straightedge, mark a line 9 1/2 inches from the square edge.

4. Working from the square edge, mark a square line across the piece 10 inches from the square end. Mark the center of this line (point A, figure 7-28).

5. Using point A as the center, scribe a circle with a 1-inch radius.

6. Mark points B and C, 6 inches from the square end.

7. Using the blade of the square as a straightedge, draw lines from points B and C to the edge of the circle.

8. Repeat steps 2 through 7 to lay out the second part on the opposite end of the lumber.

B.   USING A SPIRIT LEVEL

Construction workers use spirit levels to determine the plumbness or levelness of work they are installing. Work carefully while following the procedures in this activity.

Equipment and Materials

2-foot spirit level
Line level
Chalk line
Tape measure

Procedure

1. Mark a point near one end of a vertical surface. The surface should be at least eight feet long.

2. Use a line level to find a level point on the opposite end of the surface. Keep the line tight and move one end of it up and down slightly until the bubble in the level is centered between the marks on the vial.

3. Snap a chalk line between these two points.

4. Measure to find the midpoint of the chalk line snapped in step 3. At this point, draw a plumb line using the 2-foot spirit level and chalk.

C. LAYING OUT CORNERS

The 6-8-10 method is a quick and accurate way to check the squareness of a rectangle or square. Carpenters sometimes use this method to check the squareness of a wall they are erecting. In this activity you will lay out four corners using the 6-8-10 method.

Equipment and Materials

Four wooden stakes approximately 3 feet long
Hatchet or heavy hammer
100-foot tape measure
200 feet of mason's line

Note: Four chalk marks on a paved surface may be substituted for the wooden stakes.

Procedure

1. Drive a stake in the ground at a point designated by the instructor. Approximately 2 feet of the stake should be left above ground.

2. Drive a second stake exactly 50 feet from the first. Stretch a line between these two stakes.

3. Using the 6-8-10 method, stretch another line at right angles to the first one. Mark a point on one line 6 feet from the stake, and on the other line 8 feet from the stake. When these two points are 10 feet apart the lines are at right angles.

4. Drive a third stake 30 feet from the second one and along this right-angle line.

5. Repeat steps 3 and 4 to drive the fourth stake 30 feet from the first one.

6. Check the accuracy of the lines by measuring the diagonals of the rectangle. If the diagonals are equal, the stakes are properly located; if not, correct the error.

7. Leave these stakes in place for the next activity.

D. LEVELING CORNERS WITH THE BUILDER'S LEVEL

A cement mason may sometimes check the levelness of a concrete form. To do this, the mason measures the height at each corner of the form using a builder's level.

In this activity you will check the levelness of the rectangle measured in Activity C using a builder's level.

Equipment and Materials

Builder's level
Tripod
Target rod
Marking crayon

Procedure

1. Set up the tripod in the approximate center of the rectangle laid out in Activity C. The legs of the tripod should be approximately three feet apart and firmly set in the ground. Remove the protective cover from the head of the tripod. The tripod should be nearly level.

Note: The builder's level is a delicate instrument and should be handled with care. When not in use, it should be stored in the case designed for that purpose. All manufacturers supply instructions for setting up and using their instruments. The instructions given here are general guides only. The manufacturer's instructions should be consulted for more detail.

2. Remove the level from its case and set it in place on top of the tripod. Hand tighten the clamp screw.

3. Turn the leveling screws down so they contact the tripod plate.

4. Turn the telescope so that it is over one pair of leveling screws. Adjust these two screws so that the telescope level indicates that the telescope is level, figure 7-29.

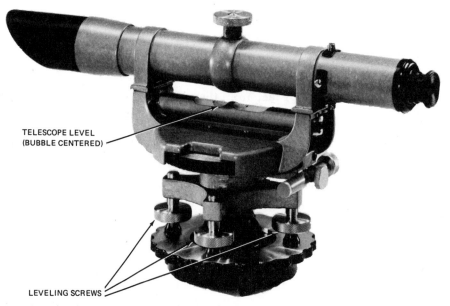

TELESCOPE LEVEL
(BUBBLE CENTERED)

LEVELING SCREWS

Fig. 7-29 Adjust leveling screws so the telescope level indicates that the instrument is level. *(Keuffel & Esser Co.)*

5. Turn the telescope so that it is over the other pair of leveling screws. Adjust these two screws so the telescope is level.

6. Repeat this over each pair of leveling screws alternately, until the telescope is level in all positions.

Note: Once the telescope has been leveled, be careful not to kick or move the tripod legs. If the tripod is accidentally moved or jarred, repeat the leveling procedure.

7. Remove the lens cap from the telescope. Have a partner hold the target rod on top of one of the stakes while the telescope is aimed and focused. The markings on the target rod should be in sharp focus.

8. Record the reading on the target rod at this stake.

9. Repeat steps 7 and 8 at each stake. *Note:* Care must be exercised not to move the tripod when aiming the telescope.

10. Mark the three highest stakes at the level of the lowest one. For example, if the target rod read 41 1/2 inches at the lowest stake and 40 inches at another stake, the higher stake should be marked 1 1/2 inch from the top, figure 7-30.

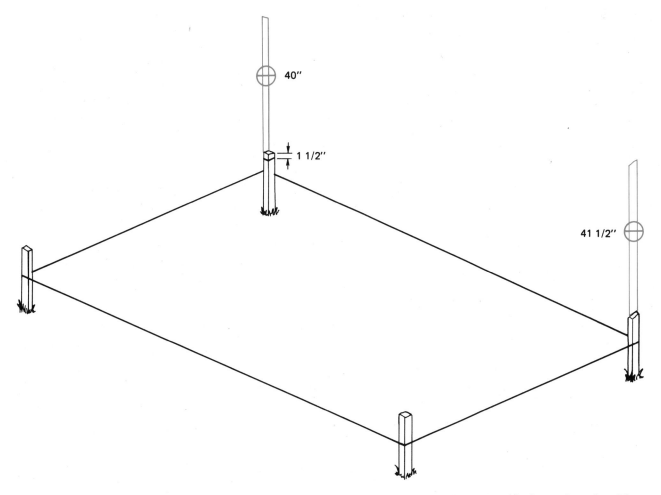

Fig. 7-30 The numbers on a level rod increase from bottom to top. The higher the reading, the lower the stake. The target on the level rod on the left is actually 41 1/2″ above the mark on the stake.

REVIEW

1. List the measurement and layout tools that would be used by workers in each of the following trades:

   a. Mason
   b. Carpenter
   c. Excavator
   d. Electrician
   e. Sheet metal worker

2. Refer to a catalog provided by the instructor and list a complete set of measurement and layout tools. Include a brief description of each, indicating important features and price.

3. Give the dimension indicated in each of the following:

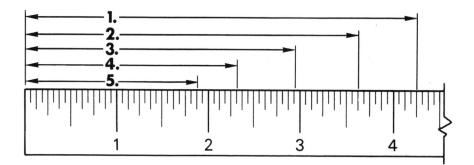

UNIT 8.

CUTTING, SAWING, AND DRILLING TOOLS

OBJECTIVES

After completing this unit, the student will be able to:

- list and identify the cutting, sawing, and drilling tools used most often by construction workers.

- name the proper tool to use for cutting, sawing, and drilling operations.

- demonstrate the proper way to perform basic operations with cutting, sawing, and drilling tools.

Most construction materials must be cut to a specified size and shape, then joined by a variety of techniques. A few materials are available from the supplier already cut to size. Examples of such materials are concrete blocks, bricks, pipe fittings, and precut studs. However, in some cases even these materials must be cut for special applications or joining techniques. While it is important for construction workers to be able to use measurement and layout tools accurately, it is equally important to be skilled in the use of cutting, sawing, and drilling tools. Any accuracy achieved through careful measurement and layout will be lost if the materials are not cut to size accurately.

CUTTING TOOLS

Cutting is an operation that is familiar to everyone. However, cutting is often confused with sawing. The operations are different in that *sawing* involves removing a small amount of material from the saw cut, while in *cutting* a sharp edge parts the material without removing chips.

The cutting principle is basically the same regardless of the material being cut. Cutting tools vary according to the materials because of the differences in the materials. For example, a thin knife-like edge may be suitable for cutting soft plastic. On the other hand, to cut hard materials, such as steel, a thicker, stronger cutting edge is required.

Fig. 8-1 Wood chisel *(The Stanley Tool Div.)*

111

Chisels

Chisels are used for making small cuts in wood, metal, and masonry materials. *Wood chisels*, figure 8-1, are fitted with a wood or plastic handle. The thin, sharp cutting edge of a wood chisel is ground with a bevel on one side only. Wood chisels are available in assorted sizes from 1/4 inch wide to 2 1/2 inches wide.

Wood chisels should never be struck with a hammer. Frequently, hand pressure is all that is required, but a soft-faced mallet can be used when additional force is needed. The depth of cut can be controlled by placing the beveled edge of the chisel against the surface of the wood, figure 8-2.

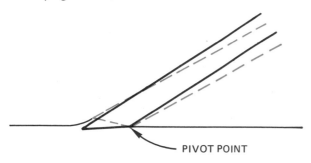

PIVOT POINT

Fig. 8-2 The depth of cut with a chisel can be controlled by placing the beveled side down and raising and lowering the handle.

Fig. 8-3 Cold chisel *(The Stanley Tool Div.)*

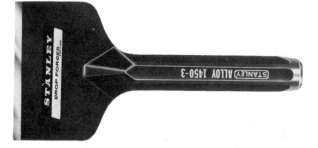

Fig. 8-4 Brick set chisel *(The Stanley Tool Div.)*

CAUTION: Wood chisels in proper condition are very sharp. Never place either hand in front of the chisel. Always cut away from the body.

Cold chisels, figure 8-3, are used for cutting metal and masonry materials. They are made of a single piece of hardened and tempered steel. Cold chisels have a blunter bevel than wood chisels, but they are still ground to a sharp edge. Cold chisels are struck with a hammer and, for this reason, do not have handles.

CAUTION: If the head of a cold chisel becomes mushroomed, the sharp edges should be ground off before the chisel is used. The sharp edges could cause an injury.

A *brick set*, figure 8-4, is quite similar to a cold chisel. Bricklayers use it to cut bricks and concrete blocks to size. The cutting edge of the brick set is the width of a standard brick. Bricks and blocks are cut by scoring each side with one sharp blow on the brick set, then breaking the unit with a final blow on this score line. Bricks and blocks can be cut with a cold chisel or a mason's hammer, but the wide edge of the brick set results in a straighter cut.

Planes

Carpenters use planes to remove a small amount of wood from the surface of a piece of lumber or millwork. *Bench planes* come in several sizes and each size is named differently. In order of their sizes from largest to smallest they are jointer, fore, jack, smooth, and block. The largest planes, *jointer planes* and *fore planes*, are used primarily for producing flat surfaces. The smallest, the *block plane*, figure 8-5, is used for planing end grain and where it is

Fig. 8-5 Block plane *(The Stanley Tool Div.)*

Fig. 8-6 Jack plane *(The Stanley Tool Div.)*

Fig. 8-7(A) At the beginning of the stroke, pressure is applied to the knob.

Fig. 8-7(B) At midstroke, pressure is applied to both the handle and the knob.

Fig. 8-7(C) At the end of the stroke, pressure is applied to the handle.

convenient to hold the plane in only one hand. The *jack plane*, figure 8-6, is the most frequently used, all-around plane.

When planing the face or edge of a piece of wood, hold the piece securely in a vise. Always plane with the grain, never across the grain. Place the front of the plane bottom on the wood and push forward while applying pressure downward on the knob, figure 8-7. As the front of the plane passes over the far end of the wood, relax the pressure on the knob but maintain pressure downward on the handle. If the plane is sharp, properly aligned, and properly used, a long smooth curled shaving should form.

To plane the end grain, precautions must be taken to prevent the far edge from splitting. This can be done by placing a piece of scrap against the far edge; chamfering the edge in the waste portion; or by planing from one edge toward the center, then from the other edge toward the center, figure 8-8.

PLANE END GRAIN
HALFWAY FROM EACH EDGE

EXCESS (WASTE) STOCK
CHAMFERED ON CORNER

WASTE STOCK BUTTED TO
FINISHED WIDTH

Fig. 8-8 Three methods of planing the end grain

Snips

It is frequently necessary for construction workers to cut sheet metal. Carpenters and masons cut sheet metal flashing to seal the joints between walls and roofs, chimneys and roofs, and other features. Sheet metal workers use large amounts of sheet metal in the ducts for heating, ventilating, and air-conditioning systems. The most common hand tool for cutting sheet metal is *aviation snips*, figure 8-9. Three types of aviation snips are available for cutting straight lines and gradual curves, cutting left-hand curves, and cutting right-hand curves.

Utility Knife

The *utility knife*, figure 8-10, is also used by workers in several of the building trades. It is often called a *Sheetrock knife* because it is used extensively for cutting *gypsum wall board* (Sheetrock®).

SAWING TOOLS

As mentioned earlier, sawing removes small chips of material from the saw cut *(kerf)*. The sawing principle is the same regardless of the material being sawed. However, different arrangements of teeth are required for different materials. Saw blades also vary depending on the kind of cut to be made. The coarseness of a saw is called its *pitch*. Saw pitch is measured in points per inch. This is the number of points of saw teeth in one inch of the blade, figure 8-11.

Crosscut Saws

Crosscut saws are used to saw wood across the grain. Crosscut saws for general purposes usually have 8 to 12 points per inch. The teeth are filed at a slight angle so that they come to sharp points at alternate sides. The top third of each tooth is *set* (bent slightly) to the sharp-pointed side, figure 8-12. Set is required in most saws to produce a kerf that is slightly wider than the thickness of the blade. This prevents the saw from binding in the kerf.

Fig. 8-9   Aviation snips *(The Stanley Tool Div.)*

Fig. 8-10   Utility knife *(The Stanley Tool Div.)*

Fig. 8-11   Saw pitch is measured in points per inch.

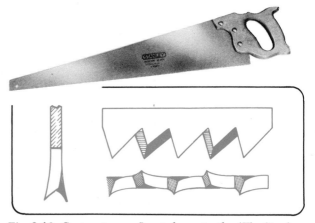

Fig. 8-12   Crosscut saw. Inset shows teeth. *(The Stanley Tool Div.)*

As the crosscut saw is pushed forward, the first parts to contact the wood are the sharp points at the sides of the kerf. This cuts the wood fibers off before they are removed. As the teeth cut deeper, the body of the tooth removes the sawdust from the kerf.

CAUTION: A properly sharpened saw should be handled with care. Keep hands away from the saw teeth. Never allow the teeth to contact metal or other hard materials.

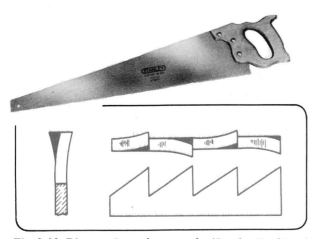

Fig. 8-13 Rip saw. Inset shows teeth. *(Stanley Tool Div.)*

Fig. 8-14 Coping saw *(The Stanley Tool Div.)*

Rip Saw

A *rip saw* is used to cut with the grain of wood. This is called *ripping*. Rip saws generally have four to eight points per inch. Rip saw teeth are filed straight across the blade, so that each tooth is chisel shaped, figure 8-13. The teeth are set much like crosscut teeth to prevent binding.

As the rip saw teeth contact the wood, the full thickness of each tooth chisels out a small amount of wood. Because the sawing is in the direction of the wood grain, it is not necessary to cut the fibers off before removing them. Rip saw teeth are usually larger than crosscut teeth because they must remove larger amounts of material in making long rip cuts.

Coping Saw

Sometimes in fitting molding to inside corners, carpenters cut the profile of one piece of molding on the end of the other. This is called *coping*. To make these intricate cuts, a coping saw is used. A *coping saw* is a small frame which holds a thin, fine-pitch crosscut blade, figure 8-14. Coping saws are useful for all kinds of sawing where intricate shapes are involved. The blade is installed so the teeth point toward the handle. The cutting action occurs as the saw is pulled, not pushed.

Compass Saw

The *compass saw* is another crosscut saw for sawing curves. A compass saw is constructed more like an ordinary handsaw, but the blade is narrower and shorter, allowing it to saw around curves, figure 8-15.

Backsaw

The *backsaw* is a short, fine-toothed crosscut saw with a reinforced back, figure 8-16. Because of their rigidity and fine teeth, backsaws are used for sawing joints in wood and other sawing where a high degree of accuracy and a smooth cut are important.

Miter Box

A *miter* is a cut at a 45-degree angle frequently used to join two pieces at a corner. To guide the saw in making miter joints, carpenters use a *miter box*. A wooden miter box can be constructed of three pieces of hardwood, forming a trough into which accurate saw kerfs are presawed.

Fig. 8-15 Compass saw *(The Stanley Tool Div.)*

Fig. 8-16 Backsaw *(The Stanley Tool Div.)*

Most carpenters and cabinetmakers use mechanical miter boxes. This is a metal frame holding a long backsaw, figure 8-17. The frame can be adjusted for any angle from 90 degrees to approximately 30 degrees. Usually a stop is provided to help locate the 90-degree, 45-degree right, and 45-degree left positions.

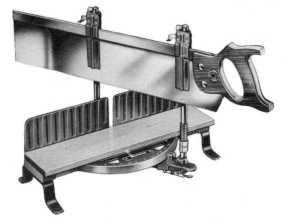

Fig. 8-17 Steel miter box and saw *(Stanley Tool Div.)*

Hacksaw

Metal can be sawed, much like wood, with a *hacksaw*. A hacksaw consists of a metal frame, often adjustable in size, with some means for attaching and tightening the blade, figure 8-18. Hacksaw blades are made of high-carbon steel with fine-pitch teeth. The teeth on a hacksaw should point away from the handle so that the cutting action occurs on the forward stroke.

Fig. 8-18 Hacksaw *(Stanley Tool Div.)*

DRILLING TOOLS

The principle used in drilling tools is similar to the cutting and sawing principles. The greatest difference is that the cutting surfaces are moved in a circle instead of a straight line. All drilling operations require two devices: the tool with the cutting edges, called a *bit*, and a device to turn the bit.

Hand Drill

The *hand drill*, figure 8-19, has a *chuck* which holds the bit and a crank with gears to increase its speed. Because most hand drills have a three-jaw chuck, they are used to turn bits with a round shank.

Bit Brace

The *bit brace*, figure 8-20, is a crank-shaped tool with a two-jaw chuck. The two-jaw chuck of a bit brace is intended for turning wood-working bits with a squared end, called a *tang*. Bit braces also have a ratchet near the chuck that allows them to be turned one way or the other. This feature is helpful where there is not enough space to swing the handle in a full circle.

Fig. 8-19 Hand drill *(The Stanley Tool Div.)*

Fig. 8-20 Bit brace *(The Stanley Tool Div.)*

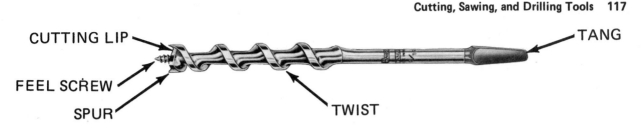

CUTTING LIP

FEEL SCREW

SPUR

TWIST

TANG

Fig. 8-21 Parts of an auger bit *(The Stanley Tool Div.)*

Auger Bit

Auger bits are used for boring holes in wood. They have a square tang that allows them to be used in the two-jaw chuck of a bit brace. The parts of an auger bit are shown in figure 8-21. As the bit is turned, the feed screw pulls it into the wood. The spurs cut off the wood fibers at the outside of the hole. The cutting lips chisel the cut wood away from the surface so the twist can carry it out of the hole.

Auger bits are available in sizes from #3 to #16. The number, which is stamped on the tang, indicates the diameter in sixteenths of an inch. For example, a #7 auger bit bores a 7/16-inch hole and a #12 auger bit bores a 3/4-inch (12/16-inch) hole.

To prevent the spurs from splintering the back of the workpiece as they cut through, two methods can be used: (1) bore through until the feed screw comes through, then finish the hole from the other side; or (2) clamp a piece of scrap wood to the back of the workpiece.

Expansive Bit

An *expansive bit*, figure 8-22, is like an adjustable auger bit. The cutting lip and spur (expansive bits have only one of each) can be adjusted to any size from approximately 7/8 inch to approximately 3 inches. Expansive bits are useful for boring holes larger than those for which auger bits are available and for odd-sized holes.

Twist Drills

Twist drills are formed of a solid, straight piece of hardened steel, figure 8-23. They have a round shank that is turned with a hand drill or

Fig. 8-22 Expansive bit with extra cutter *(The Stanley Tool Div.)*

Fig. 8-23 High-speed steel twist drill bit *(Cleveland Twist Drill, an Acme-Cleveland Company)*

CARBIDE INSERT

Fig. 8-24 Carbide-tipped masonry drill bit *(Cleveland Twist Drill, an Acme-Cleveland Company)*

electric drill having a three-jaw chuck. The cutting lips are ground at an angle. The center starts the hole and, as the bit penetrates the surface, a quarter portion of the cutting edge contacts the surface of the hole. Most twist drills are ground with a 118-degree angle between the two cutting lips. These are suitable for drilling in wood and most metal. By altering the angles of the cutting lips, twist drills can be manufactured for drilling in a variety of materials. For drilling in concrete and masonry materials, special twist drills are manufactured with *carbide* (a very hard, man-made material) cutting edges, figure 8-24.

Twist drills are sized by four systems: number sizes, letter sizes, metric sizes, and fractional-inch sizes. Most drilling done in construction uses fractional-inch drill bits. These range from 1/16 inch to 1/2 inch with straight shank and larger with the shank portion reduced in size to fit normal chucks. Most hand drills cannot hold drills over 3/8 inch in diameter.

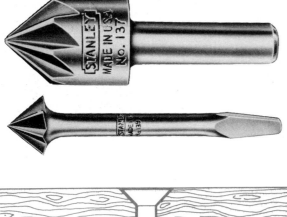

Fig. 8-25 Two types of countersinks and a countersink hole. *(The Stanley Tool Div.)*

Countersink

One operation that is performed frequently with drills is making holes for screws. One common type of screw, called a flathead screw, requires an enlarged hole near the surface of the material being fastened. This part of the hole is called a countersink and is formed with a tool called a *countersink*, figure 8-25. Countersinks can be purchased with a round shank and made

Fig. 8-26 Center punch. *(Snap On Tool Corp.)*

of tool steel for countersinking metal. They can also be purchased with a square tang for use in a bit brace. Countersinks that are intended for use in wood should never be used in metal.

Center Punch

Although they are not a type of drill, center punches are discussed here because they are frequently used in drilling operations. A *center punch* is a solid piece of tool steel, usually round, with a point ground on one end, figure 8-26. To help start a drill at a precise point, a small dimple is first made with a center punch. This holds the point of the drill in place as the hole is started.

A spring-loaded type of center punch, called a *centering punch*, can be used to locate the starting points for holes to fasten hardware to wood. The centering punch has a beveled end that fits into the countersink of the hardware. The punch is then struck with a hammer, leaving a dimple at the starting point.

ACTIVITIES

A.   CUTTING OPERATIONS

Drywall installers and sheet metal workers use a variety of cutting and measuring tools. Be particularly careful when working with sharp-edged instruments.

Equipment and Materials

Piece of gypsum wallboard, approximately 2' x 2'
Scraps of aluminum flashing or other sheet metal
Utility knife
Aviation snips
Rafter square
Dividers
Pencil

Procedure (I)

1. Lay out an 18-inch square on the face of the wallboard. The lines should extend to the edge of the wallboard.

2. Using the utility knife, cut the paper on the lines marked in step 1.

CAUTION: Do not place your hands in front of the knife.

3. Bend the wallboard away from the cutting side to break the gypsum core.

4. Cut the paper on the back of the wallboard.

Procedure (II)

1. Lay out several square corners on the sheet metal and practice cutting on these lines with aviation snips.

2. Scribe a 6-inch circle on the sheet metal and cut out this circle with the snips.

CAUTION: The edges of sheet metal are sharp. Wear gloves when handling sheet metal.

B.   SAWING AND PLANING

Sawing and planing tools are important equipment in the carpentry trade. Carpenters must know which tools will best complete a task and give the desired surface.

Equipment and Materials

Piece laid out in Unit 7, Activity A
Try square
Crosscut saw
Rip saw
Coping saw
Block plane or jack plane

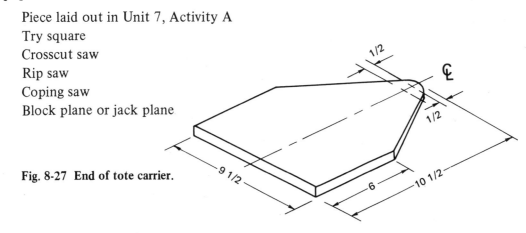

Fig. 8-27 End of tote carrier.

Procedure (refer to figure 8-27)

1. Use the crosscut saw to cut the ends square.

2. Rip the piece to within 1/4 inch of the marked width.

3. Cut the angled edges and the curved portion with a coping saw.

4. With a properly adjusted jack plane, plane the ripped edge to the line. Check frequently with a try square to be sure the edge is square.

5. Use either a block plane or a jack plane to smooth the end grain where it was sawed with the crosscut saw.

Fig. 8-28 A try square can serve as a gauge for perpendicular holes.

C.   DRILLING HOLES

Equipment and Materials

> Pieces from Activity B
> Try square
> Tape measure
> Hand drill and 3/8-inch twist drill bit
> > or
> Bit brace and #6 auger bit

Procedure

1. Lay out the centerlines of the end pieces as shown in figure 8-27.

2. On this centerline mark off two points; one 1/2 inch from the top and the other 1 inch from the top.

3. Drill a 3/16-inch hole at each of these points. Check the angle of the drill frequently with a try square, figure 8-28. Remember to take precautions to protect the back from splintering as the bit passes through.

D.   CUTTING MASONRY

Masons use brick sets and hammers to cut bricks and blocks to size. The cut must be neat and square if the course is to be accurate and attractive.

Equipment and Materials

> Several bricks
> Brick set
> Hammer
> Chalk

Procedure

1. Make a line around a brick.

2. Cut the brick on this line with a brick set. Practice until a neat, square cut can be made.

REVIEW

A.   Matching

Choose the item in the right-hand column which is associated with each item in the left-hand column.

1.	Bit brace	a) Used for sawing metal
2.	Twist drill bits	b) Used for drilling holes in metal
3.	Crosscut saw	c) Has a square tang
4.	Hacksaw	d) Used for sawing with the grain
5.	Combination drill	e) Used for sawing across the grain
6.	Hand drill	f) Used for cutting wallboard
7.	Auger bits	g) Used for sawing intricate shapes
8.	Rip saw	h) Used for drilling screw holes
9.	Coping saw	i) Has a two-jaw chuck
10.	Utility knife	j) Has a three-jaw chuck

B.   Matching

Choose the item in the right-hand column which is associated with each item in the left-hand column.

1.	Crosscut saw	a) 10 points per inch
2.	Hacksaw	b) For drilling in concrete
3.	Cold chisel	c) Thin, sharp edge
4.	Wood chisel	d) Very fine pitch
5.	Rip saw	e) Turned with a hand drill
6.	Carbide drill bit	f) Turned with a bit brace
7.	Steel drill bit	g) For cutting masonry
8.	Round shank	h) For drilling wood or metal
9.	Square tang	i) 6 points per inch
10.	Brick set	j) Blunt-angled cutting edge

C.   Tool Descriptions

Refer to a catalog provided by the instructor and list a complete set of cutting, sawing, and drilling tools used by a carpenter. Include a brief description of each, indicating important features and price.

UNIT 9.
FASTENERS, FASTENING TOOLS, AND FORMING TOOLS

OBJECTIVES

After completing this unit, the student will be able to:

- describe common types of nails and screws and the systems for sizing them.
- identify and demonstrate the proper use of the fastening and forming tools used most often by construction workers.
- explain the markings on coated abrasives.

The range of fasteners used in the construction industry is almost limitless. Hundreds of kinds of special fastening devices are available from a large number of suppliers. However, a few types of nails and screws account for most of the fasteners used.

NAILS

Numerous kinds of nails can be used for a variety of purposes. Several of the most common nails are shown in figure 9-1. Most of these are designed for a specific purpose, but a few are used for many different purposes.

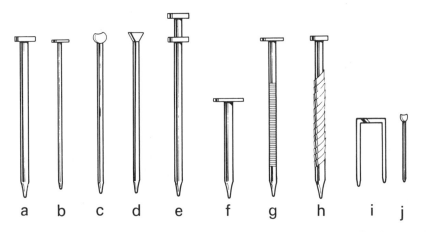

Fig. 9-1 Some of the most common kinds of nails: (a) common nail; (b) box nail; (c) finishing nail; (d) casing nail; (e) duplex-headed nail; (f) roofing nail; (g) ring-shank drywall nail; (h) screw-shank nail; (i) staple; (j) wire brad.

Common Nails

Common nails are the most frequently used of all nails. Common nails have a flat head and smooth shank. They are used for most applications where the special features of another type are not needed.

Box Nails

Box nails are similar to common nails except they have a thinner shank and thinner head. Because of their thin shank, they are less apt to split the wood used for boxes and crates. They are also useful where paint will be applied over the nailed surface. Due to their thin head, box nails do not show up as readily under paint. Frequently box nails are coated with a chemical that resists rusting and makes the box nail more difficult to withdraw.

Finishing Nails

Finishing nails have very small heads and somewhat thinner shanks than common nails. The small head of a finishing nail can be driven below the surface of the wood and concealed with putty so that it is completely hidden. Finishing nails are used for installing trim and millwork where appearance is important.

Because of their small heads, finishing nails do not have as much holding power as common nails and box nails.

Penny Size

Nail lengths are specified by *penny size*. The term penny (abbreviated d) was adopted in the early days of nailmaking. The penny size indicated the size of nails that could be purchased at the rate of 100 for a given number of pennies. Today, the penny size indicates the length of nails, regardless of the type, figure 9-2. For example, 8d common nails, finishing nails, and box nails are different diameters, but they are all 2 1/2 inches long.

Nailing Techniques

Nails can be driven in basically three ways: face nailing, toenailing, and clinching. In *face nailing*, nails are driven straight through one member and into the other. *Toenailing* is used where it is not possible to use face nailing and where resistance to withdrawal is needed. A nail is driven into the side of one member at an angle, penetrating the adjacent surface and the other member, figure 9-3. By toenailing from both sides, the members are less apt to pull apart. *Clinching* refers to driving nails through both members and bending over the points to prevent withdrawal.

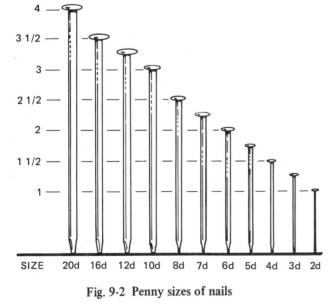

Fig. 9-2 Penny sizes of nails

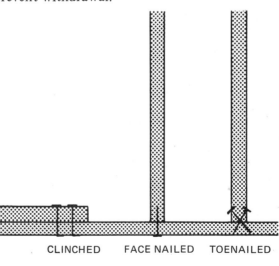

Fig. 9-3 Nailing techniques

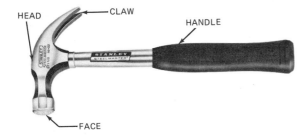

HEAD — CLAW
HANDLE
FACE

Fig. 9-4 Parts of a nail hammer *(The Stanley Tool Div.)*

Fig. 9-5 Nail set *(The Stanley Tool Div.)*

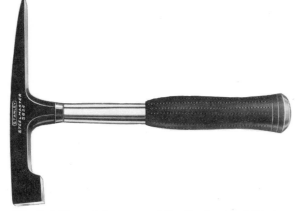

Fig. 9-6 Mason's hammer *(The Stanley Tool Div.)*

HAMMERS

Nail Hammers

Nails are driven with *nail hammers*. The parts of a nail hammer are shown in figure 9-4. The *claw* is used for withdrawing nails. Nail hammers are available with handles of wood, steel, and fiberglass and in 13-ounce, 16-ounce, and 20-ounce weights. Some carpenters prefer steel-handled hammers for their strength; others prefer wood or fiberglass for its shock-absorbing quality. The weight of the hammer depends on the kind of nailing to be done. With a heavy hammer it is easier to drive large nails, but light hammers are less apt to mar the surface of the wood.

To use the hammer, grasp it near the end of the handle and swing it with the entire forearm. The face should strike the nail head squarely. If

the nail bends (usually as a result of not striking it squarely), pull it out and start a new one. To *set* a finishing nail below the surface, use a nail set, figure 9-5, to drive the nail head about 1/16 inch into the wood.

Mason's Hammer

The *mason's hammer* (or brick hammer) has a square face and a chisel-like cutting edge, figure 9-6. Like nail hammers, mason's hammers are available with wood, steel, or fiberglass handles and in a variety of weights. The flat face of the hammer is used for occasional nailing and for striking cold chisels and brick-set chisels. The other end of the hammer can cut bricks and concrete blocks. The cutting edge of the mason's hammer is used like the brick-set chisel. The brick or block is struck on all four sides to score it, then it is broken with a final, sharp blow.

SCREWS

Screws are a common kind of fastener in construction. A variety of sizes and types of screws are available for fastening several kinds of material in a wide range of situations. Wood screws are listed according to the following:

- *Material.* Brass screws are used for exterior application, but steel screws are stronger and much less expensive.

- *Gauge Size.* The gauge size indicates the diameter of the unthreaded part of the screw. The higher the number, the larger the screw, figure 9-7.

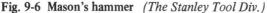

Fig. 9-7 These screws are all the same length, but different gauges.

Fig. 9-8 These screws are all #8 gauge, but different lengths.

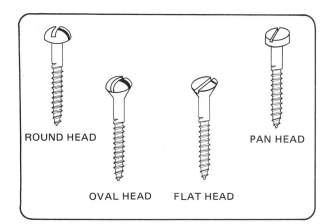

Fig. 9-9 Common screw-head shapes

- *Length.* Wood screws are available in lengths from 1/4″ to 4″, figure 9-8.

- *Head type,* figure 9-9. Flathead screws are generally used where a flat surface is desired. Round or oval heads are more difficult to conceal.

Drilling Screw Holes

Fastening two pieces of wood together with flathead screws require three operations with a drill. A shank hole just large enough to fit the unthreaded portion of the screw must be drilled in one piece. A pilot hole slightly smaller than the threaded portion of the screw must be drilled in the other piece. The chart in figure 9-10 shows suggested sizes for shank holes and pilot holes for most screw sizes. The top surface of the shank hole must be countersunk to accept the head of the screw, figure 9-11.

These operations can be combined into one operation by using a *combination drill*, figure 9-12. Combination drills are manufactured for a specific screw length and gauge. The pieces of wood to be joined are held in place while all three parts of the hole are drilled the proper size.

Screw Gauge	0	1	2	3	4	5	6	8	10	12	14	16	18
Shank Hole	$\frac{1}{16}$	$\frac{5}{64}$	$\frac{3}{32}$	$\frac{7}{64}$	$\frac{7}{64}$	$\frac{1}{8}$	$\frac{9}{64}$	$\frac{11}{64}$	$\frac{3}{16}$	$\frac{7}{32}$	$\frac{1}{4}$	$\frac{17}{64}$	$\frac{19}{64}$
Pilot Hole	$\frac{1}{64}$	$\frac{1}{32}$	$\frac{1}{32}$	$\frac{3}{64}$	$\frac{3}{64}$	$\frac{1}{16}$	$\frac{1}{16}$	$\frac{5}{64}$	$\frac{3}{32}$	$\frac{7}{64}$	$\frac{7}{64}$	$\frac{9}{64}$	$\frac{9}{64}$

Fig. 9-10 Chart of drill sizes for wood screws

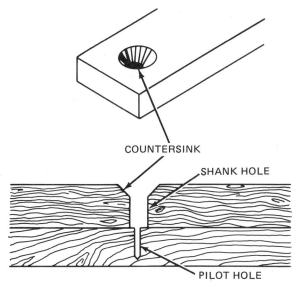

Fig. 9-11 Countersink hole

Fig. 9-12 Combination drill makes the pilot hole, shank hole, and countersink in one operation. *(The Stanley Tool Div.)*

SCREWDRIVERS

Most screws have either straight-slotted heads or Phillips heads, figure 9-13. Screwdrivers are available in a range of sizes to fit both types, figure 9-14. The screwdriver used should be large enough so the blade fills the slot in the screw head. Screwdrivers are not made of hardened steel and should not be used for prying.

WRENCHES

Although many of the fasteners used in construction do not require wrenches, most construction workers carry one or two adjustable wrenches in their tool kits. Adjustable wrenches are available in various lengths from 4 inches to 18 inches. These have one movable jaw that can be adjusted to fit any size fastener. When using an adjustable wrench, the force should be applied toward the movable jaw, figure 9-15.

Plumbers and pipefitters use *pipe wrenches* to turn pipes and pipe fittings. Pipe wrenches have a series of teeth on their jaws, figure 9-16, so they grip the round surface. Pipe wrenches are available in lengths from 6 inches to 2 feet. Usually two pipe wrenches are needed; one to turn the fitting and one to hold the pipe.

CLAMPS

Clamps are used by welders to hold parts during welding; by cabinetmakers and carpenters to glue parts together; and by plumbers, electricians, and other building tradesworkers to hold pieces in place temporarily during assembly or installation. There are many types of clamps, but most construction workers are familiar with two or three types.

C clamps, figure 9-17, are lightweight and easy to handle. Construction workers frequently use them to hold parts in place during construction. *Bar clamps* are mostly used by carpenters and cabinetmakers for clamping glued assemblies, figure 9-18. They are available in lengths ranging up to eight feet. *Hand screw clamps*, figure 9-19, are also used primarily by woodworkers. They are fast-acting and can be adjusted for nonparallel surfaces.

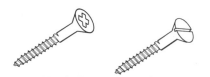

Fig. 9-13 Phillips and straight-slot screws

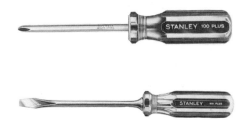

Fig. 9-14   Phillips and straight-slot screwdrivers *(The Stanley Tool Div.)*

Fig. 9-15 When using an adjustable wrench, the pressure should be applied toward the adjustable jaw.

Fig. 9-16 Pipe wrenches are used by plumbers to turn pipes and fittings. *(The Ridge Tool Co.)*

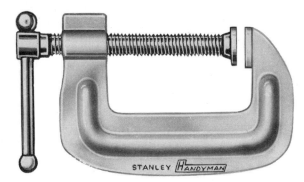

Fig. 9-17 C clamp *(The Stanley Tool Div.)*

Fig. 9-18 Bar clamps are frequently used to glue up stock. *(Adjustable Clamp Co.)*

Fig. 9-19 Wooden screw clamps can be adjusted to fit the situation. *(Adjustable Clamp Co.)*

Fig. 9-20 Floating concrete *(Portland Cement Assoc.)*

Fig. 9-21 Cement trowel

When gluing up wooden assemblies, clamps should generally be placed every few inches along the glue line. Clamps with steel clamping surfaces should be padded with scraps of softwood to prevent marring the parts being glued.

FORMING TOOLS

Many construction materials are applied while they are in a plastic state. *Plastic* means able to be formed or shaped. These materials are shaped or smoothed with *forming tools*. Most of the forming tools used in the building trades are characterized by a smooth working surface used to smooth the material.

Floats

Concrete workers use *floats* to smooth out some of the roughness in the surface of freshly placed concrete, figure 9-20. As soon as possible after the concrete is placed in the forms, it is floated. This leaves a textured but uniform surface. Floats can be made of wood, aluminum, or magnesium.

Concrete Trowels

When concrete is firm, but still plastic enough to be worked a little, it may be troweled for a smoother surface. *Trowels*, figure 9-21, are made of high-carbon steel and have a smoother working surface than floats, leaving a much

Fig. 9-22 Concrete mason finishing concrete with a power trowel *(Portland Cement Assoc.)*

Fig. 9-23 Mason's trowel

Fig. 9-24 Before the mortar sets, the mason smooths the joint with a jointer. *(Richard T. Kreh, Sr.)*

Fig. 9-25 Joint knife *(The Stanley Tool Div.)*

smoother surface. Power trowels with rotary blades are often used to trowel large areas, figure 9-22. Trowels similar to those used by concrete workers are used by plasterers in smoothing plaster on walls and ceilings.

Mason's Trowel

Mason's use another type of trowel, figure 23, for spreading mortar. The pointed shape of the *mason's trowel* is suited for applying mortar to masonry units and removing excess mortar as it is squeezed out of the joint. Mason's trowels are available in a range of sizes. Mason's who work with bricks (bricklayers) frequently select a small size, while those working with concrete blocks may select a larger size. In either case the quality of the steel and the balance of the trowel are important considerations in selecting a trowel.

Masonry Jointers

When the mortar is just hard enough to show a thumbprint, the mason smoothes the joints with the jointer, figure 9-24. This improves the appearance of the masonry job and helps make the joints watertight.

Joint Knife

After drywall mechanics install gypsum wallboard, the joints are concealed with a special compound and paper tape. The compound for this joint system is applied either with a plaster trowel or a joint knife, figure 9-25. A *joint knife* is similar to a putty knife, except that joint knives are usually 5 to 6 inches wide.

COATED ABRASIVES

Although these are not tools in the common sense, coated abrasives are included here because they are important for smoothing construction materials. Coated abrasives are frequently referred to as sandpaper, although only one type is actually sandpaper. *Coated abrasives* include all products made of a paper or cloth backing coated with sharp particles for smoothing materials.

Abrasive	Color	Description
Flint	Light tan	Relatively soft natural abrasive used for some woodwork
Garnet	Reddish brown to orange	Natural abrasive used extensively for woodwork
Aluminum oxide	Brownish grey	Very hard man-made abrasive used for metals, wood, and other materials
Emery	Dark brown	Natural abrasive commonly used for polishing metal
Silicon carbide	Black	Hard man-made abrasive used to smooth and polish metals and for wet sanding finishes

Fig. 9-26 Common abrasive materials

GARNET FINISHING PAPER
OPEN
150 A WT.

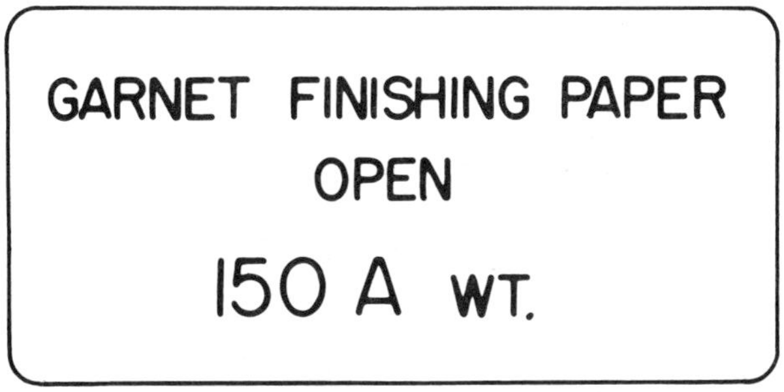

Fig. 9-27 Markings on back of coated abrasive

The grit may be natural or synthetic. The most common abrasive materials are listed in figure 9-26 with their outstanding characteristics. Garnet and aluminum oxide are the most common abrasives for smoothing wood. Emery, silicon carbide, and aluminum oxide are commonly used on metals.

The coarseness of the abrasive grains is marked on the back of the sheet with a number, figure 9-27. The number of the grit indicates the number of wires per inch in a screen through which the grains will pass. For example, if the abrasive sheet is marked with a number 120, the grains will just pass through a screen with 120 wires per inch running in each direction. Coarse abrasives, such as numbers 32 and 40, are used for sanding wood floors. Very fine abrasives, such as number 400 are used for smoothing painted surfaces. The letter marking on the back of the coated abrasive indicates the weight of the backing material. A-weight paper is used for smoothing finished woodwork. D-weight paper is generally used with coarser abrasives for heavier work.

Coated abrasives are either open coat or closed coat. *Closed-coated abrasives* have all available space covered with abrasive grains. *Open-coated abrasives* have some space between the abrasive grains. Closed-coated abrasives cut faster, but open-coated abrasives have less tendency to "plug up" when smoothing paint, varnish, or resinous materials.

———— ACTIVITIES ————

A. NAILING

Carpenters must be familiar with the different types of nails and nailing techniques. How parts are fastened together greatly influence the finished product.

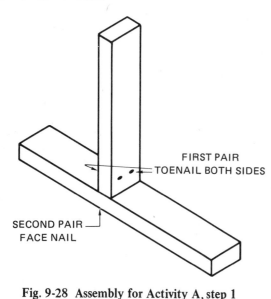

FIRST PAIR
TOENAIL BOTH SIDES

SECOND PAIR
FACE NAIL

Fig. 9-28 Assembly for Activity A, step 1

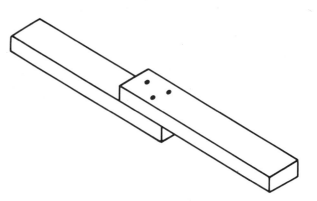

Fig. 9-29 Assembly for Activity A, steps 2 and 3

Equipment and Materials

Nail hammer
Four pieces of wood, 2″ x 4″ x 2′
Six pieces of wood, 1″ x 3″ x 2′
Supply of nails – 12d common, 6d common, 6d finish

Procedure

1. Face nail one pair of 2″ x 4″ pieces and toenail one pair of 2″ x 4″ pieces as shown in figure 9-28.

2. Lap and nail one pair of 1″ x 3″ pieces with 6d common nails as shown in figure 9-29. Clinch the nails.

3. Lap and nail one pair of 1″ x 3″ pieces with 6d finishing nails as shown in figure 9-29. Clinch the nails.

4. Hold one part of each assembly in a vise and pull the assemblies apart, noting the differences in the nails' holding power.

CAUTION: As the assemblies are pulled apart, remove the nails. Exposed nail points cause injuries.

5. Lap and nail one pair of 1″ x 3″ pieces with 6d common nails, as in step 2, but drive the nail 3/4 inch from the end of the top piece.

6. Reverse the ends of the pieces and repeat step 5. Dull the nail points first by holding the heads on a hard surface and tapping on the points with a hammer. *Note:* This is a technique frequently used by carpenters to prevent splitting.

B. FASTENING WITH SCREWS

Carpenters and other construction workers must know which drill and screw combination to use to fasten objects properly. This activity demonstrates how specific screws should be installed.

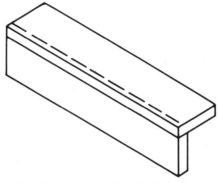

Fig. 9-30 Assembly for Activity B, step 3

Equipment and Materials

> Two pieces of wood, 1″ x 3″ x 2′
> Hand drill and set of twist drill bits
> 1 1/2 x 8 combination drill – countersink type
> 1 x 8 combination drill – counterbore type
> 1 1/2 x 8 flathead steel screws
> 1 x 8 round head steel screws
> Screwdriver
> Marking gauge

Procedure

1. Mark a line 3/8 inch from the edge of one piece of wood.

2. Refer to figure 9-10 and drill the proper size shank hole for a #8 screw on this line.

3. Hold the two pieces of wood together, as in figure 9-30, mark the location, and drill the pilot hole.

4. Countersink the shank hole.

5. Fasten the pieces with a 1 1/2 x 8 flathead steel screw.

6. With the pieces still assembled, drill a second shank hole, pilot hole, and countersink using the combination drill.

7. Drive another 1 1/2 x 8 screw.

8. Using the counterbore-type combination drill, drill the proper holes to drive a 1 x 8 round head screw with a 3/8 inch deep counterbore.

9. Drive a screw in this hole.

10. Examine the assembly. All screw heads should be tightly seated. The pieces of wood should be in tight contact along their entire length.

C.   TROWEL PRACTICE

Plasterers finish interior walls and ceilings with plaster coatings that form fire-resistant and relatively soundproof surfaces. The first step in plastering is learning how to use the trowel to produce a smooth coating.

Equipment and Materials

Gypsum wallboard or plywood, approximately 24" x 24"
Two pounds of patching plaster
Container for mixing
Plaster or concrete trowel

Procedure

1. Mix the plaster according to instructions. Patching plaster is used because it sets quickly, allowing completion of this activity in one class period. To extend the drying time, add a small amount of vinegar.

CAUTION: Plaster sets underwater. Do not dispose of unused plaster in a sink drain as it will clog the drain.

2. Dampen the surface of the wallboard or plywood. This prevents the wallboard from drawing the water out of the plaster.

3. Trowel an even coat of plaster onto the surface of the wallboard or plywood. Try to obtain a smooth coat without making ridges with the edges of the trowel.

REVIEW

A. Multiple Choice

Select the best answer for each of the following questions.

1. What kind of nail has a small diameter and thin, flat head?

   a. Box
   b. Finish

   c. Common
   d. Casing

2. Which kind of nail is most often used to install wood molding?

   a. Box
   b. Finish

   c. Common
   d. Duplex

3. Which method for nailing would be best suited for fastening the studs in figure 9-31?

   a. Face nailing
   b. Toenailing

   c. Clinching
   d. Nail setting

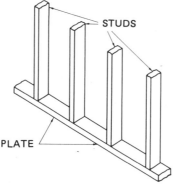

Fig. 9-31

4. What is the length of a 2 1/2 x 6 screw?

   a. 6 inches
   b. 1/6 inch
   c. 6/4 (1 1/2) inches
   d. 2 1/2 inches

5. Which screw has the largest diameter?

   a. 1 1/4 x 4   c. 2 1/2 x 6
   b. 1 1/4 x 8   d. 3 x 6

6. What should be the diameter of the shank hole for a 1 1/2 x 6 screw?

   a. 1/16 inch   c. 9/64 inch
   b. 6/32 inch   d. 3/32 inch

7. Which of the following is the coarsest coated abbrasive?

   a. 150A   c. 120D
   b. 80D   d. 120A

8. Which of the following tools is least likely to be used by a mason?

   a. Combination drill   c. Wood float
   b. Jointer   d. Pointed trowel

9. Which of the following tools is least likely to be used by a carpenter?

   a. Nail set   c. Aluminum float
   b. Screwdriver   d. Bar clamp

10. Which nail is longest?

   a. 6d box nail   c. 8d common nail
   b. 10d casing nail   d. 4d finishing nail

B.   **Identification**

Give the name of each of the tools in figure 9-32, page 134.

C.   **Tool Descriptions**

Refer to a catalog provided by the instructor to list a complete set of fastening and forming tools. Include a brief description of the important characteristics of each, including price. Also, name at least one building trade that uses each tool. It is not necessary to list fasteners and coated abrasives.

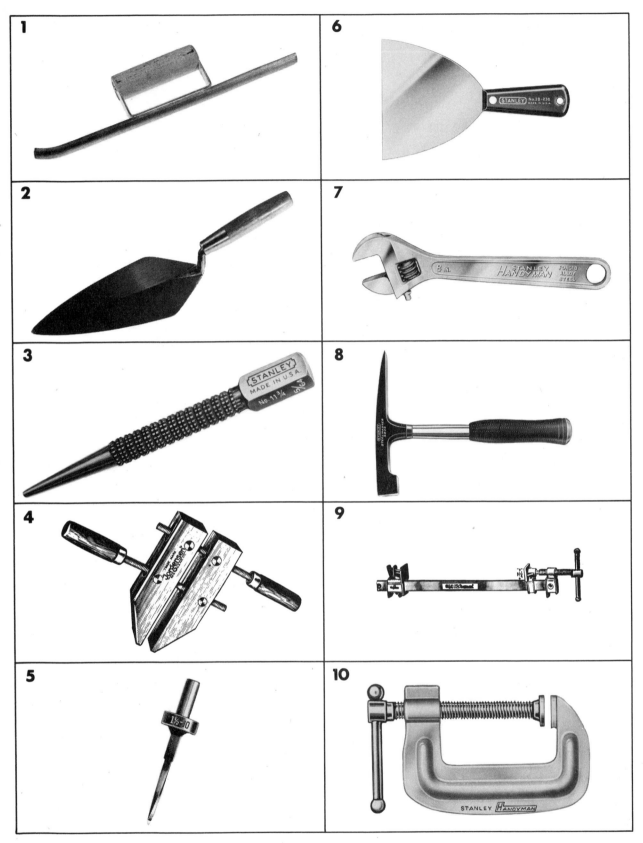

Fig. 9-32

UNIT 10.
PORTABLE POWER TOOLS

OBJECTIVES

After completing this unit, the student will be able to:

- safely perform basic operations with each of the tools listed.

- identify the most outstanding features of the power tools listed.

POWER TOOL CONSTRUCTION

Power tools perform the same basic operations as hand tools. Work can be accomplished more quickly with power tools because of the speed and power their electric motors deliver to the working parts. This increased speed of operation requires special features in the construction of power tools.

Motors

The size of the motor on most power tools is specified by the amount of electric current it uses. Electric current is measured in *amperes* (abbreviated *amps*). A typical motor size for an electric saw, for example, is 8 amps, figure 10-1. The higher the amperage, the higher the power output of the tool. Of course, higher amperage generally means more weight and greater cost.

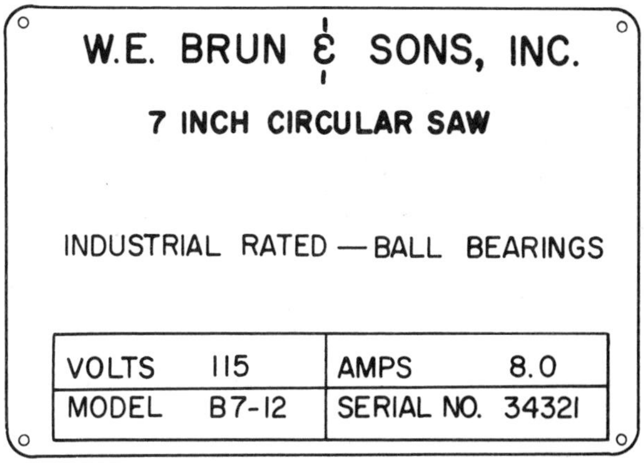

Insulation and Grounding

To protect portable power tool users from electrical shock, some power tools are double

```
┌──────────────────────────────────────────┐
│ o                                      o   │
│     W.E. BRUN & SONS, INC.                 │
│                                            │
│        7 INCH CIRCULAR SAW                 │
│                                            │
│                                            │
│     INDUSTRIAL RATED — BALL  BEARINGS      │
│                                            │
│   ┌─────────────────┬──────────────────┐  │
│   │ VOLTS    115    │ AMPS       8.0   │  │
│   ├─────────────────┼──────────────────┤  │
│   │ MODEL    B7-12  │ SERIAL NO. 34321 │  │
│ o └─────────────────┴──────────────────┘o │
└──────────────────────────────────────────┘
```

Fig. 10-1 Typical power tool identification plate

insulated. *Double-insulated tools* have two chassis. The inner one contains all of the electrical parts. The outer one is completely insulated from the inner one. In case of an electrical malfunction, no voltage can reach the operator.

Tools that are not double insulated should be connected to an electrical ground. Such tools have a three-wire power cord. The third wire is

Fig. 10-2   A three-prong grounding-type plug

attached to a grounding prong on the plug, figure 10-2. Grounded electrical outlets are connected to a satisfactory ground within the system.

Bearings

There are three kinds of bearings used in power tools. *Plain* or *sleeve bearings* consist of a smooth surface on the inside of a short sleeve, figure 10-3. These bearings have a shorter life expectancy than others and are not as widely used in top-quality tools. *Needle* or *roller bearings* are free-rolling, straight rollers which allow a shaft to roll in its support. *Ball bearings* are another kind of rolling bearings. Ball bearings are generally found where they must resist side-to-side as well as end-to-end motion.

PORTABLE POWER TOOL SAFETY

1. Tools that are not double insulated should be connected to an electrical ground.

2. Wear eye protection when operating power tools.

3. Keep all guards and protective devices in place.

4. Do not use defective tools.

5. Unplug the tool when changing bits, blades, and attachments.

6. Unplug the tool when left unattended.

7. Check to see that the cutting edge of the tool will have a clear path as it penetrates the workpiece.

8. Use power tools only after you have received instruction on their use.

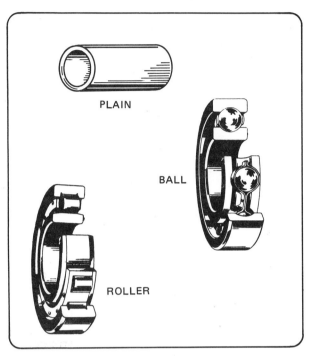

Fig. 10-3   Bearings used in tools

Fig. 10-4   Saber saw   *(Rockwell International)*

SABER SAW

The saber saw, figure 10-4, works on the same sawing principles as hand saws. An electric motor drives a gear mechanism, which in turn causes the blade to move up and down. The *shoe*, or base of the saw, adjusts to tilt the saw up to 45 degrees to either side. The blade is held in a chuck which makes it easier to change.

	Blade Length	Teeth Per Inch	Blade Width	APPLICATIONS
	3"	10	5/16"	Fast Cutting Set Tooth-Wood
	3"	6	5/16"	Faster Cutting Shark Tooth
	4 1/4"	10	1/2"	Fast Cutting Set Tooth
	4 1/4"	6	1/2"	Faster Cutting Shark Tooth
	4 1/4	10	1/4	Scroll and General Smooth Cutting Soft and Hard Grain Woods-Plywood-Masonite
	4 1/4	6	1/4	Fast Scroll and Rough Cutting Soft and Hard Grain Woods
	4 1/4	10	3/8	General Wood Cutting-Asphalt Tile Fiber-Paper-Plastic-Laminates-Lucite-Plexiglass
	4 1/4	6	3/8	General Rough Cutting Roof Rafters and General Frame Cutting-Plunge Cutting
	3 1/2	10	1/4	Smooth Scroll and Circular Cutting Masonite-Plywood-Soft and Hard Grain Trim Stock-Plastics
	3 1/2	6	1/4	Fast Scroll and Circular Cutting Solid Grain Wood-Masonite-Plastics
	3 1/2	10	3/8	General Straight and Large Curvature Cutting-Solid Grain Wood Plywood-Masonite-Plastics-Soft Aluminum Extrusions
	3	10	1/4	Smooth Scroll and Circular Cutting-Plywood, Straight Grain Wood, Masonite-Plastics-Plunge Cutting
	3	6	1/4	Fast Scroll and Circular Cutting-Plunge Cutting Straight Grain Woods-Hard Board
	3	10	3/8	General Wood Cutting, Fiber, Paper and Plastic Laminates Plexiglass, Rubber Linoleum
	3	6	3/8	Rough Cutting Wood
	2	10	13/64	Smooth Finish Cutting of Straight, Curvature, Round Finish and Trim Materials and Plunge Cutting
	2	—	5/16	Cutting-Cardboard-Cloth-Leather Rubber and Sponge Type Plastics

HIGH SPEED STEEL-FIBERGLASS CUTTING

	Blade Length	Teeth Per Inch	Blade Width	APPLICATIONS
	4 1/4	6	3/8	Cutting Fiberglass-Fiberglass Bonded to Plywood Sheet Rock-Asphalt Tile-Plastics-Plaster
	2 5/8	6	3/8	Cutting Fiberglass-Fiberglass Bonded to Plywood Sheet Rock-Asphalt Tile-Plaster

CARBIDE TIP-PROBLEM MATERIAL CUTTING

	Blade Length	Teeth Per Inch	Blade Width	APPLICATIONS
	3 1/2	6	3/8	Cutting Fiberglass, Asphalt Tile, Plastics, Sheet Rock, Plaster and General Wood Cutting

HIGH SPEED STEEL-METAL CUTTING

	Blade Length	Teeth Per Inch	Blade Width	APPLICATIONS
	3 5/8	14	3/8	Cutting Brass-Bronze-Copper and Non-Ferrous Metals 5/32 to 1/4" Thick Angle Iron-Mild Steel Sheets and Tubing 5/32 to 1/8" Wall Thickness
	3 1/2	24	1/2	Cutting Window Openings in Steel Core Fire Doors-Copper-Brass and Steel Tubing to 7/8" in Diameter
	3	10	3/8	Cutting Brass-Bronze-Copper-Aluminum to 1/2" in Thickness Steel-Cast Iron to 3/16" in Thickness
	3	14	3/8	Cutting Non-Ferrous Metals to 1/4" in Thickness-Cutting Angle Iron Mild Steel Sheets and Tubing to 1/8" Wall Thickness
	3	24	3/8	Cutting Steel Sheets to 1/8" Cutting Tubing Thin Wall to 1 3/8" Diameter
	3	24	1/4	Cutting Steel Sheets and Tubing 3/32 to 1/8" Wall Thickness
	1 3/4	14	1/4	Cutting Steel Sheets and Tubing 3/32 to 1/8" Wall Thickness
	1 3/4	24	1/4	Cutting Steel Sheets and Tubing 3/32 to 1/8" Wall Thickness

Fig. 10-5 Saber saw blades *(Rockwell International)*

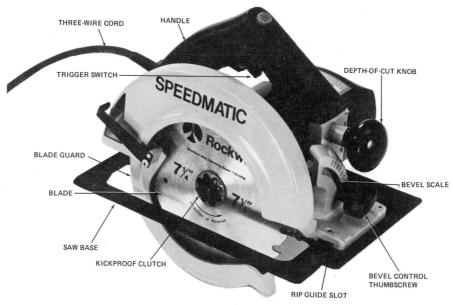

Fig. 10-6 7 1/4-inch circular saw *(Rockwell International)*

Blades of various sizes and pitches are available for a variety of sawing jobs, figure 10-5. In addition, some saws have variable-speed controls to allow even greater flexibility.

To use the saber saw, follow these steps:

1. Check to see that the proper blade is securely installed.
2. Hold the piece to be cut in a vise or clamp it securely in place.
3. Plug the saw in.
4. Turn the saw on and start the cut.
5. Avoid trying to cut too sharp a curve as this will break the blade.

PORTABLE CIRCULAR SAW

The one power tool used most frequently by carpenters is the portable circular saw, figure 10-6. It consists of a motor, a handle with a trigger switch, a shoe that tilts up to 45 degrees and moves up and down to vary the depth of cut, a blade, and a blade guard. Blades are available for different operations, figure 10-7. The blade used most often is the combination blade. This blade can be used for crosscutting and ripping, the two most commonly performed operations.

Many serious injuries are caused by improper use of circular saws and by use of defective

Fig. 10-7 Types of circular saw blades: (A) crosscut, (B) rip, (C) combination-chisel tooth, and (D) combination-planer

tive saws. To crosscut with the circular saw, follow these steps:

1. Check to see that a combination or cross-cut blade is installed securely with the teeth pointing up in front.

CAUTION: Do not overtighten the blade screw. Most saws have a special washer that allows the blade to slip if it binds. This prevents the saw from kicking back toward the operator.

2. Adjust the shoe so the blade protrudes through the bottom of the stock about 1/2 inch.

3. Check the blade guard to see that it works easily.

4. Rest the stock on saw horses so that none of the portion to be cut off is supported.

CAUTION: The stock to be cut off should not be held or supported. This may cause the blade to bind.

5. Mark a line on the stock where it is to be cut.

6. Plug the saw in.

7. Grasp the saw by the two handles provided and turn it on.

8. Rest the forward end of the shoe on the stock and push the blade into the stock slowly, but firmly. Avoid turning the saw from side to side.

9. After the cut is completed, release the trigger but hold the saw until the blade stops.

10. Unplug the saw.

ELECTRIC DRILLS

Electric drills are used by workers in most of the building trades, figure 10-8. Electric drill sizes are listed according to the maximum size bit that can be held in their chucks. The most common sizes are 1/4 inch, 3/8 inch, and 1/2 inch. Some electric drills have variable-speed controls and reversing switches. For drilling in

Fig. 10-8 Portable electric drill

Fig. 10-9 Spade bit

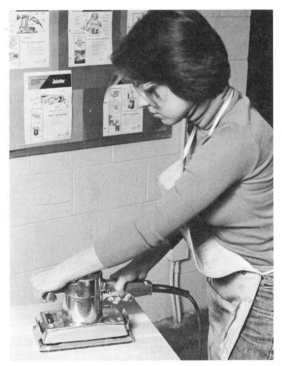

Fig. 10-10 Finishing sander

concrete and masonry, a low speed is used. For drilling in softwood, a high speed is used. The reversing switch allows the drill to be backed out of a hole.

Any of the bits that can be used in a hand drill can also be used in an electric drill. Spade bits can also be used in electric drills, figure 10-9. Spade bits are available in larger sizes than bits used in hand drills.

FINISHING SANDERS

The finishing sander, figure 10-10, is a lightweight power tool for moving coated abrasives. The abrasive is moved in one of two ways, depending on the type of sander. The *orbital sander* moves the abrasive in a small circular path. The *straight line sander* moves the abrasive in a straight, back-and-forth motion, figure 10-11.

Most finishing sanders hold either 1/3 or 1/4 of a standard sheet of coated abrasive. The abrasive paper can be torn accurately by creasing it, then tearing it over the corner of a work bench or board. The pad on the bottom of the sander has two clamps to hold the edges of the abrasive. To use the sander, it is simply turned on and moved slowly around the surface to be smoothed.

ROUTER

Carpenters and cabinetmakers use routers to shape the edges of woodwork, cut out openings in finished millwork, cut recesses for door hinges (called *gains*), and trim plastic facing material. The *router* is a high-speed motor with a chuck to hold various cutters and a base to control the router, figure 10-12. The base is moved up and down on the motor to control the amount the router bit protrudes into the work. Some type of fine-adjustment device is also included.

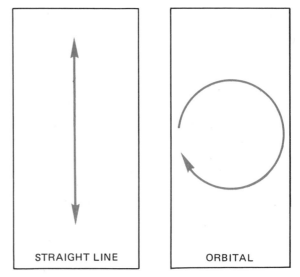

STRAIGHT LINE   ORBITAL

Fig. 10-11 Action of finishing sanders

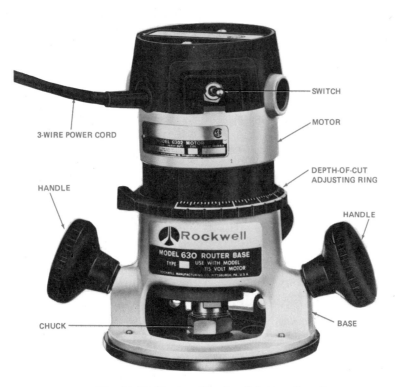

Fig. 10-12 Router *(Rockwell International)*

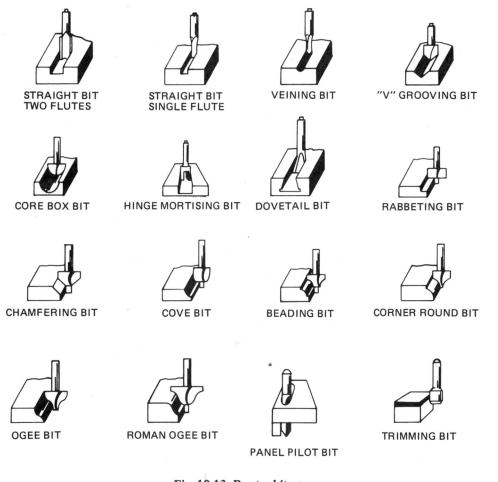

Fig. 10-13 Router bits

Router Bits

One manufacturer makes over 40 types of router bits, figure 10-13. Several shapes are available for producing a decorative edge on wood. Others are used on the face of the work for decorative or functional cuts. Some router bits are designed for piercing and cutting panels. Some trim the edge of plastic laminates used on counter tops.

Router bits used on plastics have carbide cutting edges. Bits used on wood are available with either steel or carbide cutting edges. the cost of carbide bits is higher, but they stay sharp much longer and produce smoother cuts. Some router bits have a steel or ball-bearing pilot to guide the router, figure 10-14. To use other types a guide is attached to the router, figure 10-15.

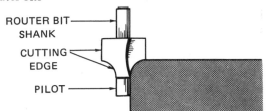

Fig. 10-14 Router bit with pilot to follow edge of stock.

Fig. 10-15 Grooving with an edge guide. (*Note:* The motor has been removed to show the position of the guide.)

Shaping an Edge with the Router

1. Insert a bit with a pilot in the router chuck.

2. Adjust the base of the router so the desired portion of the bit is exposed.

3. Clamp the workpiece to a bench so the edge to be shaped extends beyond the edge of the bench.

4. Plug the router in and turn it on.

5. Place the router base on the left end of the workpiece and move the router from left to right. If the bit does not take a full cut on the first pass, make a second pass to finish the cut.

6. Turn off and unplug the router.

Router Edge Guide

1. Insert the desired bit in the router chuck.

2. Adjust the router base for the desired depth of cut.

3. Mount the edge guide on the router base. Adjust the edge guide so the distance from the bit to the guide is equal to the desired distance from the edge of the workpiece to the cut.

4. Clamp the workpiece to a bench. Check to see that the clamps are positioned where they will not interfere with the router.

5. Plug in the router and turn it on.

6. Place the router on the end of the work with the edge guide against the edge of the stock.

7. As the router is pushed through the stock, be careful to keep the edge guide against the edge of the stock.

8. Turn off and unplug the router.

--- ACTIVITIES ---

A. SABER SAW AND ELECTRIC DRILL

Equipment and Materials

Saber saw with wood-cutting blade
Portable electric drill
1-inch spade bit
Piece of wood, 3/4" x 2 1/2" x 24" (finished size)
80-grit coated abrasive

Procedure

1. Lay out the tote carrier handle as shown in figure 10-16.

2. Saw the outside shape of the handle with a saber saw.

3. Mark the locations of the two holes for the handle, figure 10-16.

4. Drill a 1-inch hole at each of the locations marked in step 3.

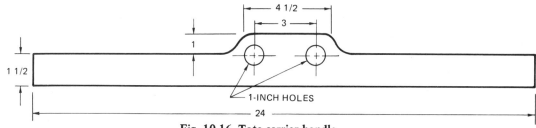

Fig. 10-16 Tote carrier handle

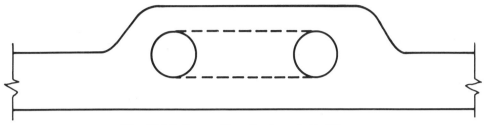

Fig. 10-17 Saw out handle along dotted lines.

5. Connect the outside edges of these holes with straight pencil lines, figure 10-17.

6. Saw out the remainder of the handle with the saber saw.

7. Smooth all sawed surfaces with a file, then 80-grit abrasive.

B.   PORTABLE CIRCULAR SAW

Equipment and Materials

Portable circular saw
Piece of wood, 3/4" x 9 1/2" x 24" (finished size)
Square
Tape measure
Straightedge and pencil
Jack plane

Procedure

1. Cut one end of the stock square with the circular saw.

CAUTION: Adjust the blade of the saw to extend through the stock a maximum of 1/2 inch.

2. Mark a second square line 24 inches from the square end.

3. Cut the stock off at this point.

4. Plane one edge of the stock if it has not already been planed.

5. Mark a line 9 1/2 inches away from the planed edge and parallel to it.

6. Rip the stock about 1/4 inch wider than the line.

CAUTION: When ripping with the circular saw, be careful not to let the saw kerf pinch the blade. Also, be sure the blade does not strike the workbench or saw horse.

7. Plane the sawed edge to the line. *Note*: This piece is the bottom of the tote carrier.

C.   SHAPING AN EDGE WITH A ROUTER

Equipment and Materials

Router
1/4-inch rounding over bit
Handle for tote carrier (cut out in Activity A)

Procedure

1. Insert the bit in the router.

2. Adjust the router base so the top of the curved cutting edge is flush with the router base.

3. Clamp the tote carrier handle to a work surface.

4. Plug in the router and shape all edges of the stock except the ends. *Note:* It will be necessary to reposition the clamps after part of the work is shaped.

5. Turn the stock over and shape the edges on the second side.

REVIEW

A. Multiple Choice

Select the best answer for each of the following questions.

1. What is the main advantage of power tools over hand tools?

    a. Power tools normally outlast hand tools
    b. Greater accuracy is possible with power tools.
    c. Power tools can perform an operation more quickly.
    d. Power tools can perform operations that cannot be performed with hand tools.

2. How is the size of the electric motor on a power tool usually specified?

    a. Torque   c. Volts
    b. Speed   d. Amperes

3. What is the purpose of the third wire on the electrical cord of a power tool?

    a. To connect the tool to an electrical ground
    b. To allow the tool to be used with 220-volt electricity
    c. To carry the electrical current if one wire breaks
    d. The third wire is the switch lead.

4. Which of the following materials cannot be cut with a saber saw?

    a. Wood
    b. Plastics
    c. Metals
    d. All of the above can be cut with a saber saw.

5. When using a portable circular saw, how much should the blade extend through the stock?

    a. 1 inch
    b. 1/2 inch
    c. It should be adjusted so the teeth just reach the far side of the stock.
    d. The depth of cut cannot be controlled on a circular saw.

6. Which direction should the teeth of a portable circular saw blade point?

    a. Up in front
    b. Down in front
    c. Opposite the direction of rotation
    d. It depends on the type of blade being used.

7. Which bit cannot be used in an electric drill?

   a. Auger bits with a square tang
   b. Twist drill bits
   c. Spade bits
   d. Combination drill bits

8. What is the advantage of carbide router bits?

   a. They last longer.
   b. They produce smoother cuts.
   c. They can be used for wood and plastics.
   d. All of the above

9. Which operation cannot be done with a router?

   a. Trim plastic laminates
   b. Cut hinge gains in doors
   c. Cut openings in millwork
   d. Trim sheet metal

10. Which portable power tool is most apt to be used by carpenters, electricians, and plumbers?

    a. Router
    b. Finishing sander
    c. Circular saw
    d. Electric drill

B. Tool Descriptions

Refer to catalogs provided by the instructor to list a set of portable power tools, including one of each of the tools discussed in this unit. Include outstanding features, size, price, and attachments available. Also, indicate which building trades are most likely to use each of the tools listed.

UNIT 11.
MACHINE TOOLS

OBJECTIVES

After completing this unit, the student will be able to:

- safely perform basic operations with each of the machine tools listed.
- identify the most outstanding features of the machine tools listed.

Machine tools perform most of the same operations as hand tools and portable power tools. Because of the many fixtures and attachments available for machine tools, they are capable of great accuracy. They are especially important in production shops, such as millwork and cabinet shops. Some machine tools may be moved to a construction site to speed the work.

Most machine tools have cast-iron frames. This makes them heavy and difficult to transport. However, cast iron has properties that are valuable in machine tools. It is an excellent sound and vibration deadening material. Cast iron is also easily machined to produce the true surfaces required for machine tables and other parts.

MACHINE TOOL SAFETY

1. Wear eye protection around machine tools.

2. Keep all guards and protective devices in place.

3. Do not operate defective machines.

4. Disconnect the electrical power before changing blades or cutters or performing maintenance.

5. Do not position hands where they will be in the path of cutters and blades.

6. Do not wear loose clothing or jewelry.

7. Stand clear of the path of the stock when ripping lumber.

8. Adjust saw blades only as deep as necessary.

9. Use machine tools only after you have had instruction on their use.

BAND SAW

Band saws are used to cut a variety of materials in the shop. The basic parts of the band saw are shown in figure 11-1. The size of a band saw is the diameter of its wheels. The table tilts up to 45 degrees for sawing bevels. The upper blade guide assembly can be raised and lowered to accommodate various thicknesses of stock.

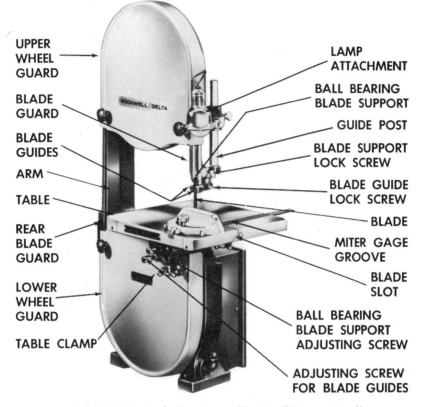

Fig. 11-1 Parts of a band saw *(Rockwell International)*

The motor is located near the lower wheel. The blade, which is a thin, continuous band of steel with teeth on one edge, rides on both wheels. The blade is completely covered by the upper and lower wheel covers and the blade guard, except for the portion that is exposed for cutting. The band saw has two blade guide assemblies; an upper blade guide assembly, figure 11-2, and an identical lower guide assembly located beneath the table. The blade guides have two guide blocks and a guide wheel. The guide blocks support the blade against side pressure. The guide wheels support the blade from being pushed backward.

Band saw blades have different pitches for different kinds of work. They are also available in various widths from 3/16 inch to 1 inch. Narrow blades are used for *scroll sawing* (sawing curves) and wide blades are used for straight sawing.

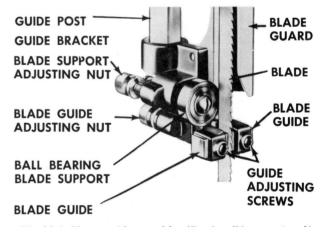

Fig. 11-2 Upper guide assembly *(Rockwell International)*

To Band Saw Curves

1. Adjust the upper blade guide to just clear the stock.

2. Check to see that the blade guides are properly adjusted.

3. Check to see that the table is properly adjusted.

4. Turn the saw on.

5. Place the workpiece on the table and feed the stock into the blade with one hand on each side of the blade.

CAUTION: Never position your hands so that they will hit the blade if you slip.

6. Plan the cut to require as little backing up as possible. It often helps to make a series of relief cuts, figure 11-3, to allow the blade to turn more sharply.

VARIETY SAW

The *variety saw* is one of the most common stationary woodworking machines. The main parts of the variety saw are the table and the arbor (shaft on which the blade is mounted), figure 11-4. The table remains stationary while the arbor can be adjusted up and down to control the depth of cut. The arbor can also be tilted to one side for sawing bevels, figure 11-5. The blades are the same as those used on other circular saws.

The variety saw has three attachments which are frequently used. The *miter gauge* slides in the groove in the table. Stock to be cut off is held firmly against the miter gauge as it is

Fig. 11-3 Make several relief cuts to prevent twisting the blade.

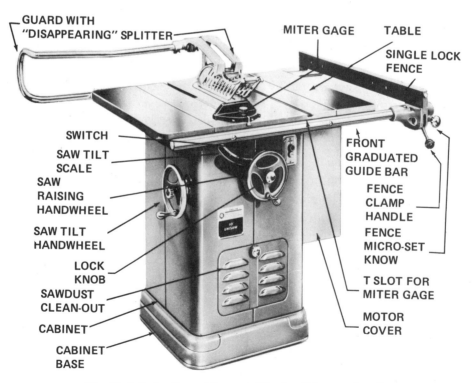

GUARD WITH "DISAPPEARING" SPLITTER

MITER GAGE   TABLE

SINGLE LOCK FENCE

SWITCH
SAW TILT SCALE
SAW RAISING HANDWHEEL
SAW TILT HANDWHEEL
LOCK KNOB
SAWDUST CLEAN-OUT
CABINET
CABINET BASE

FRONT GRADUATED GUIDE BAR
FENCE CLAMP HANDLE
FENCE MICRO-SET KNOW
T SLOT FOR MITER GAGE
MOTOR COVER

Fig. 11-4 Parts of a variety saw *(Rockwell International)*

Fig. 11-5 Sawing a bevel with a variety saw. The guard has been removed to show the position of the blade.

Fig. 11-6 Crosscutting with a variety saw

Fig. 11-7 Ripping with a variety saw

pushed across the table and past the blade. The miter gauge can be adjusted for angles of up to 30 degrees.

The *rip fence* is a straightedge that can be fastened parallel to the blade at any point on the table. For ripping, the stock is held against the rip fence and fed across the table and past the blade. The rip fence and miter gauge should not be used in combination.

The *blade guard* is another attachment to the variety saw. There are several types of blade guards currently available. Some type of guard should protect the operator from the turning blade during all operations.

Crosscutting on the Variety Saw

1. Install a combination or crosscut blade with the teeth pointing toward the operator, figure 11-6.

2. Adjust the miter gauge for a 90-degree cut.

3. Adjust the saw arbor for a 90-degree cut. The blade should protrude 1/4 to 1/2 inch above the stock.

4. Mark a line across the stock where it is to be sawed.

5. Turn the saw on.

6. Hold the stock firmly against the miter gauge and line up the mark with the blade.

7. Push the miter gauge and stock across the table.

8. Remove the stock from the table before returning the miter gauge to the starting position.

Ripping on the Variety Saw

1. Check to see that the proper blade is installed with the teeth pointing toward the operator, figure 11-7.

2. Clamp the rip fence to the table at the desired distance from the blade.

3. Adjust the arbor for a 90-degree cut. The blade should protrude 1/4 to 1/2 inch above the stock.

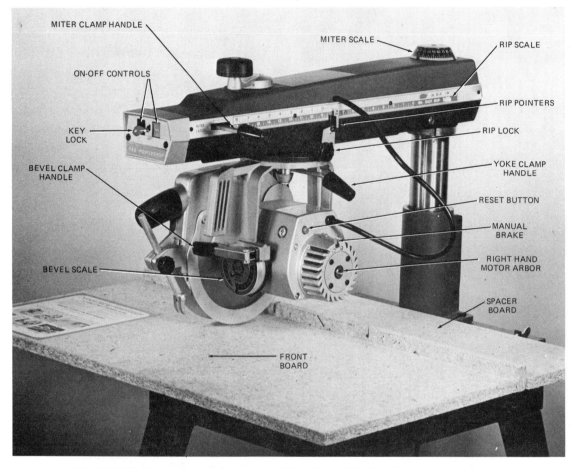

MITER CLAMP HANDLE

ON-OFF CONTROLS

KEY LOCK

BEVEL CLAMP HANDLE

BEVEL SCALE

MITER SCALE

RIP SCALE

RIP POINTERS

RIP LOCK

YOKE CLAMP HANDLE

RESET BUTTON

MANUAL BRAKE

RIGHT HAND MOTOR ARBOR

SPACER BOARD

FRONT BOARD

Fig. 11-8(A) Parts of a radial arm saw *(The Black & Decker Manufacturing Co.)*

CAUTION: Stand to one side of the path of the stock being ripped. If the stock binds between the blade and the fence, it may be thrown back toward the operator.

4. Turn the saw on and feed the stock against the fence and into the blade.

CAUTION: To rip narrow stock, a push stick should be used to feed the stock.

RADIAL ARM SAW

With attachments, the *radial arm saw* can perform most of the operations performed by other tools. It can be used for straight and scroll sawing, drilling holes, routing and shaping, and disc and drum sanding. Crosscutting, ripping, and mitering are the operations most often performed on the radial arm saw.

The parts of the radial arm saw are shown in figure 11-8. The column can be raised and lowered to control the depth of cut. The yoke rolls back and forth along the arm to make cuts. The yoke can also be turned 360 degrees and locked in any position for special cuts. In addition, the motor can be tilted up to 90 degrees in the yoke and locked in any position. The arm can also be rotated around the column and locked in any position.

The size of a radial arm saw is specified by the diameter of the largest blade that can be used. The blades for a radial arm saw are the same as for other circular saws. The blade is always installed with the teeth pointing in the direction of rotation. The direction of rotation is usually marked on the motor housing.

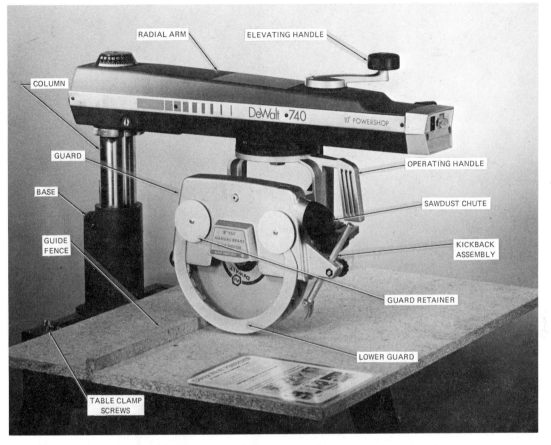

Fig. 11-8(B) Parts of a radial arm saw *(Rockwell International)*

Crosscutting with the Radial Arm Saw

1. Install a combination or crosscut blade.

2. Place the adjustable fence in the forward position.

3. Lock the arm in position at right angles to the fence.

4. Lock the yoke in position so the blade is parallel to the arm.

5. Lock the motor in position so the blade is perpendicular to the table top.

6. Lower the column until the saw teeth just penetrate the kerf in the table surface.

7. Mark the stock where it is to be sawed and hold it against the fence.

CAUTION: Keep your hands away from the path of the saw blade.

Fig. 11-9 Crosscutting with a radial arm saw

8. Turn the saw on and pull it firmly through the stock, figure 11-9. Return the saw to the rear position before removing the stock.

9. Turn the saw off.

Fig. 11-10 In-rip position on the radial arm saw

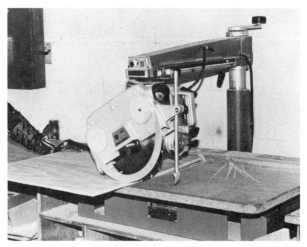

Fig. 11-11 Out-rip position on the radial arm saw

Ripping with the Radial Arm Saw

1. Install a combination or rip blade.

2. Place the adjustable fence in the forward position for ripping narrow stock or in the rear position for wider ripping.

3. Lock the motor in position so the blade is perpendicular to the table top.

4. Most ripping is done in the *in-rip position*, figure 11-10. This places the blade between the motor and the fence. Wide pieces may require that the saw be set in the *out-rip position*. The out-rip position is with the motor between the blade and the fence, figure 11-11. Lock the yoke in either the in-rip or out-rip position, depending on the width of cut to be made.

5. Lower the column until the tips of the saw teeth are just below the surface of the table.

6. Adjust the blade guard so it just clears the stock.

7. Adjust the anti-kickback device so it just drags on the stock.

CAUTION: Stand to one side of the path of the stock being ripped.

8. Turn the saw on and feed the stock into the side opposite the anti-kickback device.

CAUTION: Use a push stick to feed narrow stock, figures 11-12

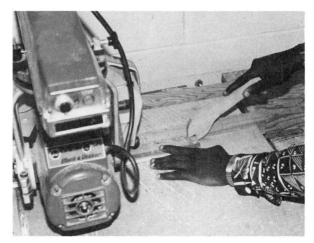

Fig. 11-12 Use a push stick to rip narrow stock.

Mitering and Beveling with the Radial Arm Saw

Miters and bevels are cut easily with the radial arm saw. The setup is the same for miters and bevels as it is for crosscutting, except for one adjustment. To saw miters, the arm is rotated by releasing the miter clamp and relocking it in the desired position, figure 11-13. For sawing bevels, the motor is tilted by releasing the bevel clamp and relocking it in the desired position, figure 11-14.

JOINTER

The *jointer* is a stationary machine that performs much of the work of bench planes. The parts of a jointer are shown in figure 11-15. The cutter head is a solid cylinder holding three

Fig. 11-13 Sawing a miter with a radial arm saw

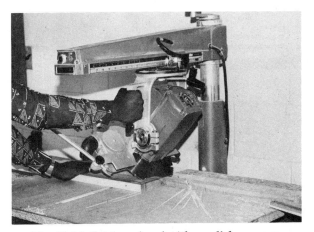

Fig. 11-14 Sawing a bevel with a radial arm saw

knives that are turned at a high speed by the motor. The infeed table can be raised and lowered to regulate the depth of cut. The outfeed table is kept at the same height as the top of the cutterhead arc, figure 11-16. The fence can be tilted for planing beveled edges. The fence can also be moved back and forth across the table to expose only the desired portion of the cutterhead. The guard is spring-loaded to keep the cutterhead covered when not in use.

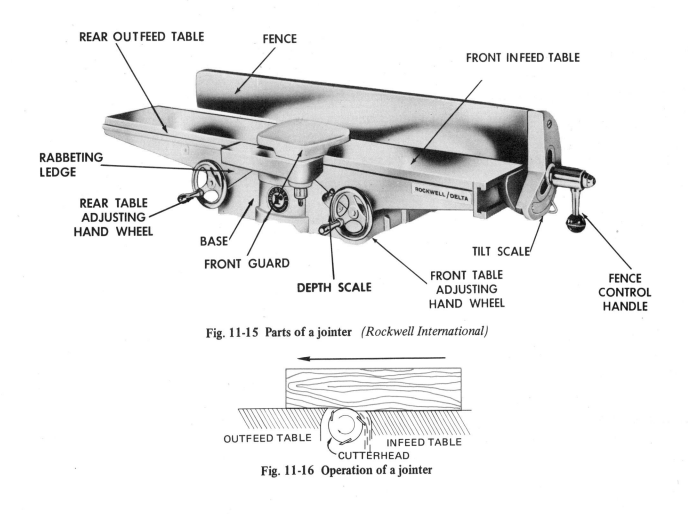

Fig. 11-15 Parts of a jointer *(Rockwell International)*

Fig. 11-16 Operation of a jointer

Fig. 11-17 Planing an edge with a jointer

Fig. 11-18 Planing a face with a jointer. Notice the push block.

The size of a jointer is specified by the length of the cutterhead. Jointers are available in sizes from 4 inches to 30 inches.

Planing an Edge with the Jointer

1. Adjust the infeed table for a 1/32-inch to 1/16-inch cut, figure 11-17.

2. Position the fence so that just enough of the cutter is exposed to plane the edge.

3. Adjust the fence so that it is at right angles to the table.

4. Turn the jointer on and hold the stock against the fence.

CAUTION: The operator's hands must not pass below the top of the guard.

5. Feed the stock from the infeed table to the outfeed table.

6. Turn the jointer off.

Planing a Face with the Jointer

1. Adjust the infeed table for a 1/64-inch to a 1/32-inch cut, figure 11-18.

2. Position the fence so that just enough of the cutter is exposed to plane the surface.

3. Use a push block to feed the stock.

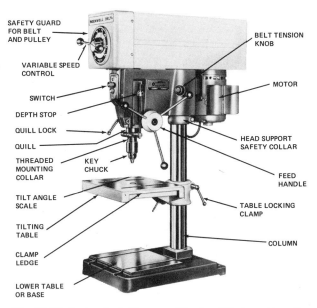

Fig. 11-19 Parts of a drill press *(Rockwell International)*

4. Feed the stock from the infeed table to the outfeed table.

5. Turn the jointer off.

DRILL PRESS

The *drill press* performs the same operations as other drills but with greater accuracy. The main parts of a drill press are shown in figure 11-19.   The chuck is mounted on a movable quill. The quill is connected to the motor by a V-belt and pulley system. The quill is raised and lowered by the feed handle to feed the drill bit into the work. The table can be locked in any position on the column with the table locking clamp. In addition, the table on most drill presses can be tilted from side to side for angle drilling. Most drill presses also have an adjustable stop to position the quill at the desired depth.

The speed of the drill press is controlled in one of two ways. Some drill presses are equipped with a variable speed drive. On these machines the speed is selected while the machine is running. Other drill presses use a system of stepped pulleys, figure 11-20. Before changing speeds on this type of machine, the electrical power should be disconnected. The speed is changed by moving the belt to different steps on the pulleys. In general, small bits should be used at a high speed and larger bits at a low speed.

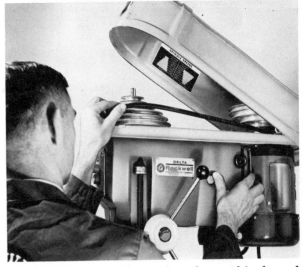

Fig. 11-20 On some drill presses, the speed is changed by repositioning the drive belt. *(Rockwell International)*

CAUTION: Small pieces of wood and all metal pieces should be clamped to the table or held in a drill press vise. Be sure the drill bit will not strike the table as it passes through the workpiece.

ACTIVITIES

A. BAND SAWING

Equipment and Materials

　　Band saw
　　Scrap wood

Procedure

1. Lay out the scroll sawing exercise on the scrap wood as shown in figure 11-21.

2. Adjust the upper blade guide assembly to clear the stock by approximately 1/4 inch.

3. Make several relief cuts from the edge of the stock to the sharp curve in the layout line.

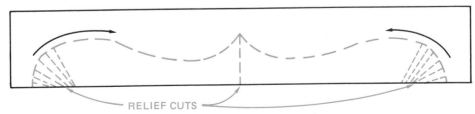

RELIEF CUTS

Fig. 11-21 Scroll sawing exercise

CAUTION: When backing out of the relief cut, be careful not to pull the blade from between the guide blocks.

4. Saw the stock on the layout line. Be careful not to twist the blade.

B.   MACHINE SQUARING STOCK – VARIETY SAW AND JOINTER

Equipment and Materials

> Portable circular saw or hand crosscut saw
> Variety saw
> Jointer
> Piece of lumber, 3/4" x 6" x 25 1/2" (finished size)
> Tape measure or folding rule

Procedure

1. Cut the stock to a rough length of 26 1/2 inches with the portable circular saw or hand saw.

2. Follow the instructions on page 154 to plane one edge of the stock on the jointer.

CAUTION: Do not position your hands where they will pass below the top of the cutter guard.

3. Follow the instructions on page 149 for crosscutting on the variety saw and cut a small amount from one end of the stock. The trued edge should be against the miter gauge. If one end of the stock is already square, this step is not necessary.

4. Mark off the finished length (25 1/2 inches) from the square end and cut the stock to finished length. Remember to keep the trued edge against the miter gauge.

5. Follow the instructions on page 149 and rip the stock to a width of 6 1/16 inches on the variety saw. (1/16 is allowed for planing.)

6. Plane the sawed edge on the jointer.

C.   MACHINE SQUARING STOCK – RADIAL ARM SAW AND JOINTER

Equipment and Materials

> Radial arm saw
> Jointer
> Piece of lumber, 3/4" x 6" x 25 1/2" (finished size)
> Tape measure or folding rule

Procedure

1. Follow the instructions on page 151 for crosscutting on the radial arm saw and cut the stock to a rough length of 26 1/2 inches.

CAUTION: Do not place your hands in the path of the blade. The force of the blade tends to pull the saw into the stock.

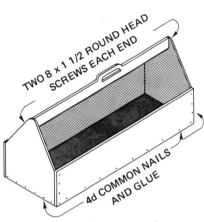

Fig. 11-22 Tote carrier.

2. If the stock does not have a smooth square edge, follow the instructions on page 151 for planing an edge on the jointer.

CAUTION: Do not position your hands where they will pass below the top of the guard.

3. Place the trued edge of the stock against the radial arm saw fence and cut a very small amount from one end. If one end is already square, this step is not necessary.

4. Mark off the finished length (25 1/2 inches) from the square end and cut the stock to finished length. Remember to keep the trued edge against the fence.

5. Follow the instructions on page 152 to rip the stock to a width of 6 1/16 inches on the radial arm saw. (1/16 inch is allowed for planing.)

6. Plane the sawed edge on the jointer.

7. *Note:* The dimensions used for Activities B and C are for the sides of the tote carrier. When all pieces are produced, the carrier can be assembled as shown in figure 11-22.

REVIEW

A. Multiple Choice

Select the best answer for each of the following questions.

1. Which of the following operations would probably be performed with a band saw?

   a. Cutting framing materials to length on a job site
   b. Scroll sawing parts for trim
   c. Accurately ripping pieces for stair construction
   d. Cutting an opening in wall paneling for an electrical outlet

2. What is the purpose of the blade guide wheels on a band saw?

   a. To prevent the blade from being pushed toward the back of the table
   b. To keep the blade on the wheels
   c. To keep the blade in a straight line
   d. To help the operator control the path of the blade

3. For which operation might a carpenter use a variety saw?

   a. Sawing large curves in plywood
   b. Cutting sheet metal for heating ducts
   c. Cutting openings in paneling for electrical outlets
   d. Ripping lumber for a concrete form

4. What direction should the teeth on a variety saw blade point?

   a. Away from the operator
   b. Toward the operator
   c. Up
   d. Down

5. How should the blade guard on a radial arm saw be adjusted for ripping stock?

   a. Parallel to the table
   b. The outfeed side just clears the stock
   c. The infeed side rides on the stock
   d. The infeed side just clears the stock

6. When ripping with the radial arm saw, which way is the stock fed into the machine?

   a. From the side with the anti-kickback device
   b. From the front
   c. From the side opposite the anti-kickback device
   d. From the rear

7. How should narrow stock be fed into a variety saw or radial arm saw for ripping?

   a. It should be pushed with only one hand.
   b. It should be pushed with a push stick.
   c. It should be ripped partway, then turned around and completed from the opposite end.
   d. It should be pulled through from the far side of the saw.

8. At what depth should the jointer be set for planing an edge?

   a. 1/2 inch
   b. 1/4 inch to 3/8 inch
   c. 1/16 inch to 1/8 inch
   d. 1/32 inch

9. Which of the following adjustments can be made on most drill presses?

   a. Speed
   b. Height of the table
   c. Angle of the table
   d. All of these can be adjusted.

10. What is the main advantage of the drill press as compared to a portable electric drill?

    a. Greater speed
    b. Greater accuracy
    c. Larger pieces of material can be drilled
    d. Some materials that cannot be drilled with a portable electric drill can be drilled with a drill press.

B. Identification

Give the name for each of the parts indicated.

1. Variety saw, figure 11-23
2. Radial arm saw, figure 11-24
3. Drill press, figure 11-25
4. Jointer, figure 11-26

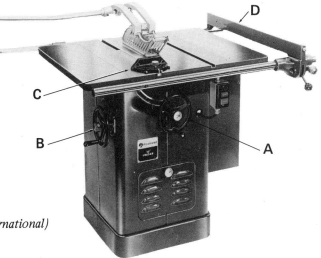

Fig. 11-23 Variety saw *(Rockwell International)*

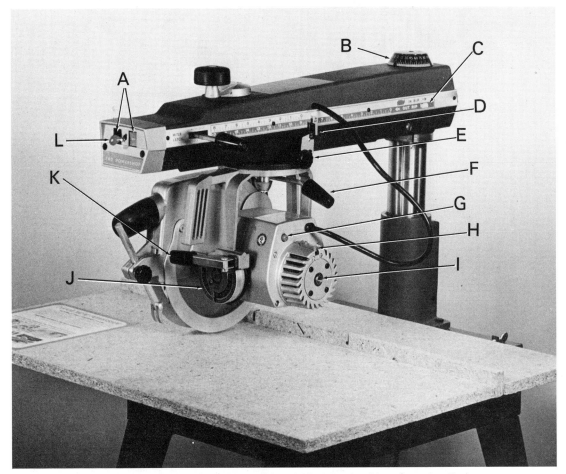

Fig. 11-24 Radial arm saw. *(The Black & Decker Manufacturing Co.)*

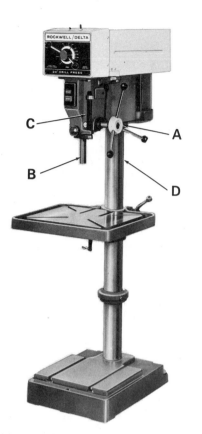

Fig. 11-25 Drill press *(Rockwell International)*

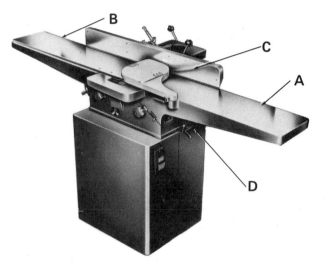

Fig. 11-26 Jointer *(Rockwell International)*

SECTION 4
SECTION 4
SECTION 4
SECTION 4

LIGHT CONSTRUCTION

UNIT 12.
SITE WORK

OBJECTIVES

After completing this unit, the student will be able to:

- interpret a plot plan.
- lay out building lines and erect batter boards.

PLOT PLANS AND BUILDING CODES

The building codes of most communities regulate the placement of a house on a building site. In some communities, this is based on the setback of neighboring houses. *Setback* is the distance that a building is from the street. Codes of this type insure that a new house is not built closer to the street than surrounding houses. Codes that do not base setback regulations on existing structures may specify a minimum setback.

Local governments usually require that a plot plan, figure 12-1 be included as a part of the set of working drawings. The *plot plan* indicates the location of the proposed building, location of trees to remain on the site, and the finished grade. The *finished grade* is the elevation above sea level of the site after construction is completed. The plot plan, or site plan, for large construction projects is prepared by the architect or surveyor. However, in residential construction, working drawings are often obtained from a planning service and the architect never sees the construction site. In this case, the general contractor frequently prepares a plot plan.

LAYING OUT BUILDING LINES

After the plot plan is submitted and a building permit is obtained, the position of the new building is staked out. Stakes are driven into the ground where the corners of the building will be.

Usually the front line of the building is established first. If the building is to be parallel with the street, this line can be found by measuring from the curb or centerline of the street. A line is stretched between two stakes to indicate where the front building line will be. The stakes are driven at the locations of the front corners of the building, figure 12-2.

The sides of the building are found by laying out lines at right angles to the front line. Right angles can be measured by the 6-8-10

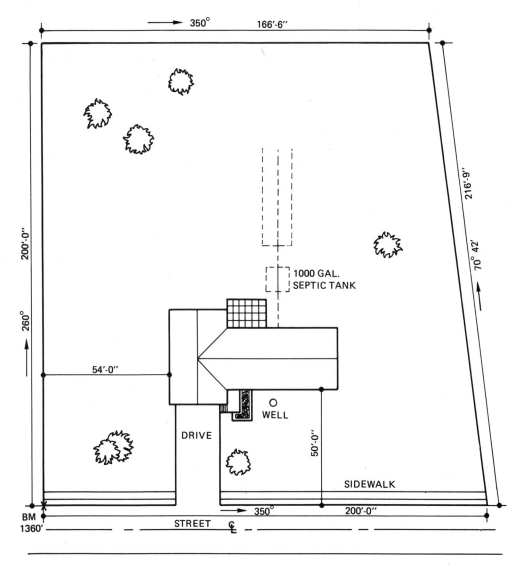

Fig. 12-1 Typical plot plan

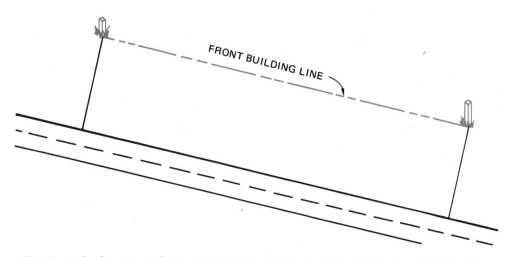

Fig. 12-2 The first step in laying out a building is to drive stakes for the front building line.

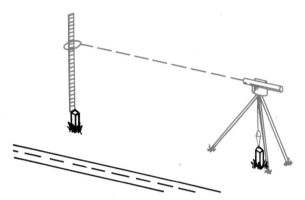

Fig. 12-3 The level or transit is first lined up on the front building line stakes.

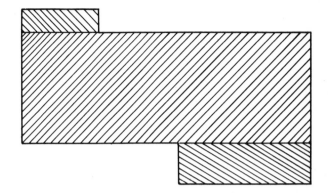

Fig. 12-4 Irregularly shaped buildings are divided into smaller rectangles, then each part is laid out separately.

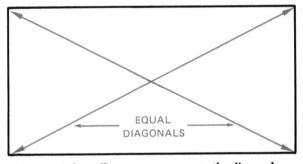

Fig. 12-5 When all corners are square, the diagonals are equal.

method explained in Unit 7. However, corners are usually laid out by using a builder's level or transit. The instrument is set up over a corner stake. If the builder's level is used, it is then focused on a target rod held over the other front corner stake, figure 12-3. The advantage of a transit for laying out corners is it can be aimed directly at the stake, eliminating the target rod. With the level or transit in this position, the 360-degree scale is adjusted to zero. Then the telescope is turned so the scale reads 90 degrees. The telescope is now aimed at the side building line.

When both side lines have been established, the back corners are found by measuring from the front corners. If the building is irregular in shape, it is divided into several smaller rectangles and laid out in the same way, figure 12-4.

The squareness of the layout should be checked by measuring the diagonals. If all of the corners are 90 degrees, the diagonals are equal, figure 12-5. It is extremely important for the building lines to be accurate. If the lines are not correct, many materials will have to be cut during construction, wasting a great amount of labor.

ERECTING BATTER BOARDS

Batter boards are usually erected under the direct supervision of the general contractor. Batter boards allow the corner stakes to be removed without loosing the building lines.

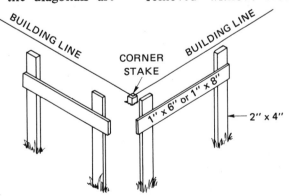

Fig. 12-6 Batter boards are erected at each corner.

Batter boards are erected at each corner about 5 feet outside the building lines. By placing them away from the building lines, they are not disturbed when the *excavation* (earth moving) is done. Four 2″ x 4″ stakes are driven into the ground and two pieces of 1″ x 6″ or 1″ x 8″ lumber are nailed to them, figure 12-6. A line stretched over the corner stakes is used to mark the building lines on the batter boards. To insure that the line is directly over the corner stake, a plumb bob is suspended over the stake, figure 12-7. When the building line has been accurately marked on the batter boards, a saw kerf about 1/4 inch deep marks it permanently. The batter boards will be used to guide the excavation and construction of the foundation.

EXCAVATION

Even small buildings have considerable weight. The weight of the building must be supported by the earth or rock directly beneath it. This fact makes it important to give special consideration to the soil the building will rest on.

If the area has been a landfill site, the earth and fill may not be fully compacted. Landfill sites also often contain *organic materials* (materials that will decompose, such as wood and garbage) that will eventually cause the area to settle. Some kinds of earth compact more easily than others.

Most soil contains some moisture. In many parts of the country, this moisture freezes during the winter. As the ground freezes, it swells just as water does. When it thaws in the spring, it contracts. The depth to which earth freezes in winter is called the *frost line*. This swelling and contracting creates severe problems if it occurs under the building.

To overcome these problems of unstable soil, the building rests on a base below the frost line and on solid earth. To construct this base, the earth must be *excavated* (dug out), figure 12-8. Frequently, a cellar area is excavated and included in the structure. Buildings that do not have cellars either have a concrete

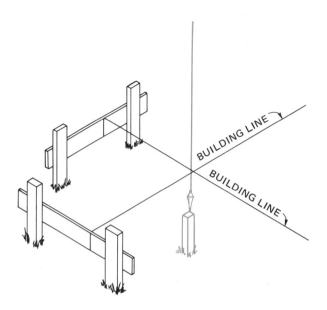

Fig. 12-7 A plumb bob is suspended over the corner stake to find the point where the building lines cross.

Fig. 12-8 Excavating for a foundation *(Deere & Co.)*

floor directly on the soil or a *crawl space* big enough to permit access to electrical and mechanical systems under the floor.

The excavation is usually done by an excavating contractor. Excavating contractors use a variety of heavy equipment to complete the excavation. If the earth must be removed, the excavating contractor generally hauls it away in dump trucks. Excavators must know how to interpret plot plans and use a builder's level to accurately measure the excavation.

Fig. 12-9 A bench mark may be an official marker or any fixed object of known elevation.

GRADING

The excavator usually grades the land surrounding the building lines to the rough grade. The *rough grade* is the elevation and slope of the finished grade minus a few inches for top soil. If the finished grade is substantially different from the *existing grade* (grade before construction) a surveyor indicates where the finished grade will be. The surveyor uses a bench mark as a starting point. *Bench marks* are fixed points indicating the elevation above sea level at that point, figure 12-9. The surveyor

Fig. 12-10 Grade stakes tell the excavator where the finished grade should be.

determines grade lines by adding to or subtracting from the elevation at the bench mark.

If additional *fill*, or earth, is required to bring the area up to finished grade, the surveyor marks the desired level on *grade stakes*, figure 12-10. When earth must be removed, or *cut*, the surveyor indicates the required depth of excavation on the grade stakes.

─── ACTIVITIES ───

A. ESTABLISHING BUILDING LINES

Before excavation begins, the corners of the proposed structure must be staked. A surveyor usually marks the building lines of large commercial projects. On lighter commercial buildings and residential construction, the general contractor often does this work.

Establishing these points requires accurate measurements. Work carefully to lay out the building in this activity.

Equipment and Materials

100-foot tape measure
Ball of line
4 wood stakes, 2″ x 2″ x 2′
16 wood stakes, 2″ x 4″ x 4′
8 boards, 1″ x 6″ x 4′

4-pound hammer
Plumb bob
Hand crosscut saw

Procedure

1. Drive two stakes 20 feet apart and 10 feet back from the property line. The front property line will be designed by the instructor.

2. Use the 6-8-10 method to lay out the side building lines.

3. Drive stakes on the side building lines and 30 feet from the front line. These stakes should be 20 feet apart.

4. Check the diagonals to be sure the building lines are square.

5. Drive four 2″ x 4″ stakes about five feet outside the building lines at each corner. Refer to figure 12-6.

6. Nail a 1″ x 6″ board to each pair of stakes to complete the batter boards. The 1″ x 6″ pieces should be nearly level to make it easier to locate the building lines.

7. Attach a line to one batter board and stretch it over the corner stakes.

8. Hold a plumb bob over the corner stakes to check the position of the lines.

9. Repeat steps 7 and 8 for all four sides of the building.

10. Saw a kerf approximately 1/4 inch deep to mark the location of the building lines on the batter boards.

B.   PLOT PLAN

When planning a project, the architect or surveyor prepares a plot plan. This shows where the building and other features are located on the site. It also indicates the finish grade for each main corner of the building so the excavator knows how much to fill or cut. The general contractor also uses the plot plan to stake out the house and locate such features as the sidewalks, wells, gas and water lines, and landscaping.

Equipment and Materials

Architect's scale
Paper and pencil
30-60-90° triangle

Procedure

Draw a plot plan for a house, 26 feet wide (front and back) and 48 feet long, situated on a 200 foot by 200 foot lot. The house is to face a street on the south side of the lot. The setback is to be 50 feet and the house is to be centered between the east and west boundaries. The elevation at a bench mark on the edge of the street is 474 feet. The finished grade is to be 478 feet at the front of the house and 477 feet at the back of the house. The northeast corner of the lot is at 470 feet and the northwest corner is at 467 feet. Include a 3-foot sidewalk beside the street and a 3-foot walk leading to the front entrance, 24 feet from the west end of the house. A 9-foot driveway leads to a garage in the front of the west end. Draw the plot plan to a scale of 1/16″ = 1′-0″.

REVIEW

1. Refer to figure 12-11 to determine the amount of *cut* (earth removed) and *fill* (additional earth) required for the new building in figure 12-12. Write the number of feet and the word "cut" or the word "fill" for each of the lettered points.

2. List all of the occupations that were probably involved with the site planning, site preparation, and earthwork for your school.

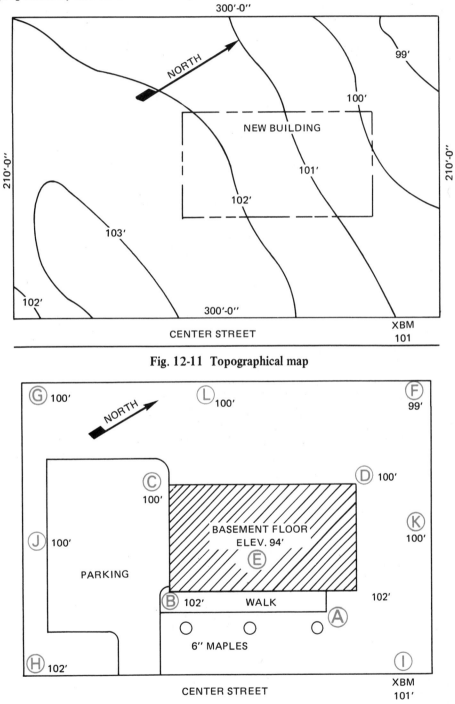

Fig. 12-11 Topographical map

Fig. 12-12 Plot plan

LUNIT 13.

FOOTINGS AND FOUNDATIONS

OBJECTIVES

After completing this unit, the student will be able to:

- explain the importance and function of footings.

- explain the most important design considerations for the foundation of a house.

- construct a concrete block foundation.

FUNCTION OF FOOTINGS

In Unit 12, it was pointed out that soil conditions can vary and, therefore, the base of the building must allow for these conditions. In the construction of most houses, this base is properly called a *spread footing*. It is called this because it "spreads" the weight of the house over a larger area. All of the weight of a house is supported by the foundation walls. These walls vary in thickness from 6 inches to 12 inches. The pressure these walls apply to the ground is greatly reduced by resting the walls on a concrete footing that is wider than the thickness of the wall, figure 13-1. Similarly, where posts support the weight of beams in the interior of the basement, footings spread their pressure over a greater area, figure 13-2.

FOOTING DESIGN

In general practice, the excavation for the foundation is done to a depth below any loose

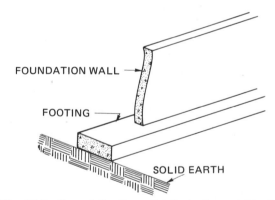

Fig. 13-1 Spread footings distribute the weight of the structure over a larger area than the foundation wall.

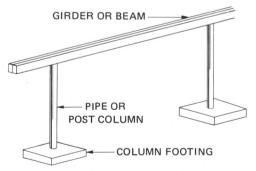

Fig. 13-2 Pipe columns or posts which support girders or beams rest on concrete footings.

Footings

Sec. 2907. (a) **General.** Footings and foundations, unless otherwise specifically provided, shall be constructed of masonry or concrete and in all cases extend below the frost line. Footings shall be constructed of solid masonry or concrete. Foundations supporting wood shall extend at least 6 inches above the adjacent finish grade. Footings shall have a minimum depth below finished grade as indicated in Table No. 29-A unless another depth is recommended by a foundation investigation.

(b) **Bearing Walls.** Bearing walls shall be supported on masonry or concrete foundations or piles or other approved foundation system which shall be of sufficient size to support all loads. Where a design is not provided, the minimum foundation requirements for stud bearing walls shall be as set forth in Table No. 29-A.

TABLE NO. 29-A—FOUNDATIONS FOR STUD BEARING WALLS MINIMUM REQUIREMENTS

NUMBER OF STORIES	THICKNESS OF FOUNDATION WALL (Inches)		WIDTH OF FOOTING (Inches)	THICKNESS OF FOOTING (Inches)	DEPTH OF FOUNDATION BELOW NATURAL SURFACE OF GROUND AND FINISH GRADE (Inches)
	CONCRETE	UNIT MASONRY			
1	6	6	12	6	12
2	8	8	15	7	18
3	10	10	18	8	24

NOTES:

Where unusual conditions or frost conditions are found, footings and foundations shall be as required in Section 2907 (a).

The ground under the floor may be excavated to the elevation of the top of the footing.

Fig. 13-3 Most building codes include a section on footing design. *(Reproduced from the 1976 edition of The Uniform Building Code, Copyright 1976, with permission of the International Conference of Building Officials)*

fill, soft organic material, and the frost line. Excavation must extend below the frost line because the forces of freezing and thawing cannot be practically controlled. However, in some cases, it may not be practical to excavate to the depth at which the soil can support the building on conventional sized footings. This is particularly true in wet areas, such as many parts of the southeastern United States. For this reason, footing designs must be varied to suit the conditions. Usually footing design is specified by building codes, figure 13-3.

Where footing design is not specified by a building code, it is up to the architect to indicate the size of the footing. The footing is shown on the foundation plan by a broken line, figure 13-4. Usually a note is included to indicate the dimensions of the footing. When the footing is not designed by the architect and no building code is available, the builder relies on experience. Typical footings for residential and light commercial construction are twice as wide as the thickness of the foundation wall and the same depth as the thickness of the foundation

wall. For example, if the foundation wall is 10 inches thick, the footing is built 20 inches wide and 10 inches high.

PLACING FOOTINGS

The excavator digs to the depth of the basement floor if one is included in the plans. Otherwise, the excavation is dug to the bottom of the foundation walls. In either case, the excavation extends approximately 2 feet outside the building lines. This provides space for carpenters to erect forms for concrete work and for masons to lay concrete blocks. The excavation for the footings is finished by hand with shovels by construction laborers, figure 13-5. It is done by hand to prevent going beyond the depth of the footings.

On some jobs, the ditches for the footings are dug carefully and the concrete is placed directly in them without the need for forms. On other jobs, lumber is used to construct forms in the ditches.

If the concrete is placed directly in the ditch, grade stakes are driven every few feet in

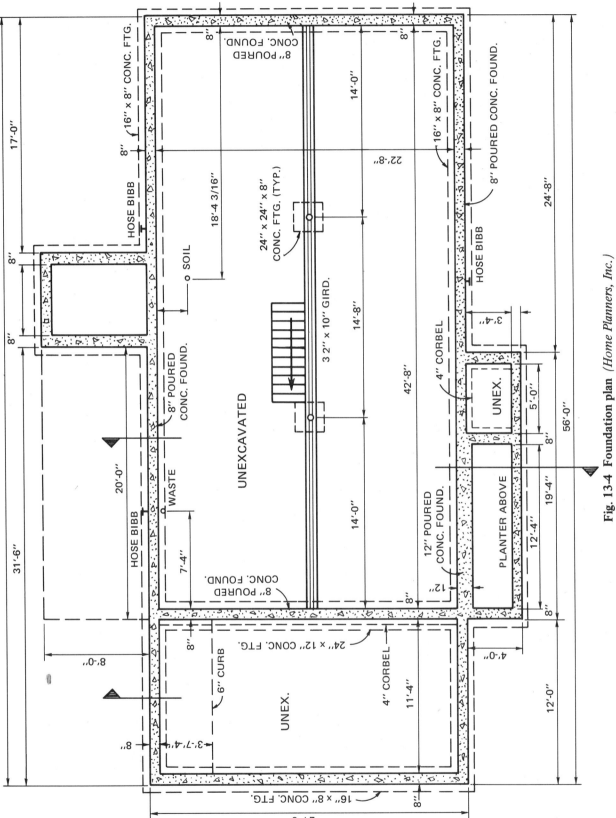

Fig. 13-4 Foundation plan *(Home Planners, Inc.)*

Fig. 13-5 The bottom of the footing excavation must be flat.

Fig. 13-6 Footing forms are leveled as they are constructed, then concrete is leveled with the top of the forms. *(Portland Cement Assoc.)*

the center of the ditch. The height of these stakes is measured with a builder's level. When the concrete is flush with their tops, the footing is level. If side forms are used, they are leveled as they are built. As the concrete is placed it is leveled with the top of the forms, figure 13-6.

As the concrete is *placed* (since concrete is not considered liquid, it is not "poured"), it is screeded off. A *screed* is a straightedge used to push excess concrete into low spots. The concrete is not smoothed beyond screeding. The rough surface left by screeding provides for better bonding of the mortar in which concrete blocks are set.

FOUNDATION DESIGN

The most obvious function of a foundation is to support the weight of the building. Other factors must be considered by the architect. In many homes, the basement is an area for future expansion. In some home designs, the basement is an important living space, figure 13-7. Certain characteristics are necessary if the basement is to be a living space. There must be adequate headroom and the area must be dry. It is also desirable to have good ventilation and some windows for natural light. These features and included on the architect's foundation plan.

Fig. 13-7 Finished basement living space *(Masonite Corp.)*

Fig. 13-8 All-weather wood foundation *(National Forest Products Assoc.)*

Foundations are usually constructed of concrete or concrete block. However, a type of specially treated wood foundation is gaining popularity. The wood for these foundations is treated with preservative under pressure to prevent it from decaying. It is further protected by covering it with a thin sheet of plastic during construction, figure 13-8.

When a concrete foundation is used, carpenters erect forms of plywood or metal. *Form carpentry* is an important branch of the carpentry trade, figure 13-9. As soon as possible after the concrete cures, the forms are *stripped* (removed), cleaned, and stored for use on the next job.

Concrete blocks are also a popular material for foundations. Although a concrete block foundation takes somewhat longer to build, the materials are less expensive. Concrete blocks are laid by masons.

Fig. 13-9 Erecting forms for a concrete foundation

Fig. 13-10 Mortar is usually mixed in power mixers.
(Richard T. Kreh, Sr.)

LAYING A CONCRETE BLOCK FOUNDATION

When the concrete blocks are delivered to the construction site, they are stacked at several points around the footings. The lime, sand, and cement (or masonry cement) are stacked near where they will be mixed. The cement is protected from rain by a tarp.

Before any mortar is mixed or blocks are laid, the masons mark the location of the wall on the footing with a chalk line. Then the wall is measured to determine if it will be necessary to cut any blocks. The most common length of concrete blocks is 16 inches and it may be necessary to cut one block in every course to build the planned wall.

The mortar is mixed, usually in a power mixer, by masonry laborers, figure 13-10. The mixed mortar is transferred to mortar pans located next to the footing. The masons take their mortar from these pans. A full bed of mortar is spread along the footing for a length of several blocks. The blocks are set in the mortar bed with mortar spread on the head joints (end joints). As each block is laid, it is check for levelness and plumbness with a spirit level, figure 13-11.

Fig. 13-11 A mason checks blocks for plumbness.

Fig. 13-12 These masons are laying blocks to a line.

The corners are constructed first so the main portion of each wall can be laid to a line. As each course of blocks is laid, a length of mason's line is stretched between the tops of the corner blocks for that course, figure 13-12. The masons use this line as a guide in setting that course to the right height. The plumbness is still checked with a spirit level.

The blocks for a foundation are usually laid in *running bond*. This means that the head joints are located over the center of the block below, figure 13-13. With 8" x 8" x 16" blocks, this is accomplished by alternating the blocks at the corner. If blocks of any other size are used, it is necessary to cut the corner blocks.

When the mortar is just hard enough so that it leaves a thumbprint when pressed with the thumb, the joints are tooled. The most common jointing tool is the *convex jointer*; it produces a concave joint. Portions of the foundation that will be hidden by earth on the outside may not be tooled.

Fig. 13-14 Parging the foundation wall with portland cement mortar (*Richart T. Kreh, Sr.*)

Fig. 13-13 Foundations are usually laid in running bond so the end joints are over the center of the block below.

DAMPPROOFING AND DRAINAGE

To help prevent moisture from seeping through the foundation walls, they are damp-proofed. This frequently consists of *parging* (coating) the wall with a 1/2-inch coat of portland cement and lime plaster and covering this with asphalt waterproofing, figure 13-14. Dampproofing does not extend above the finished grade line. For a more waterproof job, some foundations are covered with a *waterproof membrane* (thin sheet of material) and hot tar.

As ground water reaches the coated foundation, it runs down to the bottom of the foundation. Plastic or clay drain pipes are placed around the footing to carry this water away from the building. Plastic drain pipe has holes to allow the water to enter. Clay drain tiles have loose joints that allow the water to enter. These pipes are buried in crushed stone to permit a free flow of water, figure 13-15.

Fig. 13-15 Perforated drain pipe partially covered with stone (*Richard T. Kreh, Sr.*)

—— ACTIVITIES ——————————————————————————

A. FOOTING DESIGN

Structural engineers design the load-carrying parts of a building. They must know how each type of footing will settle on a particular type of soil. To do this, they work closely with the architect to find the amount of weight on the building. They also consult soil engineers for facts about the soil on the site. Using this data, they then decide the size and depth of the footings for the building.

Equipment and Materials

Container at least 1' x 1' x 1'
Sand
Peat moss
Lumber, 2" x 6" x 10"
Lumber, 2" x 4" x 10"
Tape measure or folding rule
Concrete block, 8" x 8" x 16"

Procedure

1. Fill the container with sand to a depth of at least one foot.

2. Place the 2" x 6" x 10" piece of lumber on edge on the sand.

3. Place the concrete block on the 2" x 6" piece as a weight.

4. Measure the depth to which the 2" x 6" piece settles in the sand.

5. Repeat steps 1 through 4, but place the 2" x 4" lumber on its 4-inch surface under the 2" x 6" lumber.

6. Repeat steps 1 through 5 using peat moss instead of sand.

7. What effect does the footing have in each type of soil?

B. LAYING CONCRETE BLOCKS

(This activity should be done by a team of 4-8 students.) A sound concrete block foundation depends upon a mason's skill and accuracy. Masons must be able to lay blocks in a straight line and in proportion. Their work must be uniform. All blocks must have a 3/8-inch joint and be firmly set in place. Good construction depends on a sound foundation.

Equipment and Materials

Tape measure or folding rule
Chalk line
112 concrete blocks, 8" x 8" x 16"
Sand-lime training mortar
Trowels
Spirit level
Mason's line and line blocks
Convex jointer

Procedure

1. Lay out a square with 9'-4" sides on the floor or pavement.

2. While some students are laying out the activity, others should mix the mortar.

3. With the students working alone or in pairs, spread mortar inside the square at each corner and lay the first course of blocks.

4. Level and plumb each block leaving 3/8-inch joints. Any excess mortar should be cut off with a trowel and returned to the supply.

5. Build each corner four courses high, figure 13-16. Care should be exercised to see that all joints are 3/8 inch and that all blocks are level and plumb.

6. When all corners are built, stretch the mason's line between two corner blocks of the same course. Figure 13-17 shows how the line is tied to the line blocks.

7. Lay the remaining blocks to the line. These blocks must be plumbed with a spirit level.

8. At the end of each class session during which blocks are laid or when the mortar is thumbprint hard, strike the joints with a convex jointer.

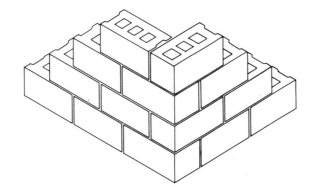

Fig. 13-16 Four-block high corner

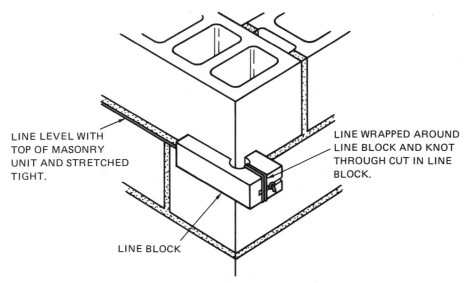

LINE LEVEL WITH TOP OF MASONRY UNIT AND STRETCHED TIGHT.

LINE WRAPPED AROUND LINE BLOCK AND KNOT THROUGH CUT IN LINE BLOCK.

LINE BLOCK

Fig. 13-17 Line tied to line block

REVIEW

A.   Multiple Choice

1. What is the purpose of the footings for a house?

    a. To spread the weight over a larger area
    b. To provide a strong base for the foundation walls
    c. To prevent the foundation from settling
    d. All of the above

2. Who is most apt to be concerned with designing footings?

    a. Building code official   c. Carpenter
    b. Mason   d. Excavator

3. Who is most apt to construct footings?

    a. Excavator   c. Carpenter
    b. Mason   d. Architect

4. What is the most common size for footings for an 8-inch foundation?

    a. 20″ wide x 10″ deep   c. 8″ wide x 16″ deep
    b. 16″ wide x 16″ deep   d. 16″ wide x 8″ deep

5. What is the most common size for footings for a 12-inch foundation?

    a. 30″ wide x 16″ deep   c. 24″ wide x 12″ deep
    b. 24″ wide x 8″ deep   d. 12″ wide x 24″ deep

6. How is the top of the footing leveled?

    a. By measuring from the top of the excavation
    b. By measuring from the bottom of the excavation
    c. Footings are not leveled; leveling is done later with mortar
    d. By driving grade stakes in the footing excavation

7. Which of the following materials is used to construct foundations?

    a. Pressure treated wood   c. Concrete blocks
    b. Concrete   d. All of the above

8. Which is the most likely order of work on a concrete block foundation?

    a. Each course is completed before the next is begun.
    b. The main portion of the wall is completed before the corners.
    c. The corners are completed before the rest of the wall.
    d. Each side of the foundation is completed before another is begun.

9. What is parging?

    a. A special cement used in foundations
    b. A portland cement plaster applied to foundations
    c. A waterproof membrane
    d. A mixture of tar and cement

10. How is the plumbness of blocks checked as a foundation is constructed?

    a. With a mason's line   c. With a builder's level
    b. With a spirit level   d. With a straightedge

B.   Factors to Consider

List four important things an architect considers in designing a basement that may be used as living space in the future.

UNIT 14.

FLOOR CONSTRUCTION

OBJECTIVES

After completing this unit, the student will be able to:

- identify and describe the function of floor framing members.
- explain the 4-inch module used in building construction.
- explain how bridging works.

Many houses that do not have basements have a concrete floor placed directly on well-compacted earth. However, most homes have a basement or crawl space and framed floors. The floor framing consists of all of the construction from the top of the foundation to the *subfloor* (the first layer of flooring). The girders and posts, which support the floor framing, are also considered part of the floor framing.

FOUR-INCH MODULE

To understand the reasons for the size and spacing of many building materials, it is necessary to understand the *4-inch module*. Using 4 inches as a standard module, 4-foot wide building panels are exactly 12 modules wide, and 8-foot long panels are 24 modules long, figure 14-1. Some building panels are manufactured in 2-foot widths, so they are 6 modules wide. Likewise, the length is often varied in 2-foot increments to conform with the 4-inch module.

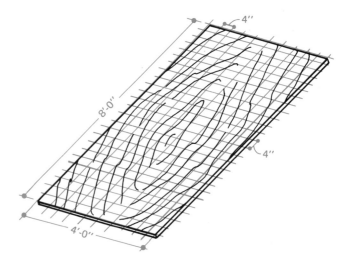

Fig. 14-1 4′ x 8′ building panels are coordinated with the 4-inch modules.

Most building panels, such as plywood, gypsum wallboard, and particleboard, require support in three or four spaces for each 4-foot width. This requirement is easily accommodated by the 4-inch module. If framing members are spaced on 24-inch centers, 4-foot panels are

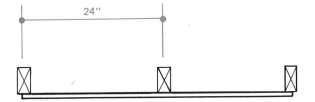

Fig. 14-2 Four-foot panel on 24″ O.C. framing

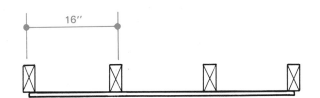

Fig. 14-3 Four-foot panel on 16″ O.C. framing

supported in three places, figure 14-2. If framing members are spaced 16 inches on center, (O.C.) the panels are supported in four places, figure 14-3.

To avoid extra cutting and wasting of materials, buildings are generally designed around 24-inch major modules (six 4-inch modules), figure 14-4. Although it is not always possible to design rooms around the 24-inch module, the overall dimensions of the building are easily held to this standard. With this system, if a 2-foot piece of wall material (1/2 of a 4-foot panel) is left over at one end of the wall, it can be used on the opposite wall.

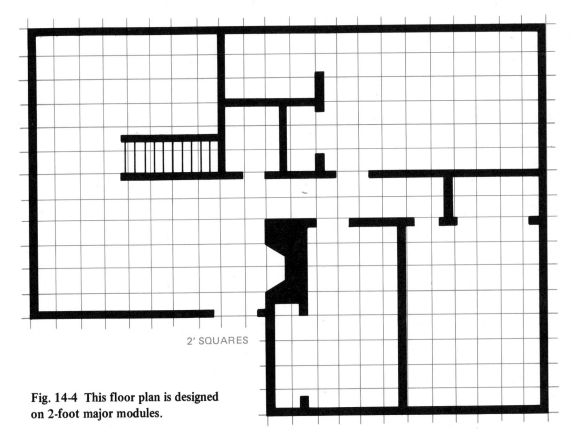

2′ SQUARES

Fig. 14-4 This floor plan is designed on 2-foot major modules.

THE SILL

The *sill* is the wood member directly on top of the concrete or masonry foundation, figure 14-5. It provides a base for fastening the building frame to the foundation. The sill is usually 2″ x 6″ or 2″ x 8″ lumber. The method of anchoring depends somewhat on the kind of foundation. In concrete foundations, anchor bolts are inserted into the fresh concrete as it is placed. Then the carpenters drill holes in the sill at the location of each anchor bolt. The same method can be used with concrete block foundations if the top courses of blocks are filled with concrete. Another method of anchoring the sill to masonry foundations is to use solid blocks for the top course, then nail the sill in place with hardened nails.

GIRDERS AND POSTS

Usually buildings are too wide for continuous pieces of lumber to span the full width. The floor framing is supported by one or more *girders* (beams) running the length of the building. The girder is supported at regular intervals by wood or metal posts or masonry columns called *piers*, figure 14-6. Metal posts called *pipe columns* are used most frequently.

The girder may be one of several types. Steel beams are often used where strength is a critical factor. Built-up wood girders are constructed on the site by the carpenters. These consist of two or three pieces of 2″ x 8″ or 2″ x 10″ nailed together with staggered joints to form larger beams, figure 14-7. Recently, many buildings have been constructed with *box beams*. These beams are made up of a solid wood frame covered with plywood, figure 14-8. The plywood skin adds rigidity to the box beam, although a relatively small amount of material is used. Box beams are also used in several other applications throughout the construction industry. They may be built on the site by carpenters or prebuilt in a millroom. A *millroom* is a shop that makes wood parts for buildings.

Fig. 14-5   A wood sill rests on top of the foundation.

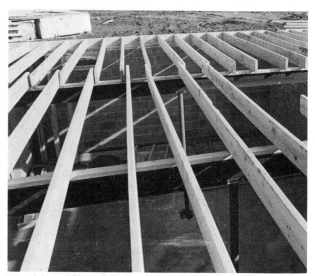

Fig. 14-6   Floor framing is supported by girders. The girders are supported by wood or metal posts or masonry piers. *(Richard T. Kreh, Sr.)*

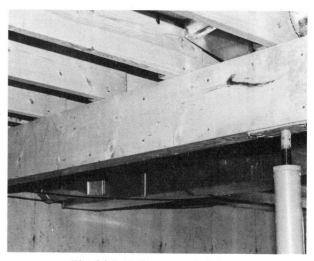

Fig. 14-7   Built-up wood girders

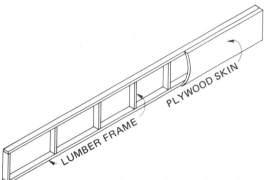

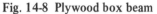

Fig. 14-8 Plywood box beam

Fig. 14-9 Metal joist hangers

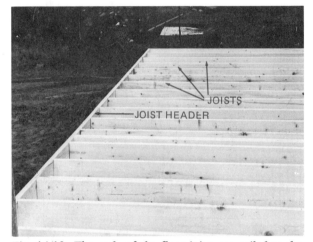

Fig. 14-10 The ends of the floor joists are nailed to the joist headers.

JOISTS

The framing members that rest on the wood sill and support the first layer of flooring (*subfloor*) are called *floor joists*. In a typical house with one girder, the inner ends of the joists either overlap on top of the girder or butt against it. When the joists butt against the girder, they are supported by metal joist hangers or a ledger nailed to the girder, figure 14-9. The outer ends rest on the sill and are nailed to the *joist header*, sometimes called the *band*, figure 14-10.

Traditionally, wood has been the standard material for house framing, including the joists. However, as wood supplies become scarcer and engineered materials become more readily available, many architects specify metal framing members, figure 14-11. Metal joists for house framing are installed the same way as wood joists except for the method of fastening them.

Fig. 14-11 Metal joists are sometimes used instead of wood framing members.

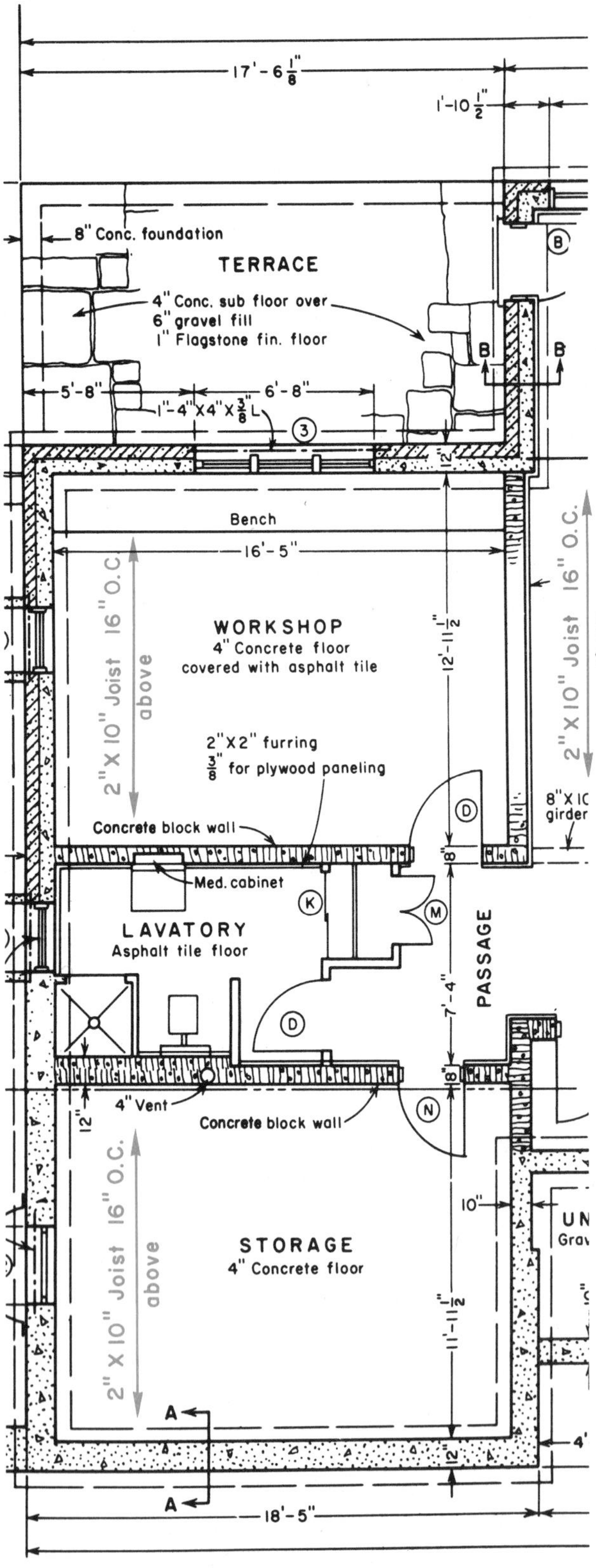
17'-6 1/8"
1'-10 1/2"
8" Conc. foundation
TERRACE
4" Conc. sub floor over
6" gravel fill
1" Flagstone fin. floor
5'-8"
6'-8"
1'-4"X4"X3/8"L
Bench
16'-5"
WORKSHOP
4" Concrete floor
covered with asphalt tile
2"X2" furring
3/8" for plywood paneling
Concrete block wall
2"X10" Joist 16" O.C. above
12'-11 1/2"
8"X10 girder
Med. cabinet
LAVATORY
Asphalt tile floor
PASSAGE
7'-4"
4" Vent
Concrete block wall
STORAGE
4" Concrete floor
11'-11 1/2"
18'-5"
Top of this foundation
to be 5" lower than

Fig. 14-12 Joist callouts for the first floor are shown on the foundation plan.

Metal joists are fastened to the foundation with powder-actuated stud drivers. These tools, powered by an explosive cartridge, drive a nail-like fastener, called a *stud*, through the framing member and into the concrete or masonry foundation. The subfloor is later fastened in place by self-drilling, self-tapping screws and power screwdrivers.

The size and spacing of the floor joists are shown on the working drawings, figure 14-12. The spacing is usually either 16 inches on center or 24 inches on center. Wood floor joists used in houses are usually 8, 10, or 12 inches deep. If the spacing is to be 16 inches on center, the carpenters mark the joist header every 16 inches from one end of the building. The first joist, called a *stringer joist*, is placed on the outside edge of the end wall of the foundation. Each successive joist is centered on the 16-inch marks. Where partitions are to be located, the joists may be doubled for added strength. Around openings for chimneys and stairs, the ends of the joists are nailed to a *double header*. The joists at each side are doubled with a *trimmer joist*, figure 14-13.

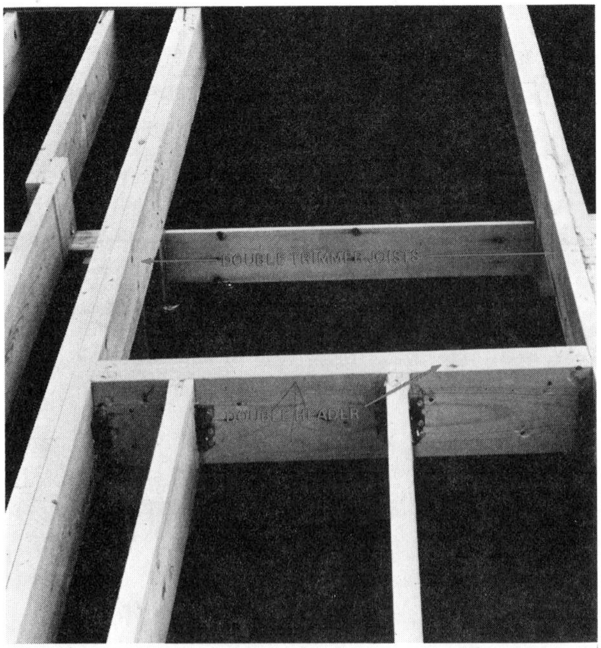
DOUBLE TRIMMER JOISTS
DOUBLE HEADER

Fig. 14-13 Double framing members are used around openings for stairs and chimneys.

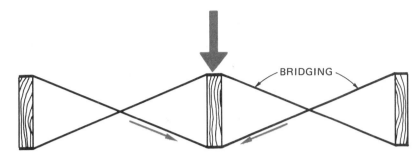

Fig. 14-14 When a load is placed on one joist, the bridging pulls down on the adjacent joists.

Fig. 14-15 (A) Solid wood bridging

Fig. 14-15 (B) Diagonal wood bridging

BRIDGING

The floor joists must be strong enough to support the load that is expected on the floor they support. However, one of the sometimes useful characteristics of wood is its ability to flex and adjust to various forces. In a floor this characteristic could result in a springy floor. Bridging prevents this from happening.

Bridging stiffens the floor framing by resisting two tendencies of wood floor joists. When a load is placed on one joist, the bridging transfers part of that load to the joists on each side, figure 14-14. Bridging also prevents the floor joists from twisting to one side or the other. Bridging may be one of three types, figure 14-15: (A) solid wood bridging, (B) diagonal bridging, or (C) diagonal metal bridging.

Fig. 14-15 (C) Diagonal metal bridging

Fig. 14-16 Carpenters install subflooring over the floor joists. *(American Plywood Assoc.)*

The top end of diagonal bridging is nailed in place before the subfloor is applied. After the subfloor and wall framing are in place, most of the eventual load is on the floor framing. The bottom end of the diagonal bridging is then nailed to the joists.

Fig. 14-17 Single-floor system uses thick plywood and framing members 4 feet on centers. *(American Plywood Assoc.)*

SUBFLOORING

The *subflooring* is the first layer of material applied over the floor joists, figure 14-16. Once the subfloor is in place, carpenters and other construction personnel have a smooth platform on which to work. Most subflooring used in residential construction is plywood. In conventional floor systems, 1/2-inch or 5/8-inch plywood is nailed to the floor joists. Then an *underlayment,* which is a second layer of plywood or particleboard, or wood flooring is laid over the subfloor.

Through their efforts to devise more efficient ways to use plywood, the American Plywood Association (APA) has developed a *single-floor system.* In this type of construction, a single layer of thicker plywood with tongue and groove edges is substituted for the subfloor underlayment system. This single-floor system reduces the labor involved in laying flooring. Because this system allows the joists to be spaced up to 48 inches on center, less labor and material is required for the framing, figure 14-17.

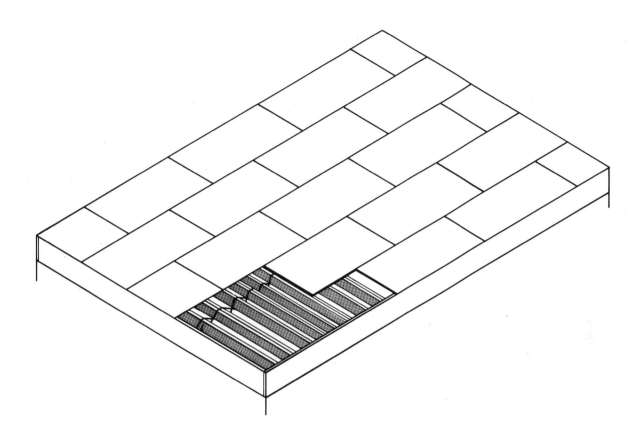

Fig. 14-18 The joints in plywood subflooring are staggered.

Plywood subflooring is installed with the long (usually 8-foot) edge spanning several joists. The joints are staggered, figure 14-18. If metal joists are used, the subflooring is installed with screws. If wood joists are used, the subflooring is nailed in place. In either case, glue may be applied to the joists first. This prevents floors from squeaking and nails from popping later.

ACTIVITIES

A.   DRAWING A JOIST PLAN

A *joist plan* is a drawing showing the location of exterior walls, girders, and the arrangement of joists as seen from directly above. Architects sometimes include a joist plan with the working drawings for a house, figure 14-19. Sometimes the building contractor or carpenter's foreman sketches a joist plan to help plan the carpenters' work before they begin.

Equipment and Materials

> Architect's scale
> Plastic triangle
> Pencils and paper

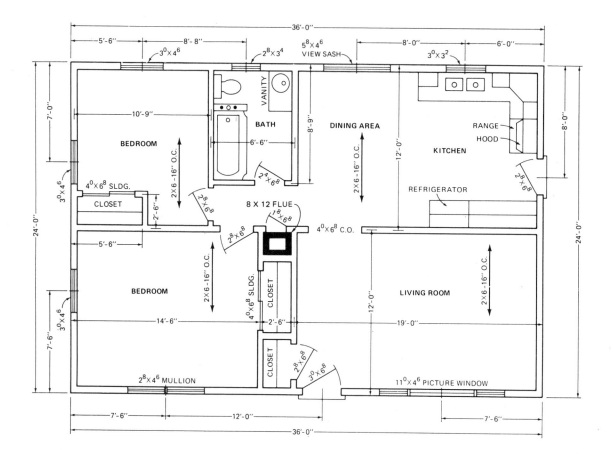

Fig. 14-19 (A) Floor plan

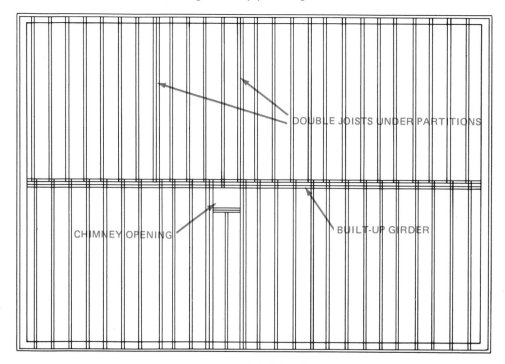

Fig. 14-19 (B) Joist plan

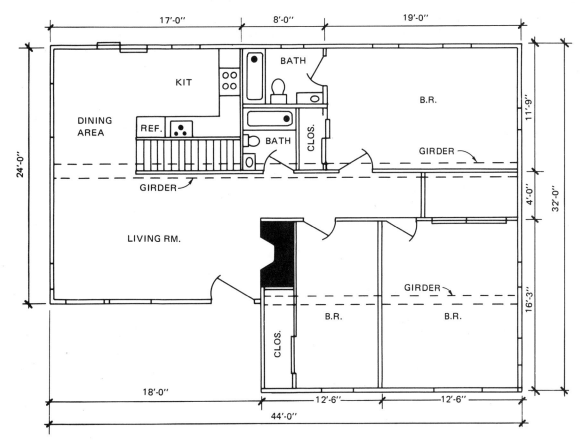

Fig. 14-20 Draw a joist plan for this floor plan.

Procedure

Draw a joist plan for the building in figure 14-20. Use a scale of 1/4″ = 1′-0″. Remember to double all headers and trimmers around openings and double the joists under walls.

B. FLOOR FRAMING AND BRIDGING

Framing carpenters construct the subfloors in a building. They must study the building plans and select the specified lumber and materials. Then, according to the plans, they install the posts, girders, sills, joists, and bridging.

Equipment and Materials

Seven pieces of 1″ x 3″ lumber
One sheet of 1/4-inch plywood
Eight pieces of 20 gauge sheet metal 3/4″ x 9″
Supply of 6d common nails and 4d common nails
Claw hammer
Saw
Framing square
Tape measure or folding rule
Chalk line

Procedure

1. Construct the floor module as shown in figure 14-21. Fasten the plywood with only one nail at each corner. Do not nail the bridging to the bottom of the joists.

2. Support the assembly on concrete blocks at each corner.

3. Stretch a chalk line between diagonally opposite corners, then have a student stand in the center of the assembly. Measure the distance that the floor sags below the chalk line.

4. Turn the floor module over and nail the bridging to the bottom of the joists.

5. Repeat step 3.

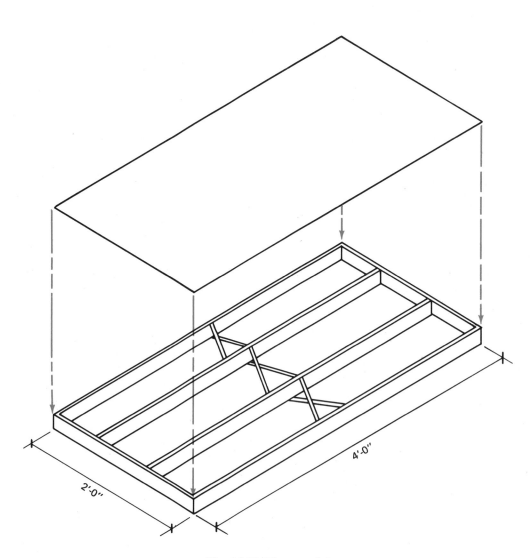

Fig. 14-21 Floor module

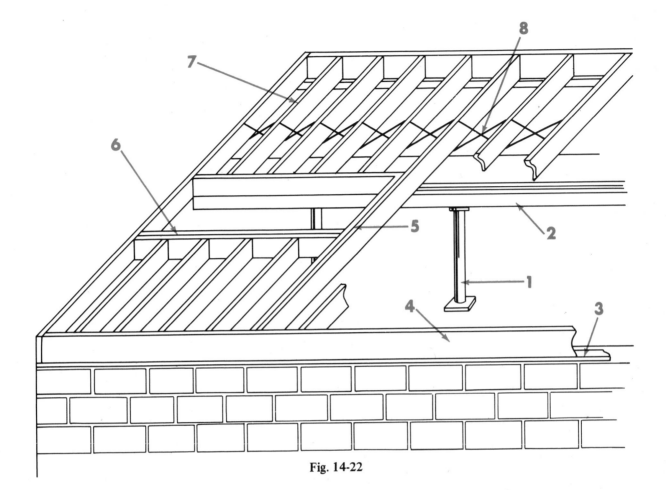

Fig. 14-22

REVIEW

A. Identification

Identify each of the numbered parts in figure 14-22.

B. Matching

Choose which item in the right-hand column is associated with each item in the left-hand column.

1. Box beam
2. Single-floor system
3. Pipe column
4. Built-up beam
5. Four-inch module
6. Subfloor
7. Anchor bolts
8. Steel beam
9. Bridging

   a. Steel post to support a girder
   b. Basic unit in building design
   c. Available in great lengths
   d. Conserves material and makes light-weight, strong girders
   e. Stiffens the floor
   f. Uses thick plywood
   g. Solid wood girder built by a carpenter
   h. First layer of flooring
   i. Fastens the sill in place

UNIT 15.
WALL FRAMING

OBJECTIVES

After completing this unit, the student will be able to:

- identify and describe the function of wall-framing members.
- explain the layout and construction of wall framing.
- cut and assemble members for a section of a wall.

The walls in a house serve many purposes. Some walls support the weight of the structure above them. These are called *load-bearing walls*. Other walls, called *partitions*, do not support weight but divide the house into separate rooms for privacy and convenient living. *Exterior walls* provide protection from the weather and make indoor living comfortable. All the walls of a house must create a pleasing appearance. The architect considers all of these functions in planning the design of a residence.

Walls may be constructed of masonry, concrete, or with wood or metal frames. In residential construction most walls are of the wood-frame type. Wood-frame walls are relatively inexpensive, easy to alter, and have adequate strength for light construction. With wood building materials becoming scarcer, metal-framing members are becoming more popular. Construction with both materials is very similar.

WALL-FRAMING MEMBERS

The basic components of a wall frame are the top and bottom plates and the studs, figure 15-1. The *plates* are the horizontal members at the top and bottom of the wall. They hold the

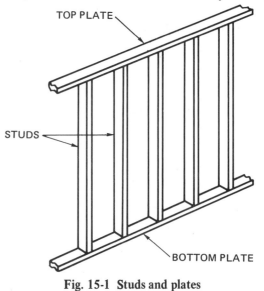

Fig. 15-1 Studs and plates

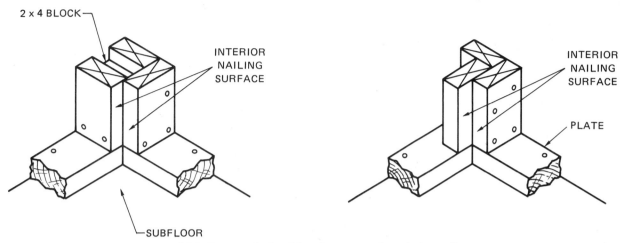

Fig. 15-2 Two methods of framing corners in exterior walls

ends of the studs in place and provide a surface to fasten the wall in place on the floor framing. In most walls the plates and studs are made of 2″ x 4″ lumber.

The wall frame also provides a surface on which to nail the inside and outside wall covering. Where two exterior walls meet at a corner, an extra stud must be added to provide this nailing surface. Figure 15-2 shows two types of corner post construction.

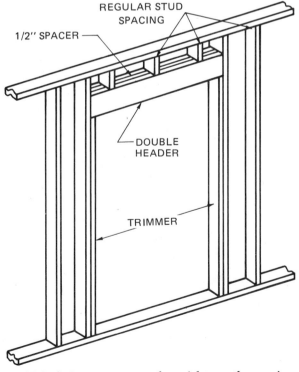

Fig. 15-3 The header supports the weight over the opening.

Where an inside partition meets another wall, studs must be located to provide a nailing surface on both sides of the partition. Walls are usually built flat on the floor, then tilted up into place. For this reason, it is important that the carpenter who lays out the wall framing understands architectural drawings and works accurately. If extra studs for nailing surfaces are not properly located, the error will have to be corrected later at a great expense.

One or more of the studs must be cut off in the window and door openings. The weight ordinarily supported by those studs must be transferred to the studs at the sides of the *rough opening* (the framed opening into which the door or window is placed). The *header* distributes this load to the sides of the opening, figure 15-3. Headers are usually constructed of two pieces of 2-inch lumber placed on edge. *Spacers*, usually scraps of plywood, are inserted between the two pieces to build the header up to the 3 1/2 inch thickness of a 2″ x 4″ wall. The greater the width of the rough opening, the wider the lumber for the header must be, figure 15-4.

Maximum Span	Header Size
3′-6″	2 x 6
5′-0″	2 x 8
6′-6″	2 x 10
8′-0″	2 x 12

Fig. 15-4 Table of typical header sizes

To support the extra weight, the header transfers to the sides of the opening, a second stud is used. This stud, called a *trimmer*, is cut just long enough to fit under the ends of the header, (see figure 15-3). The trimmer supports the header and strengthens the full stud.

The framing for windows is the same as that for doors, except the rough opening does not extend all the way down to the floor for the windows. At the bottom of the rough opening for a window, a horizontal member, called a *sill*, extends from one stud to the other, figure 15-5. Short lengths of framing, called *jack studs*, are installed below the rough sill. The jack studs provide a nailing surface for the interior and exterior wall covering.

SHEATHING

The wall sheathing is not actually part of the wall framing. It is included here because it is usually installed by the carpenters as the framing is done. The *sheathing* is the first layer of wall covering on the exterior of the walls. Boards

may be used, but the most common sheathing materials are plywood, fiberboard, and rigid plastic foam boards. These materials are available in large sheets that allow the carpenters to enclose the structure more quickly. In addition, plywood makes the entire structure more rigid. If fiberboard or rigid foam board is used, it is common practice to use plywood sheathing at the corners of the building to brace the walls, figure 15-6. When boards are used, they are installed diagonally to brace the walls. In addition to making the wall frame more rigid, the sheathing provides a surface on which to nail the finished siding.

CONSTRUCTING WALLS AND PARTITIONS

The first step in constructing the walls and partitions in a building is to determine their location and mark this on the subfloor. In large construction crews, the layout is done by the foreman or a senior carpenter. However, the carpenters who erect the walls usually lay them out. Wall and partition layout requires the ability to read plans and measure accurately. The location of each wall or partition is marked on the subfloor with a chalk line, figure 15-7.

With the location marked on the floor, two straight pieces of framing lumber are cut to length for the top and bottom plates. Next, the locations of the centers of all door and window openings are marked on the plates. From these marks the sides of the rough openings can be measured. The location of the centers of all studs are marked on the top and

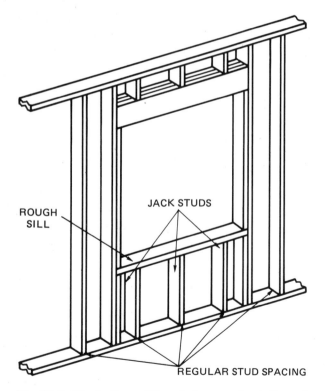

ROUGH SILL

JACK STUDS

REGULAR STUD SPACING

Fig. 15-5 The bottom of the window opening is formed by the rough sill. Jack studs are installed under the sill.

Fig. 15-6 Plywood is often used on corners when there is fiberboard wall sheathing. *(Richard T. Kreh, Sr.)*

Fig. 15-7 This carpenter is using a chalk line to lay out the location of partitions.

Fig. 15-8 The wall must be square before the sheathing is applied.

Fig. 15-9 When the wall section is assembled, it is tilted up and positioned on the floor.

bottom plates. If the studs are to be 16 inches on center, a mark is made every 16 inches from the end of the plate. Tape measures and carpenter's folding rules usually have a mark every 16 inches to help the framing carpenter lay out 16-inch centers. The location of extra studs for corners at adjoining walls is marked.

If the walls are to be any height other than 8 feet, the carpenter must cut the materials for studs to the proper length. If the walls are to be 8 feet high, precut studs measuring 2″ x 4″ x 7′-9″ are available to eliminate the need for cutting them to length. When 2-inch nominal size framing material (1 1/2 inch actual size) is used, the two plates added to a 7′-9″ stud makes an 8-foot wall.

The material is laid out on the subfloor, and the plates and studs are nailed together. Two 16d common nails are face-nailed through the plates into the ends of the studs. Headers, trimmers, sills, and jack studs for openings are nailed into position.

The wall can be tilted up into place at this time, but most carpenters prefer to nail the wall sheathing on first. The large panels used for sheathing are easier to handle with the wall frame laying flat than after it is upright. It is important for the carpenter to make sure the wall is square before the sheathing is applied. The sheathing panels make the wall frame rigid so that it cannot be squared later. The squareness of the wall frame can be checked by measuring the diagonals, figure 15-8.

Once the wall framing is completely assembled with the sheathing in place, it is tilted up and slid into position according to the chalk line on the subfloor, figure 15-9. The bottom plate is nailed to the floor framing with 16d common nails. The wall sections are plumbed with a spirit level and braced to hold them plum until the framing is completed, figure 15-10. The corners are then nailed together.

After all of the framing is in place, the second member of the double top plate is nailed into position. The corners of the top member of the double plate are lapped over the bottom members, figure 15-11. This helps tie the walls together and makes the structure stronger.

Fig. 15-10 Temporary braces hold the wall plumb.

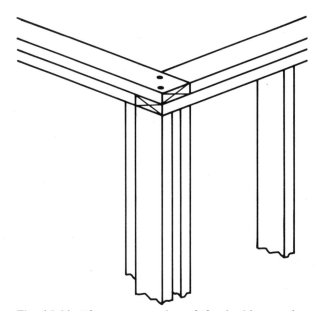

Fig. 15-11 The upper member of the double top plate overlaps the lower member at the corners.

SPECIAL WALL-FRAMING CONSIDERATIONS

As the carpenters build the walls for a building, they must allow for features that will be added later. Openings sometimes have to be framed for heating, ventilating and air-conditioning (HVAC) ducts. This may require cutting studs and installing headers, figure 15-12. The design may call for 4-inch pipes to be installed by the plumbers. This requires thicker walls that are framed with 2″ x 6″ lumber instead of 2″ x 4″ lumber. Sometimes it is necessary to install special framing on which cabinets will be mounted. It is often easier to install this as the wall is framed than to add it later.

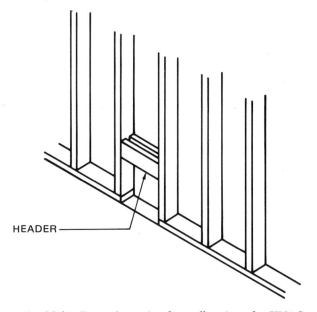

HEADER

Fig. 15-12 Framed opening for wall register for HVAC

——— ACTIVITIES ———————————

A.   DRAWING A WALL-FRAMING ELEVATION

Elevations are not normally drawn for the wall framing in a residence because the construction of walls is practically standardized. Nearly all walls for residential and light commercial construction are made as described in this unit. However, to gain experience in laying out the members in wall framing, drawing an elevation is a useful technique.

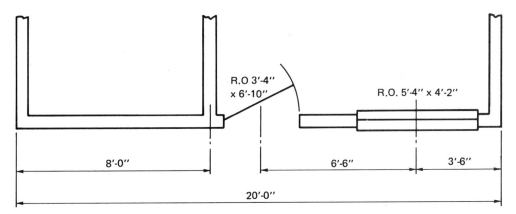

Fig. 15-13

Equipment

    Paper and pencils
    Architect's scale
    Drafting triangle

Procedure

    Draw an elevation of a wall frame using a scale of 1/2″ = 1′-0″ and figure 15-13. Dimension the location of all members.

B. BUILDING A WALL FRAME

    The framing carpenter must keep in mind how the wall will fit the frame. Carpenters must follow architectural drawings and measure accurately. Carpentry mistakes add unnecessary costs to a project.

Equipment

    56 linear feet of 1″ x 2″ lumber
    3 linear feet of 1″ x 3″ lumber
    Supply of 6d common nails
    Tape measure or folding rule
    Saw
    Hammer
    Rafter square

Procedure

1. Use a scale of 6″ = 1′-0″
2. Cut all members to length.
3. Select two pieces to be used as plates and mark the location of all studs 16 inches O.C.
4. Face nail all studs in place.
5. Construct the header over the rough opening.

6. Install the trimmers at the sides of the rough opening. These should be as long as the opening is high, figure 15-14.

7. Install the rough sill.

8. Install the bottom part of the trimmers and the jack studs.

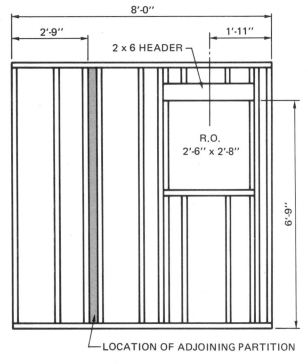

NOTE: STUDS 16″ O.C.

Fig. 15-14 Wall-framing elevation for Activity B.

Fig. 15-15

REVIEW

A. Identification

Identify the parts of the wall frame in figure 15-15.

B. Matching

Choose the item in the right-hand column which is associated with each item in the left-hand column.

1. Specially constructed to provide a nailing surface for interior wall covering
2. Wall that supports the weight of the structure above
3. Divides space but supports no weight
4. Transfers the weight from above to the sides of a rough opening
5. Is nailed to the floor framing
6. Is overlapped at the corners
7. Vertical members installed under a rough sill
8. Makes the entire wall frame rigid

a. Sheathing
b. Load-bearing wall
c. Bottom plate
d. Partition
e. Double top plate
f. Jack studs
g. Header
h. Corner post

L UNIT 16.
ROOF CONSTRUCTION

OBJECTIVES

After completing this unit, the student will be able to:

- identify the most common types of roofs used on residences.
- explain the function of roof-framing members.
- apply asphalt shingles.
- compare conventional rafters with trussed rafters.

The roof of a house protects the structure and its occupants from rain and snow. The style of the roof should be in keeping with the architectural design. The roof must also be capable of supporting a heavy load, especially where several feet of snow may fall on the roof. Carpenters who construct roofs must be familiar with various roof designs and their construction.

TYPES OF ROOFS

There are five types of roofs that are commonly used in residential construction, figure 16-1. Variations of these may be used to create certain architectural styles.

Gable Roof. The *gable roof* is one of the most common types used on houses. The gable roof consists of two sloping sides which meet at

the ridge. The triangle formed at the ends of the house between the top plates of the wall and the roof is called the *gable*.

Gambrel Roof. The *gambrel roof* is similar to the gable roof. On this roof, the sides slope very steeply from the walls to a point about halfway up the roof, then they have a more gradual slope.

Hip Roof. The *hip roof* slopes on all four sides The hip roof has no exposed wall above the top plates. This results in all four sides of the house being equally protected from the weather.

Mansard Roof. The *mansard roof* is similar to the hip roof, except the lower half of the roof has a very steep slope and the top half is more gradual. This roof style is used extensively in commercial construction, such as on stores.

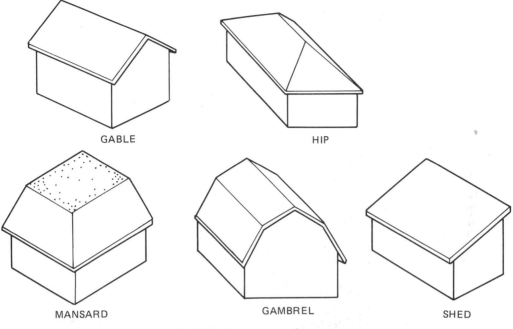

GABLE

HIP

MANSARD

GAMBREL

SHED

Fig. 16-1 Common roof types

Shed Roof. The *shed roof* is a simple sloped roof with no ridge. Although the shed roof is not as common as other types for residential construction, it is used on some modern houses and additions to houses.

CONVENTIONAL RAFTER FRAMING

The roof-framing members that extend from the wall plates to the ridge are called *common rafters*. On a shed roof the common rafters span the entire structure.

Ceiling Joists

Before the carpenters can begin setting rafters, *ceiling joists* must be installed, figure 16-2. These are similar to floor joists. The ceiling joists perform two functions. They provide a surface on which to attach the ceiling and they prevent the rafters from pushing the walls outward. The size and direction of the ceiling joists are shown on the plan for the floor directly below in the same way floor joists are indicated, figure 16-3. The ceiling joists are either toenailed to the double top plate or fastened with special metal anchors.

Fig. 16-2 The ceiling joists rest on the double top plate.

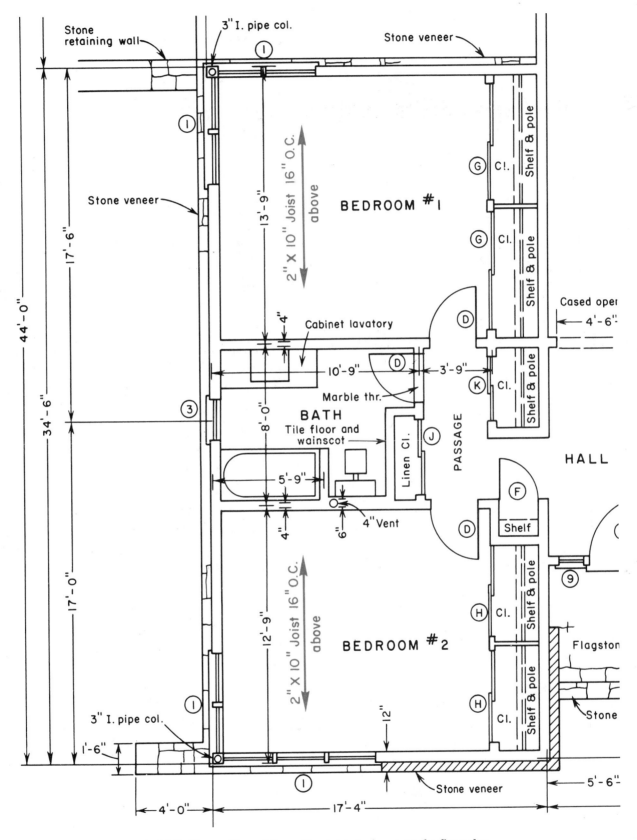

Stone retaining wall

3" I. pipe col.

Stone veneer

Stone veneer

I

I

I

44'-0"

17'-6"

34'-6"

2" X 10" Joist 16" O.C. above

13'-9"

BEDROOM #1

G Cl. Shelf & pole

G Cl. Shelf & pole

Cased open

4'-6"

D

Shelf & pole

4"

Cabinet lavatory

10'-9"

D

Marble thr.

3'-9"

K Cl.

Shelf & pole

3

8'-0"

BATH

Tile floor and wainscot

Linen Cl.

J

PASSAGE

HALL

5'-9"

4"

6"

4" Vent

F

Shelf

D

9

17'-0"

2" X 10" Joist 16" O.C. above

12'-9"

BEDROOM #2

H Cl. Shelf & pole

H Cl. Shelf & pole

Flagston

Stone

3" I. pipe col.

1'-6"

12"

Stone veneer

5'-6"

I

4'-0"

17'-4"

Fig. 16-3 The position of the ceiling joists is shown on the floor plan.

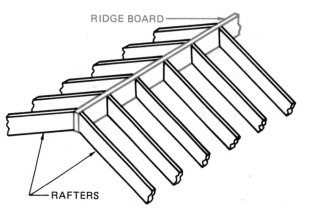

Fig. 16-4 The ridge board runs the length of the roof.

Roof-Framing Terms

The main parts in a roof above the ceiling joists are the rafters and the ridge board. The *ridge board*, figure 16-4, runs the length of the roof between the rafters of the two sides. The ridge board is nailing surface for the tops of the rafters.

When the rafters are ready to be cut, the first one is carefully laid out and used as a pattern. A few terms must be understood for any discussion of how rafters are laid out, figure 16-5.

- *Span* is the total width to be covered by the rafters. This is usually the distance between the outside walls of the house.

- *Run* is the width covered by one rafter. If the roof has the same slope on both sides, the run is one half the span.

- *Rise* is the height from the top of the wall plates to the top of the roof.

- *Measuring line* is an imaginary line along the center of the rafter. This is where the length of the rafter is measured.

- *Plumb cuts* are the cuts made at the top and bottom of each rafter. These cuts are plumb (vertical) when the rafter is in place.

- *Tail* is the portion of the rafter that extends from the wall outward to create the *overhang* at the eaves.

- *Pitch* is the steepness of the roof. This is usually expressed in terms of the number of inches of rise per foot of run. For example, if the height of the roof changes 4 inches for every 12 inches horizontally, the pitch is referred to as 4 in 12.

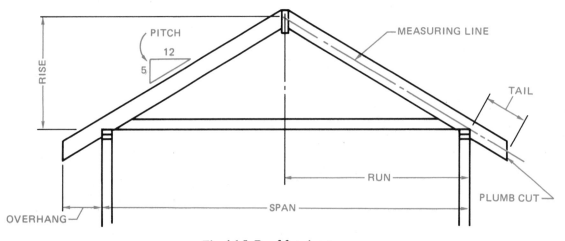

Fig. 16-5 Roof framing terms

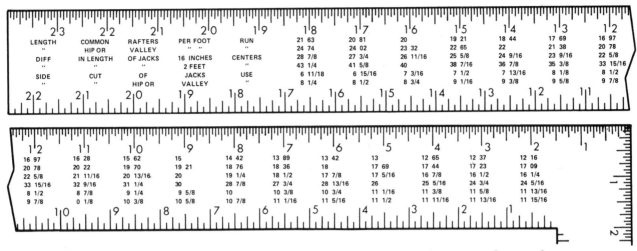

Fig. 16-6 Rafter table on the face of a square. The top line is the length of common rafters per foot or run.

Rafter Tables

Carpenters use rafter tables to determine the length of the rafters. These tables are available in handbooks and are usually printed on framing squares, figure 16-6. To find the length of a common rafter:

1. Find the number of inches of rise per foot of run at the top of the table. These numbers are the regular graduations on the square.

2. Under this number, find the length of the rafter per foot of run. A space between the numbers indicates a decimal point.

3. Multiply the length of the common rafter per foot of run (the number found in step 2) by the number of feet of run.

4. Add the length of the tail and subtract one half the thickness of the ridge board. This is the length of the common rafter as measured along the measuring line.

Note: If the overhang is given on the working drawings, it can be added to the run of the rafter instead of adding the length of the tail.

Example: Find the length of a common rafter for the roof in figure 16-7. (Refer to the rafter table in figure 16-6.)

1. Rise per foot of run = 4″

2. Length of common rafter per foot of run = 12.65″

3. Run of one rafter including overhang = 16′-0″

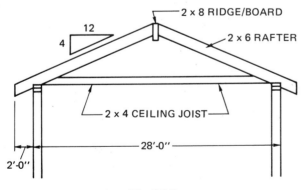

Fig. 16-7

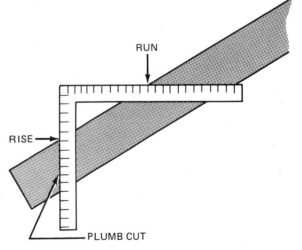

Fig. 16-8 The rafter square is used to lay out a plumb cut.

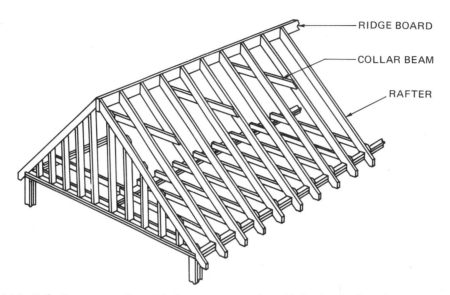

RIDGE BOARD

COLLAR BEAM

RAFTER

Fig. 16-9 Collar beams are often added to every second or third pair of rafters for extra strength.

4. 16 x 12.65″ = 202.40″ (round off to 202 1/2″)

5. Subtract 1/2 the thickness of the ridge board. 202 1/2″-3/4″ = 201 3/4″

Building the Roof Frame

When the length of the rafters has been determined, the carpenter cuts one rafter. This rafter is labeled as a pattern to lay out the rest. One end is marked for a plumb cut. The number 12 on the blade of the square is placed at the edge of the rafter. The number on the tongue, which corresponds to the rise per foot of run, is lined up with the edge of the rafter, figure 16-8. Stair gauges are helpful if several rafters are to be laid out. The end of the rafter is cut at this line. The opposite end is cut in the same manner and is parallel to the first end. Finally a notch, called a *bird's mouth*, is cut where the rafter rests on the wall plate.

The ridge board is temporarily held in place by braces. The rafters are then nailed to the ridge board and the wall plates.

It is common practice to install collar beams on every other or every third pair of rafters. *Collar beams* are horizontal members that brace the rafters about halfway up the roof, figure 16-9.

TRUSSED RAFTERS

Through engineering advances, a system has been devised that speeds roof framing, reduces material needs, and produces stronger roofs. This is the use of trussed rafters. Trussed rafters, commonly called *roof trusses*, are units assembled in a shop. These units are then transported to the construction site and set on the walls, figure 16-10.

This is the system of roof construction used most often today. The top members of a truss, corresponding to rafters, are the *top chords*. The *bottom chord* is on the bottom of the truss and corresponds to the ceiling joists in

Fig. 16-10 Hoisting a roof truss into place *(GNH Lumber)*

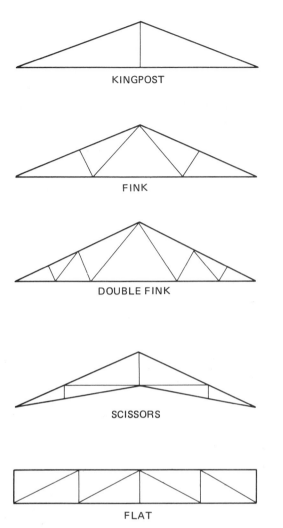

KINGPOST

FINK

DOUBLE FINK

SCISSORS

FLAT

Fig. 16-11 Some common types of roof trusses

conventional rafter framing. Depending on the design of the truss, there are several braces, called *webs*, between the top and bottom chords. Figure 16-11 shows several roof truss designs.

GABLE FRAMING

Whether conventional framing or roof trusses are used, the triangular ends of a gable roof must be filled in with framing. If the architect specifies a trussed roof, gable trusses are set on the end walls, figure 16-12. In conventional framing, gable end studs are placed directly above the regular wall studs. Gable end studs are toenailed to the top wall plate and notched to fit against the end rafter.

RAKE FRAMING

When the roof overhangs at the ends, special framing is required. This involves the use of *gable plates* and *lookouts*. The overhanging rafter is nailed to the ends of the lookouts. The lookouts rest on top of the gable plates, figure 16-13.

The final member of the roof frame is the *fascia header*. This is a piece of lumber the same size as the rafters nailed to the ends of the rafters. The fascia header will support trim to be added later.

Fig. 16-12 The gable truss has studs over which sheathing and siding are applied.
(Richard T. Kreh, Sr.)

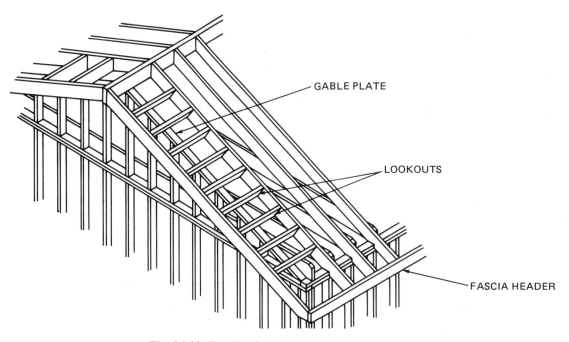

GABLE PLATE

LOOKOUTS

FASCIA HEADER

Fig. 16-13 Framing for an overhang at the gable end

ROOF COVERING

Most types of roof coverings require that the roof frame be covered with boards or plywood first. This is called the *roof sheathing* or *roof decking*. Roof sheathing is applied over the rafters in the same way that subflooring is applied over the floor joists.

The roof covering is applied by *roofers* (people who specialize in this field of work) or carpenters. Roofers and carpenters who do roofing must be comfortable working in high places. Most roofing contractors work on both residential and commercial construction.

The first step in covering the sheathing is to apply roofing underlayment. *Roofing underlayment* serves two purposes: It prevents chemical reactions between the resins in the wood and the roof covering material; and it provides additional weather protection. Asphalt-saturated felt is the most common roofing underlayment material.

The most common roof coverings for residential construction are asphalt-rolled roofing, asphalt shingles, and wood shingles and shakes. Asphalt strip shingles are the most common. Asphalt shingles and rolled roofing are available in several weights. The weight is specified according to the weight of material required to cover one square. (A *square* is 100 square feet of roof.) Underlayment felt is generally a 15-pound weight. Strip shingles are generally 225- to 240-pound asphalt.

Shingles are applied starting at the eaves and working toward the ridge. Each row of shingles across the roof is called a *course*. The first course of shingles is a solid starter course or a strip of 240-pound rolled roofing. A course of regular roofing shingles is applied directly over the starter course. The next course is laid with the bottom edge lined up with the tops of the tabs of the first course (A *tab* is the part that is exposed to the weather.) The first shingle of the second regular course has half a tab cut off. This insures that none of the cutouts between the tabs will fall over an end joint in the course

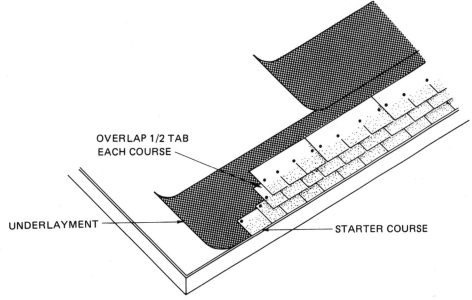

OVERLAP 1/2 TAB
EACH COURSE

UNDERLAYMENT

STARTER COURSE

Fig. 16-14 Arrangement of asphalt strip shingles

beneath. Figure 16-14 shows the arrangement of shingles on a roof. After every few courses the roofers strike a chalk line to be sure that the courses are straight and parallel with the ridge.

At the ridge, the tops of the shingles are lapped over the ridge. When both sides of the roof are completely shingled, ridge shingles are applied, figure 16-15. Ridge shingles can be purchased precut, or they can be made by cutting strip shingles apart at each tab.

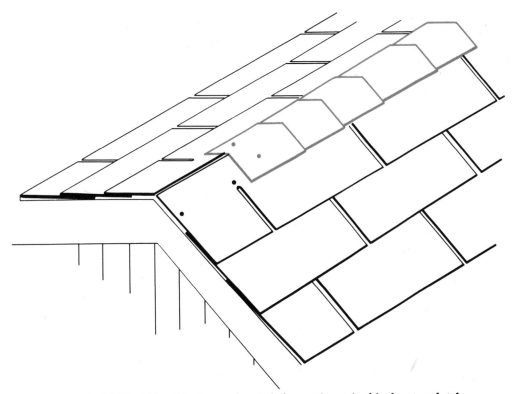

Fig. 16-15 Ridge shingles can be made by cutting strip shingles at each tab.

—— ACTIVITIES ——

A.   LAYING OUT RAFTERS

The first thing roofers do when building a roof is to cut out one rafter as a pattern. With this as a guide, they can then lay out the entire roof.

Equipment and Materials

Piece of 2″ x 4″ lumber at least 4 feet long
Framing square
Tape measure or folding rule

Procedure

Lay out a common rafter for a roof with the following dimensions:

Span of roof – 6'-0″
Pitch -   3 ⟍12
Ridge board – 2″ x 6″
Overhang – 0'-6″

B.   BUILDING ROOF TRUSS

Equipment and Materials

8 pieces of plywood, 1/4″ x 10″ x 16″
2 pieces of 2″ x 4″ lumber, 8 feet long (rafter from Activity A can be substituted for one piece)
Supply of 2d box or common nails
Hammer
Framing square
Saw
Tape measure or folding rule

Procedure

1. Cut the top chords, bottom chord, and web to length according to figure 16-16. The ends of the bottom chord can be laid out with the framing square, figure 16-17.

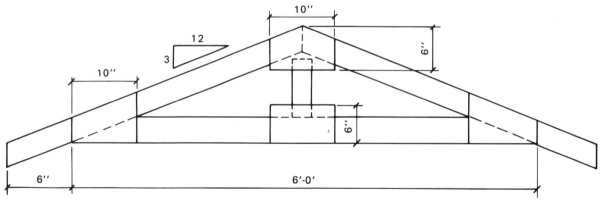

Fig. 16-16

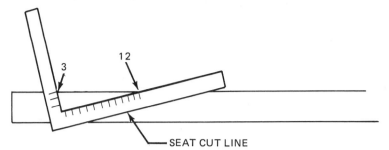

Fig. 16-17 Laying out the bottom chord

2. Mark the length of the tail on each top chord. The tail length can be found by finding the length of a common rafter for 1/2 foot of run.

3. Position all members on a flat surface and trace the shape of the *gussets* (the plywood reinforcements at joints.)

4. Being careful to keep the parts aligned, nail the gussets in place. Drive four nails into each member of the truss at each gusset.

C. SHINGLING

Roofers work with a variety of building materials and hand tools. They must be safety conscious because they work in high places and in unusual positions.

Equipment and Materials

Sheet of 1/2 to 3/4-inch plywood
Bundle of asphalt strip shingles
15-pound saturated felt
Supply of 3d smooth shank drywall nails*
Hammer
Utility knife (to cut shingles)
Square
Chalk line

*Asphalt shingles are normally applied with galvanized roofing nails. However, smooth shank drywall nails are suggested for this activity to make removal and salvage easier.

Procedure

1. Nail scrap pieces of lumber to the back of the plywood. By doing this, the nails used for shingling will not penetrate through the plywood into the surface below.

2. Cover the plywood with underlayment.

3. Nail one course of inverted shingles to the edge of the plywood. Inverted shingles are commonly used as a substitute for starter shingles.

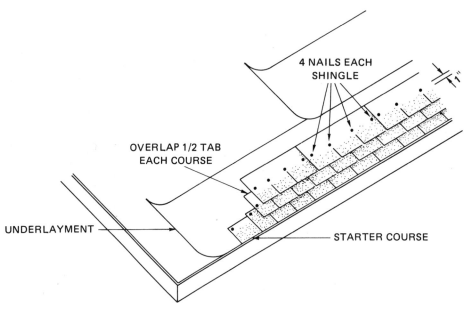

Fig. 16-18

4. Apply the first course of regular shingles with four nails in each shingle, figure 16-18.

5. Cut away half of a tab from the first shingle for the second course.

6. Continue to shingle the plywood according to figure 16-18. Strike a chalk line along the tops of the cutouts of every third course.

REVIEW

A.   Identification

What type of roof is indicated in each drawing in figure 16-19?

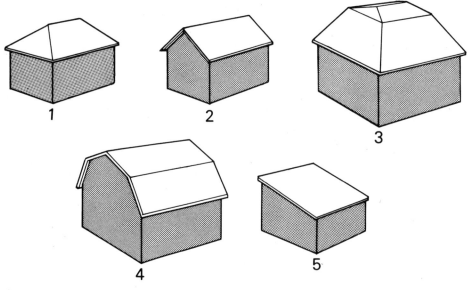

Fig. 16-19

B. Identification

Show where these items are indicated in figures 16-20 and 16-21:

Top chord
Common rafter
Ridge board
Web member
Gusset
Gable stud
Bottom chord
Span
Tail
Fascia header

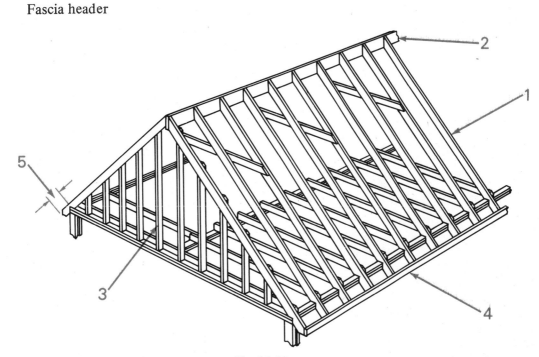

Fig. 16-20

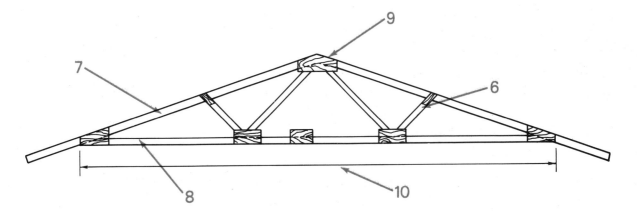

Fig. 16-21

C.   **Fill-Ins**

Fill in each blank with the proper term.

1. A _____ cut is made at the end of the rafter so the end will be vertical when in place.

2. The height from the top of the wall plates to the top of the roof is the _____.

3. The total width covered by a pair of rafters is the _____ .

4. The width covered by a single rafter is the _____ .

5. The imaginary line along which a rafter is measured is the _____ .

6. The portion of a rafter that extends outside the wall plates is the _____ .

7. The steepness of a roof is the _____ .

8. A rafter which extends all the way from the wall plate to the ridge board is called a _____ .

UNIT 17.
ENCLOSING THE STRUCTURE

OBJECTIVES

After completing this unit, the student will be able to:

- describe the various functions of siding or masonry veneer, doors and windows, and exterior trim.
- compare a variety of materials used to finish residential building exteriors.

CORNICE

The trim at the edge of the roof makes up the *cornice*. The *eaves cornice* is the construction where the rafters meet or overhang the walls. Where the cornice follows the slope of the rafters, such as at the ends of a gable roof, it is called a *rake cornice*.

The cornice is usually constructed of wood or a combination of wood and aluminum. Wood cornices are constructed by carpenters. On many jobs this is done by finish carpenters. Finish carpenters install trim and millwork after the framing carpenters have completed the basic frame of the structure. Finish carpenters work to close tolerances and must do very neat work. When aluminum trim is used in the cornice, it is installed by aluminum siding and trim installers.

There are basically three types of cornices used in residential construction. A *closed cornice* is used where there is no overhang. An *open*

cornice is used with overhanging eaves and exposed rafters. A *boxed cornice* completely encloses the rafters, figure 17-1.

Fig. 17-1 The cornice covers the framing at the eaves and end of the roof. *(Richard T. Kreh, Sr.)*

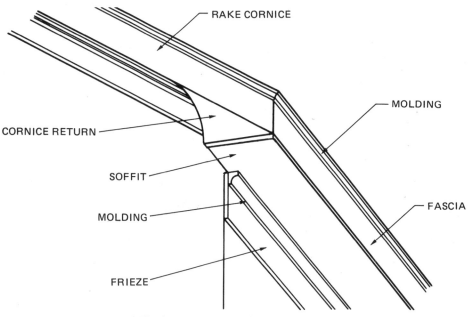

RAKE CORNICE

MOLDING

CORNICE RETURN

SOFFIT

MOLDING

FASCIA

FRIEZE

Fig. 17-2 Parts of a boxed cornice

Fig. 17-3 Sloping cornice

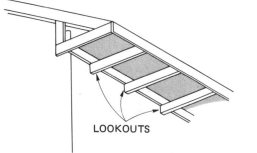

LOOKOUTS

Fig. 17-4 The soffit is nailed to lookouts which extend from the wall to the fascia.

The main parts of a cornice are the frieze, soffit, and fascia, figure 17-2. The *frieze* is a horizontal piece against the wall of the building. The *soffit* is the covering on the underside of the rafters on a boxed cornice. The *fascia* is nailed to the ends of the rafters at the eaves or to the side of the rake rafters. In addition, molding may be used to create a pleasing appearance.

Boxed cornices may be constructed with the soffit fastened directly to the underside of the rafters, figure 17-3. This type is called a *sloping cornice*. Another type of boxed cornice is the *level cornice*, such as the one in figure 17-1. On a level cornice, *lookouts* are installed from the ends of the rafters to the wall of the building. The soffit is nailed to these lookouts, figure 17-4.

The soffit has openings to allow air to flow into the space between the rafters, figure 17-5.

Fig. 17-5 This perforated aluminum soffit provides attic ventilation.

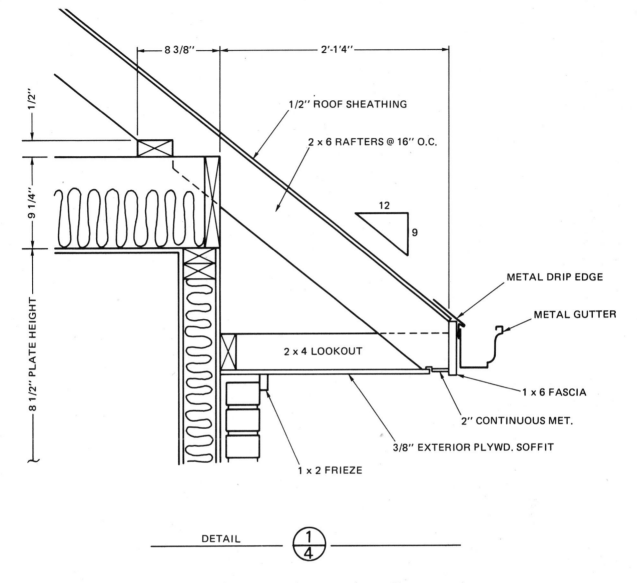

8 3/8″

2'-1'4″

1/2″

9 1/4″

1/2″ ROOF SHEATHING

2 x 6 RAFTERS @ 16″ O.C.

12

9

METAL DRIP EDGE

METAL GUTTER

8 1/2″ PLATE HEIGHT

2 x 4 LOOKOUT

1 x 6 FASCIA

2″ CONTINUOUS MET.

3/8″ EXTERIOR PLYWD. SOFFIT

1 x 2 FRIEZE

DETAIL $\frac{1}{4}$

Fig. 17-6 Typical cornice detail drawing *(Home Planners, Inc.)*

This prevents ice from building up at the eaves. The free flow of air also helps ventilate the attic.

The working drawings almost always include detail drawings of the cornice, figure 17-6. Carpenters and siding and trim installers consult these detail drawings before beginning work on the cornice.

EXTERIOR DOORS

Exterior doors provide protection and privacy. They are also an important part of any architectural design. They may be of the swing type or sliding type. The main entrance is usually a decorative swing-type door. Where the door opens into an entrance hall with no other windows, the door assembly frequently includes *side lites* (small windows beside the door) and a glazed door. A *glazed door* has a window. Several styles of exterior doors are shown in figure 17-7.

Flush doors have a smooth facing that is glued to a solid or hollow core, figure 17-8.

Fig. 17-7 Several styles of main entrances: (A) panel door with glazing; (B) flush door with side lites; (C) panel door with side lites

Panel doors have two or more panels in a framework of stiles and rails, figure 17-9. *Stiles* are the vertical members and *rails* are the horizontal members.

Doors are made of wood, aluminum, and steel. Wood has long been the standard material for doors, but metal doors are becoming increasingly popular.

Doors are hung on hinges in a door frame. The door frame consists of four main parts and the trim, figure 17-10. The side jambs and head jamb are cut to the proper length for the

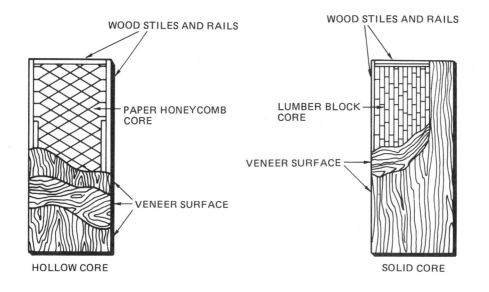

Fig. 17-8 Construction of flush doors

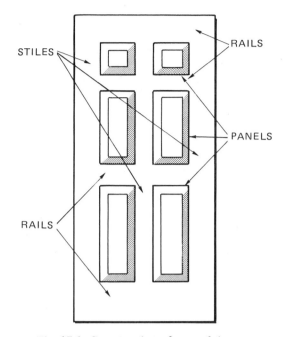

Fig. 17-9 Construction of a panel door

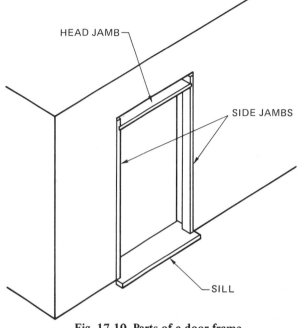

Fig. 17-10 Parts of a door frame

door and the necessary width to fit flush on both sides of the wall. The sill is made of either oak or metal to resist wear. The interior and exterior trim is called *casing*.

The floor plans show the size and location of the doors. Usually a schedule of doors and windows are also included to give additional information, figure 17-11. The *hand* of a door refers to the direction it opens. To determine the hand of a door, stand facing the door so that it opens toward you. If the door opens from the left, it is a left-hand swing; if it opens from the right, it is a right-hand swing.

DOOR SCHEDULE					
Mark	Quantity	Size	Type	Material	Remarks
A	1	1 3/4" x 3'-0" x 6'-8"	See Elev.	Pine	Paint
B	8	1 3/8" x 2'-6" x 6'-8"	Flush	Birch	Hollow Core
C	3	1 3/8" x 2'-6" x 6'-8"	Louvered	Pine	
D	1	1 3/4" x 2'-6" x 6'-8"	10 Lights	Pine	
E	3	1 3/8" x 5'-0" x 6'-8"	Folding	Pine	Louvered
F	1	1 3/8" x 2'-0" x 6'-8"	Flush	Birch	Hollow Core
G	1	1 3/4" x 2'-6" x 6'-8"	Lights	Pine	See Rear Elevation

Fig. 17-11 The door schedule gives information about the doors.

In some construction, prehung doors are specified. *Prehung doors* include the door, door frame, and all of the necessary hardware. These units are simply set in the rough opening, plumbed and leveled with a spirit level, and nailed through the casing into the studs at the sides of the opening, figure 17-12.

Fig. 17-12 Setting a prehung door in the rough opening *(C-E Morgan)*

When the doors are not prehung, the carpenter installs the individual parts and fits the door. Hanging doors require a skilled carpenter and careful work. The door jamb and sill are first assembled and fitted into the opening. Next, the door is trimmed to fit the opening with a plane. Then gains are cut for the hinges. A *hinge gain* is a recess made in both the door edge and the jamb that accepts the hinge. The hinges are installed and the door is hung in the jambs. If the jambs do not include a door stop rabbet, stop molding is nailed to the jambs. Finally, the lock set is installed.

WINDOWS

Windows consist of the sash and the frame. The *sash* is the glass and the frame that holds it. The *frame* of a window holds the sash in the wall.

Windows are named according to the way they open, figure 17-13. The simplest kind of window has a *fixed* sash that does not open. *Double-hung* windows have two sashes which slide up and down. A *sliding* window is similar to a double-hung window turned on its side. Sliding sashes slide from side to side. *Casement* windows are hinged on the side and swing out like doors. *Awning* windows are hinged at the top so the bottoms swing outward.

Fig. 17-3 Different styles of windows include: (A) double-hung, (B) sliding sash, (C) casement, and (D) awning. *(Courtesy Andersen Corp., Bayport, MN 55003)*

The size of windows is usually referred to by sash size. Other sizes sometimes referred to are glass size and rough-opening size, figure 17-14. The floor plan shows the location and sash size of the windows. The type of window is also indicated on the floor plan by the symbol used. Additional information about the windows is given in the specifications and on the window schedule.

Windows are installed by carpenters in much the same way as doors. The complete window unit without the interior casing is slid into the rough opening, figure 17-15. *Shims* are placed under the window sill to level the window. The unit must be perfectly level and square to operate properly. When the window is accurately positioned, finishing nails or casing nails are driven through the exterior casing and into the studs. These nails are set below the surface of the wood and covered with plastic wood or putty.

EXTERIOR WALL COVERINGS

The purpose of exterior wall covering is to make the structure weathertight and to create an attractive appearance. The kind of exterior wall covering on a house plays a very important part in the overall architectural style. Exterior wall coverings used on most residences can be classified as either siding or masonry veneer.

Wood Siding

Wood siding can be either vertical or horizontal. Horizontal siding creates a more traditional appearance. Vertical board and batten siding creates a contemporary appearance. Whether the siding is vertical or horizontal, it must be applied so that water can run down the wall without running behind the siding. Each kind of wood siding pictured in figure

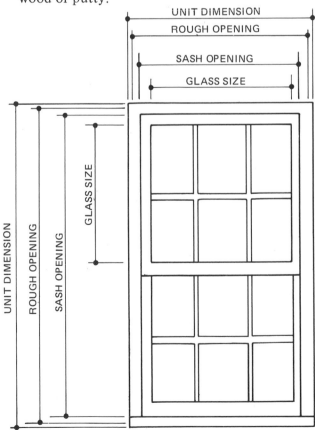

Fig. 17-14 The size of a window can be measured in several ways. The size usually listed is the sash opening.

Fig. 17-15 The carpenter first positions the window unit in the opening, then nails through the casing and into the sheathing and studs. *(Courtesy Andersen Corp., Bayport, MN 55003)*

Fig. 17-16 Types of siding include: (A) horizontal beveled siding, (B) horizontal novelty siding, (C) vertical tongue-and-groove siding, and (D) vertical board-and-batten siding. *(Western Wood Products Assoc.; Weyerhaeuser Co.)*

17-16 will shed water as it runs from top to bottom.

Horizontal wood siding is installed starting at the bottom of the wall. The first piece is leveled with a spirit level, then nailed to the wall frame with aluminum or galvanized nails. Ordinary steel nails are not used because they would rust and stain the painted siding. The second course of siding is applied so that a specified amount of the first course is left uncovered. This is called the *exposure* of the siding. Wood siding is manufactured in widths from 6 inches to 10 inches, depending on the intended exposure. After every few courses, a chalk line is snapped to guide the siding installers.

Fig. 17-17 Horizontal siding is butted against the edge of the corner board.

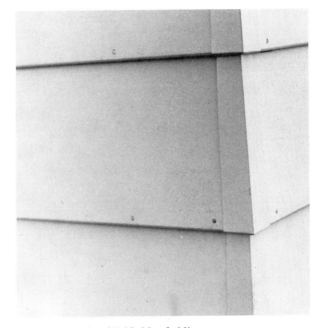

Fig. 17-18 Metal siding corners

For appearance and weather protection it is important that the siding be accurately measured and cut. Large joints between the ends of two pieces would allow water to seep through. At the corners the siding is either butted snuggly against corner boards or covered with metal corners, figures 17-17 and 17-18.

Vertical siding is plumbed with a spirit level as it is applied. Tongue-and-groove siding is nailed with finishing nails driven at an angle through the tongue. Board-and-batten siding is nailed near the edges where it will be covered by the battens. The battens are face-nailed with aluminum or galvanized nails.

Metal Siding

Many homes are covered with steel or aluminum siding. This eliminates the need for painting and reduces maintenance. Metal siding is manufactured in a wide range of styles to duplicate the appearance of most kinds of wood siding, figure 17-19. These sidings are painted at the factory and do not generally require repainting for many years. Trim to be used with metal siding is factory painted to match the siding.

Fig. 17-19 Aluminum siding can be made to look like wood siding.

The first step in applying horizontal metal siding is to nail a starting strip to the bottom of the wall. Metal channels, called *J channels*, are nailed around windows and doors. Corners may be trimmed with metal corner posts or covered with metal corners. The siding is cut to length. Where additional length is required, the pieces

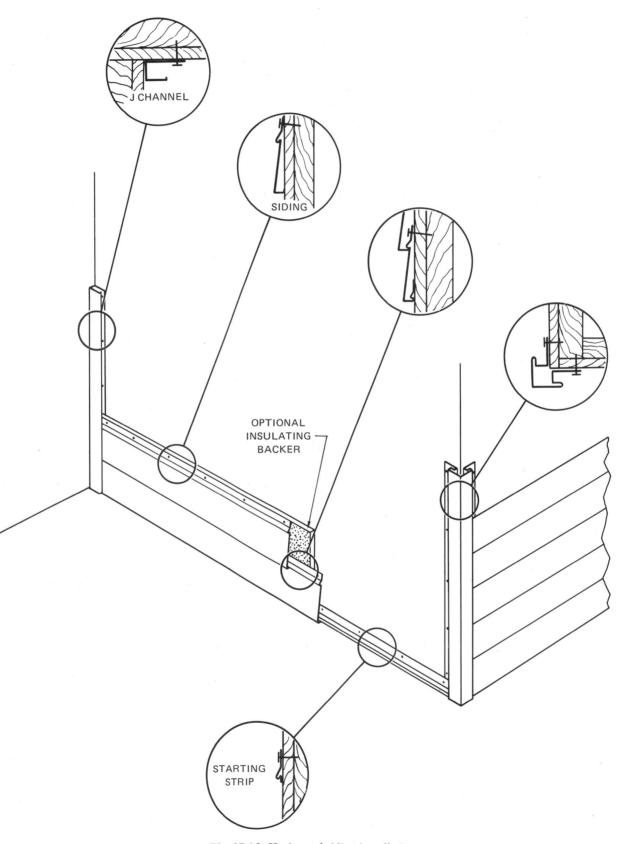

Fig. 17-20 Horizontal siding installation

are overlapped slightly. The bottom of the first piece is slid up onto the starting strip, then the top edge is nailed. The top edge of the siding is shaped to hold the bottom of the next piece. For additional insulation, *backer boards* may be slipped into the back of the siding. Figure 17-20 shows a typical metal siding installation.

Sheet Siding

Plywood and hardboard are manufactured with special patterns for use as exterior wall coverings. These are usually a vertical pattern, figure 17-21. They make attractive, weather-tight coverings and reduce the amount of labor involved. Most sheet sidings are simply face-nailed to the building.

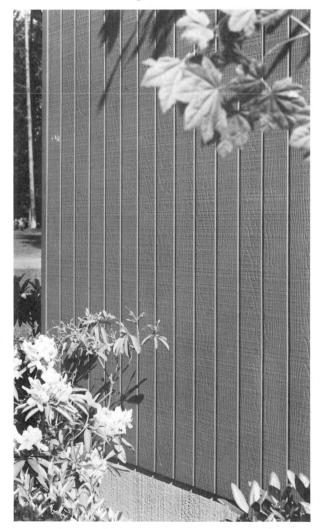

Fig. 17-21 Hardboard siding *(Weyerhaeuser Co.)*

Masonry Veneer

Masonry veneer consists of covering a structure with masonry materials, such as brick or stone. Most houses that appear to be of brick construction are actually brick veneer. Masonry veneer is attractive and requires almost no maintanance.

Unlike other kinds of wall covering, masonry veneer requires that the foundation be designed for this kind of wall covering. The weight of the masonry veneer is more than most soil can support, so it must rest on the foundation, figure 17-22.

Masonry veneer is built by masons after the building frame is completed. The masonry units are laid in mortar, just as masonry units are for foundation walls. Architects may specify special arrangements of bricks in veneer construction to create decorative effects, figure 17-23. The arrangement of bricks to create a pattern is called a *bond*. Masons must know how to lay bricks in a variety of bond patterns.

To prevent the masonry veneer from pulling away from the building frame, wall ties are used. *Wall ties* are metal devices that are nailed to the wall sheathing and embedded in the mortar joints of the veneer.

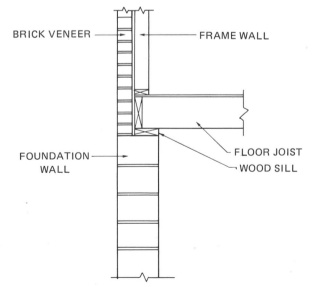

Fig. 17-22 For masonry veneer construction, the foundation walls must be thick enough to provide a base for the veneer.

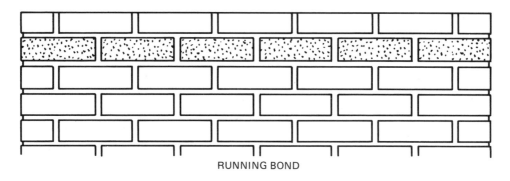

RUNNING BOND

STACK BOND

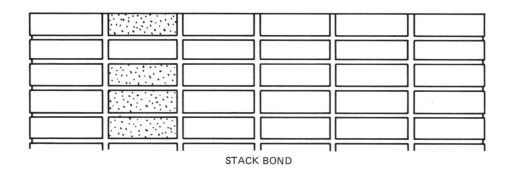

ENGLISH BOND

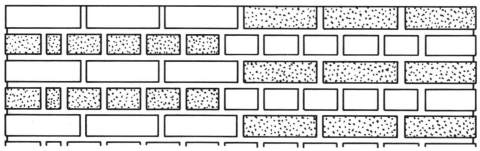

GARDEN WALL BOND. SHADED PORTIONS SHOW ANOTHER PATTERN CREATED BY THE BONDING.

Fig. 17-23 A variety of effects can be created by using different bonding arrangements.

─────── ACTIVITIES ────────────────────────────────────

A.   CONSTRUCTING A BOXED CORNICE

Finish carpenters install wood cornices. Their work must be accurate if the completed project is to look neat and attractive. Finish carpenters must be able to read architectural drawings. These drawings show how the exposed trim is installed.

Equipment and Materials

Roof and wall frame module
Lumber: 2″ x 4″ x 2′
          1″ x 2″ x 4′
          1″ x 4″ x 4′
          1″ x 8″ x 4′
3/4-inch cove molding, 4 feet long
Square
Tape measure or folding rule
Saw
Hammer
Supply of 6d finishing nails

Procedure

1. Cut and install 2″ x 4″ lookouts on each rafter.

2. Cut all cornice materials to length and install them with 6d finishing nails according to figure 17-24. Remember that the cornice is part of the exposed trim on the house. Neatness is the mark of a fine carpenter.

B.   HANGING A DOOR

Door information is also included in the working drawings. The floor plans show the size and location of doors. The door schedule tells which type of door and kind of material to use.

Hanging doors requires a skilled carpenter. The carpenter must measure, cut, and trim carefully to hang the door in the frame properly.

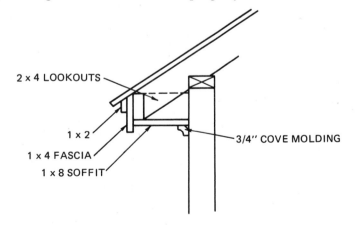

Fig. 17-24 Cornice detail for Activity B

Equipment and Materials

Lumber: 1″ x 4″ x 6′-6″
              1 x 8 x 4′
One pair 2-inch butt hinges
Wood chisel or router
Jack plane
Square
Hammer
Saw
Supply of 6d common nails
Screwdriver
Tape measure or folding rule

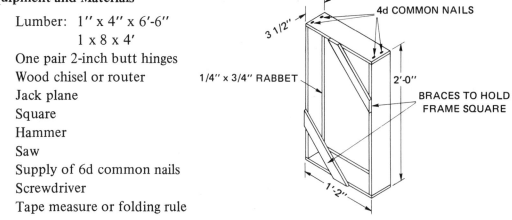

Fig. 17-25 Simulated door frame for Activity B

Procedure

1. Construct the simulated door frame shown in figure 17-25.

2. Glue two 4-foot pieces of 1″ x 8″ together to make a panel slightly larger than the opening. This will be the door.

3. Trim the door to fit the opening. Saw off large amounts of excess, then plane the door for an accurate fit.

4. Mark the location of the hinges on the door edge. The hinges should be three inches from the top and bottom of the door.

5. Using a chisel or electric router, cut the hinge gains in the door edge, figure 17-26.

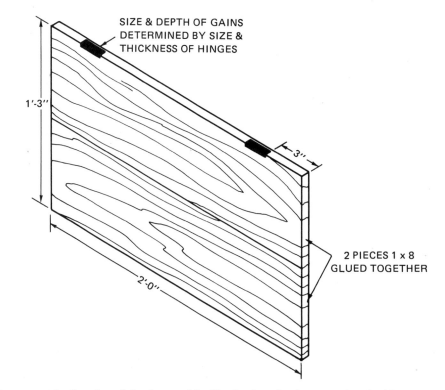

Fig. 17-26 Gains are cut in the edge of the door and inside the door jambs to receive the hinges.

CAUTION: If a chisel is used, review its use in Unit 8. If an electric router is used, review its use in Unit 10.

6. Install the butt hinges on the door edge.

7. Place the door in the opening and mark the location of the hinges on the jamb.

8. Cut the hinge gains in the jamb.

9. Install the door in the door frame and plane any areas that bind.

C. INSTALLING ALUMINUM SIDING

Like all construction people, aluminum siding and trim installers must be aware of safety hazards in their work. When they cut siding with aviation or tin snips, for instance, a very sharp edge is formed. To protect themselves, installers wear gloves when they work.

Equipment and Materials

Sheet of 1/2- to 3/8-inch plywood with 2-foot square opening
Aluminum siding to cover plywood
12-foot J channel for siding
8-foot starting strip for siding
Tape measure or folding rule
Framing square
Aviation snips
Utility knife
Chalk line
Hammer
Supply of aluminum siding nails

Procedure

1. Nail J channel along both ends and around the opening in the plywood.

2. Nail starting strip along the bottom edge of the plywood.

3. Apply siding to the plywood.

4. Siding can be cut as follows: Cut formed edges with aviation snips or tin snips, then score one side of the siding and bend to break along the score line.

CAUTION: The cut edges of metal siding are sharp. Wear gloves.

5. To form a beaded edge at the top of a cut piece of siding, slip the bead from the top edge over the cut edge, figure 17-27.

REVIEW

A. Questions

Give a brief answer for each question.

1. List three types of cornice construction.

2. Name the worker who applies wood trim to a house.

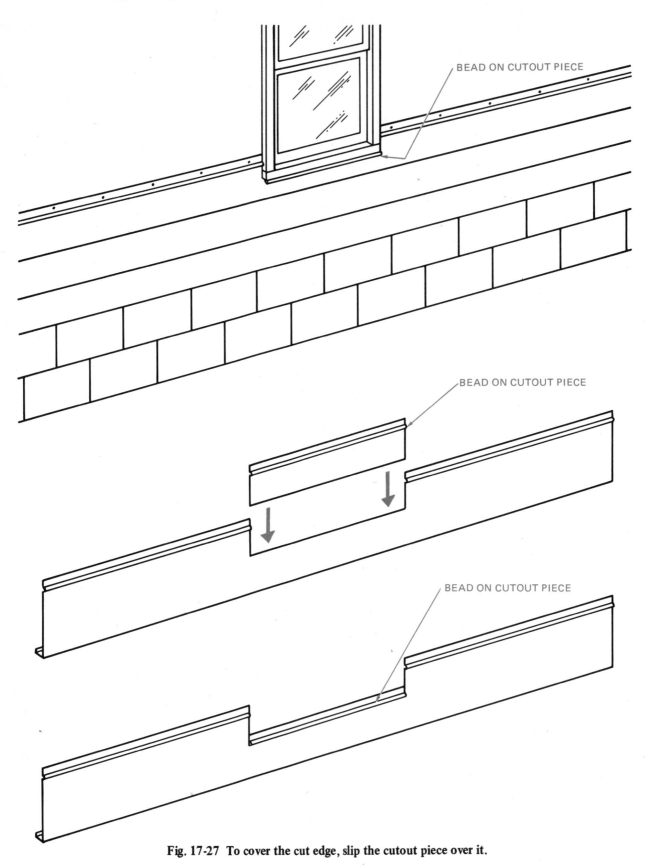

BEAD ON CUTOUT PIECE

BEAD ON CUTOUT PIECE

BEAD ON CUTOUT PIECE

Fig. 17-27 To cover the cut edge, slip the cutout piece over it.

3. Name the worker who applies masonry veneer.

4. Name the worker who installs aluminum cornices.

5. What is a glazed door?

6. What is a prehung door?

7. What is a sash?

8. Name two important functions of siding.

9. What is the difference between a foundation for a masonry veneer building and a building to have siding?

10. What is the function of wall ties?

B. Identification

1. Label the lettered parts of the cornice in figure 17-28.

2. Identify the kinds of windows in figure 17-29.

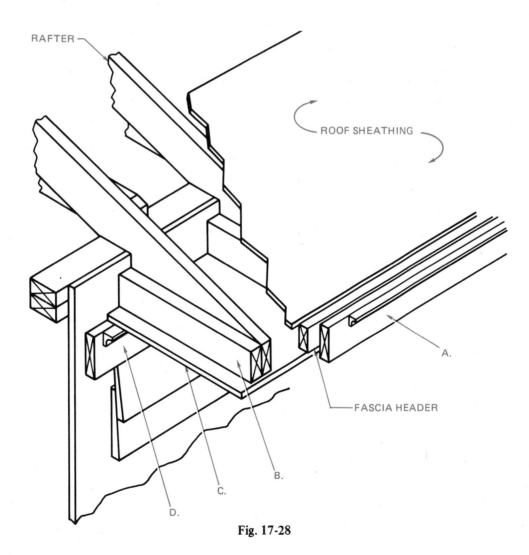

RAFTER

ROOF SHEATHING

A.

FASCIA HEADER

B.

C.

D.

Fig. 17-28

Fig. 17-29 (A)

Fig. 17-29 (B)

Fig. 17-29 (C)

Fig. 17-29 (D)

SECTION 5
SECTION 5
SECTION 5
SECTION 5

HEAVY CONSTRUCTION

LUNIT 18.

SOILS AND SPECIAL FOUNDATIONS

OBJECTIVES

After completing this unit, the student will be able to:

- describe the important engineering characteristics of soil.
- explain the principles of piers, pilings, steel-grillage, and mat foundations.
- outline the steps in designing and constructing foundations.

Large commercial and industrial structures require more carefully engineered foundations than do residences. A reinforced concrete building or a steel-frame structure places much more weight on its foundation. Equally important are the characteristics of the ground which must support the foundation.

Early in the design stages, the building planners obtain soil surveys, figure 18-1. Usually these are available from the Soil Conservation Service, U.S. Department of Agriculture. The soil survey tells the designers some important facts about soil conditions on that site. In order to understand the design of heavy-construction foundation, some knowledge of soil characteristics is necessary.

SOIL CHARACTERISTICS

Shrinking and Swelling

Some soils swell considerably when they are wet and shrink when they are dry. These are

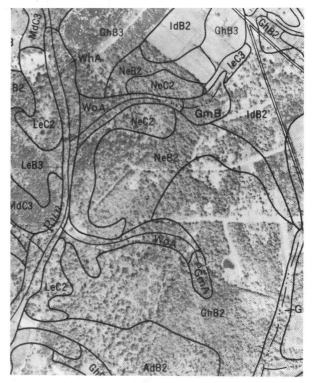

Fig. 18-1 Soil survey maps are prepared by soil scientists. *(USDA Soil Conservation Service)*

233

Fig. 18-2 A soil scientist examines damage to foundation wall. It cracked because of shrinking and swelling of the soil on which it is built. *(USDA Soil Conservation Service)*

Fig. 18-3 This excavation is in a poor drainage area. *(USDA Soil Conservation Service)*

soils with a high content of clay. In extreme cases this shrinkage and swelling may be enough to crack concrete or masonry walls, figure 18-2. Soil engineers calculate shrinkage and swelling by first measuring a sample of wet soil, drying it in an oven, and then measuring the dried soil.

Drainage

Some soils allow water to drain off more readily than others. Poor drainage can cause several problems. Soil that is saturated does not support heavy construction machinery and excavations may become flooded, figure 18-3. In extreme cases, there may be a flood hazard after construction.

The drainage characteristics of soil can be determined by pouring a measured amount of water into a hole and measuring the time it takes for the soil to absorb it. This is called a *percolation test*.

Depth to Bedrock

The surface of the earth is made up of a hard rock crust, called *bedrock*, covered with a thin layer of soil, figure 18-4. This layer of soil varies from a few inches to hundreds of feet deep. Some kinds of soil will support the weight of buildings. However, skyscrapers and other types of heavy construction are supported by bedrock when possible. The engineers designing

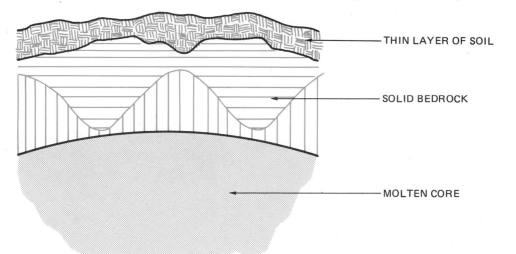

THIN LAYER OF SOIL

SOLID BEDROCK

MOLTEN CORE

Fig. 18-4 Construction of the earth's surface

the structure must know how deep the soil is so they can design the foundation.

Several methods are used to determine the depth of the bedrock. One of the simplest is the *sounding rod method*. Sections of steel rod

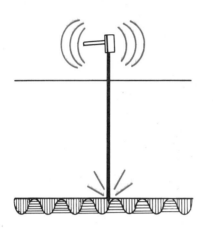

Fig. 18-5 When the sounding rod strikes bedrock, it "rings up".

Fig. 18-6 This soil scientist is making a soil map of an area where construction is planned. *(UDSA Soil Conservation Service)*

Fig. 18-7 Soil samples are taken from great depths by a soil auger. *(Schroeder Brothers Corp.)*

are driven into the ground with a sledge hammer. As each section is driven into the surface, another section is screwed onto it. When the rod strikes bedrock, it makes a ringing sound, figure 18-5. Several soundings are made to make sure the rod does not hit a boulder.

Bearing Capacity

In some locations the bedrock is too deep to reach with the foundation of a structure. In this case, soil engineers determine the bearing capacity of the soil. The *bearing capacity* is the weight that a certain area of the soil will support.

Soil engineers obtain information about soil-bearing capacity on the site and in laboratories, figure 18-6. On-site bearing capacity tests are conducted by placing a load on the soil and observing the effect. However, this is not a reliable test so samples are also tested in a laboratory. Soil samples for these tests are taken from great depths by a soil auger, figure 18-7.

FOUNDATIONS

Structural engineers design the load-carrying parts of structures, including the foundation. Throughout the design process, the structural engineers calculate the weight of the parts of the structure. Each structural component is designed to support the *load* (weight) placed on it. The entire weight of the structure is the *foundation load*. The foundation load plus the weight of the foundation itself is supported by the soil beneath it.

In residential construction the load on the soil is relatively small, so simple spread footings are adequate. In heavy construction much greater loads are carried by the soil, so the foundation design must be more complex.

The structural engineer works closely with the architect during the design stages to keep track of building loads and to design an adequate structure. The structural engineer also consults with soil engineers to design the foundation. Generally, soil survey maps are available to give some information. Soil tests are conducted

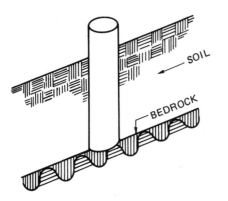

Fig. 18-8 Piers carry their load to a stable base.

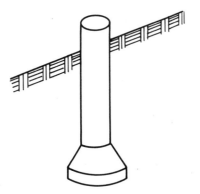

Fig. 18-9   Where bedrock cannot be reached, bell piers may be used.

at the site, however, to get more accurate information. Depending on conditions, the engineer designs one of four kinds of foundations: pier, pile, steel grillage, or mat foundation.

Piers

When the soil is not capable of supporting the structure for several feet below the surface, a pier foundation is used.   A *pier* is a column, usually concrete, which carries the load down to a suitable depth, figure 18-8. The most common type is a round, reinforced concrete pier. When a greater bearing capacity pier is needed, a *bell-bottom pier* is used, figure 18-9. The flared bottom spreads the load over a greater area.

Piers are generally cast into place in the ground. A hole is bored with a soil auger, then the reinforcement is set in this hole. However, the sides of the boring may cave in. To prevent this, steel or wooden forms extend at least below loose soil. Steel reinforcement rods are placed inside the form and tied with wire to hold them in place. Concrete is placed inside the casing (form), which may or may not be left on the pier.

Piers are spaced several feet apart. *Grade beams* are placed on top of them, figure 18-10. Grade beams may be made of timber, steel,

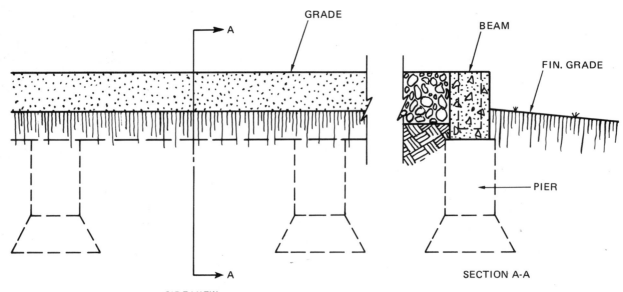

SIDE VIEW

SECTION A-A

Fig. 18-10 Grade beam on piers

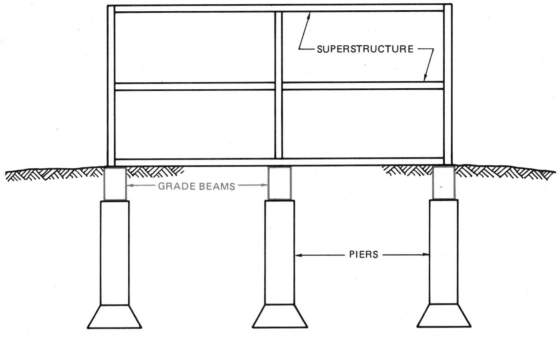

Fig. 18-11 The building superstructure rests on the grade beams.

or reinforced concrete. The *superstructure* (all of the above-ground structure) rests on the grade beams, figure 18-11.

Fig. 18-12 A pile driver drops a huge weight on the pile to drive it into the ground. *(Bucyrus-Erie Co.)*

Pile Foundations

Piles are similar to piers, except they are usually smaller in diameter and often longer than piers. Piles are made of concrete, steel, or wood. While piers are cast of concrete in a hole in the ground, piles are driven into undisturbed soil, figure 18-12. Piles may be driven very deep to bedrock, figure 18-13. When the bedrock is too deep, tapered piles are used. *Tapered piles* support their load by friction against the soil. As the tapered pile is driven, it compacts the soil along its

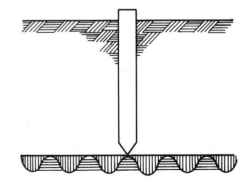

Fig. 18-13 Straight piles rest on bedrock.

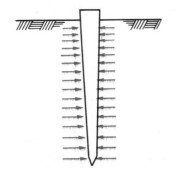

Fig. 18-14 Tapered piles are supported by friction with the soil.

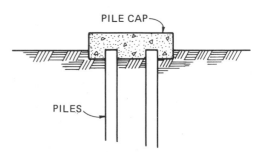

Fig. 18-15 Concrete pile cap

sides. This compacted soil bears the load of the pile, figure 18-14.

Piles are used in clusters. When the piles are driven, they are cut off at the proper height. A concrete cap is cast around the top of each cluster of piles, figure 18-15. In some construction, entire floor areas are supported by pile caps, figure 18-16. Piers or grade beams rest on the pile caps.

Steel Grillage

Where columns place a very heavy load on the foundation, steel grillage may be used. *Steel grillage* is a kind of spread footing. In lighter construction the column load is spread by the use of a steel plate. However, when very heavy loads exist, the footing must spread more. In steel grillage, short steel beams form the footing, figure 18-17. Steel-grillage foundations are

constructed on top of concrete footings or pile caps by ironworkers.

Mat Foundations

Lighter-weight buildings on low-bearing capacity soil may be built on mat foundations. A *mat foundation* spreads over a very large area so that it "floats" on the soil. A good example of a mat foundation is a building on which the basement floor is the footing, figure 18-18. As the soil moves, the entire structure moves with it.

COFFERDAMS

Frequently it is necessary to hold back earth or water at the edge of an excavation. When deep excavations are near existing structures, the sides of the excavation are braced by a

Fig. 18-16 The entire ground floor of this building will be supported by piles. *(Community College of the Finger Lakes)*

cofferdam. Construction in waterways and very wet areas is possible by using a cofferdam to keep the water out, figure 18-19. Cofferdams are usually constructed of steel-sheet piles that are driven into the ground and interlocked at their edges.

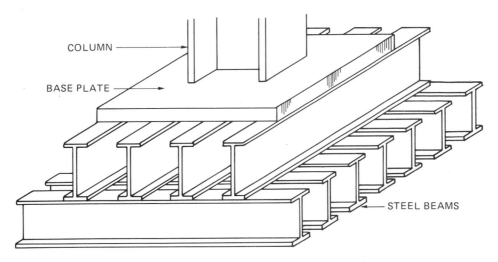

Fig. 18-17 Steel-grillage foundation

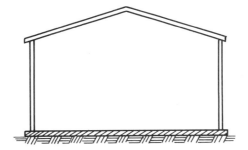

Fig. 18-18 A mat foundation spreads
the load over a very large area.

Fig. 18-19 This sheet-steel cofferdam keeps water out of the construction area. *(Bethlehem Steel Corp.)*

───── ACTIVITIES ─────

A.   PERCOLATION TEST

Before a foundation can be designed, the soil on the construction site must be studied. Soil engineers measure shrinkage and swelling. They test the soil's drainage and load-bearing capacity. The depth of the bedrock is also determined. All this information helps the structural engineers design an adequate foundation.

Equipment and Materials

Dirt shovel
5-gallon bucket
Folding rule or yardstick

Procedure

1. Dig a hole 12 inches in diameter by 30 inches deep.

2. Pour five gallons of water into the hole and measure the time required for the water level to drop one inch. This is the percolation time for that area.

B.   KINDS OF FOUNDATIONS

Locate several large structures in your community and find out what kind of foundation they have. Locate at least three different kinds of footings. Sketch a cross section of each and label the important parts.

REVIEW

A.   Multiple Choice

Select the best answer for each of the following questions.

1. Which of the following information is given on a soil survey map?

   a. Property boundaries
   b. Areas that may flood
   c. Location of buildings
   d. Best crops to plant in an area

2. Which type of soil swells and shrinks the most?

   a. Sand   c. Gravel
   b. Loam   d. Clay

3. What causes soil to swell?

   a. Wetting   c. Heating
   b. Drying   d. Cooling

4. What is measured by a percolation test?

   a. Bearing capacity
   b. Drainage
   c. Swelling and shrinking
   d. Depth to bedrock

5. Why do engineers need to know the depth to bedrock?

    a. To predict earthquakes

    b. To determine drainage characteristics

    c. To figure the depth of water mains

    d. To figure the depth of the foundation

6. Which of the following has the highest bearing capacity?

    a. Clay   c. Wet sand

    b. Bedrock   d. Loam

7. What professional determines the load on a foundation?

    a. Structural engineering

    b. Architect

    c. Mechanical engineer

    d. Soil engineer

8. What type of foundation uses grade beams?

    a. Piles   c. Piers

    b. Steel grillage   d. Mat

9. What type of foundation relies on friction against the soil?

    a. Piles   c. Piers

    b. Steel grillage   d. Mat

10. What type of foundation is best where earthquakes may occur?

    a. Piles   c. Piers

    b. Steel grillage   d. Mat

B. Constructing a Foundation

    Arrange the following in the proper order for constructing the foundation in figure 18-20.

1. Carpenters build forms for pile caps.

2. Piles are driven.

3. Steel casings for piers are set in place.

4. Construction surveyor lays out building lines.

5. Soil survey maps are ordered.

6. Cement masons place concrete for piers.

7. Cement masons place concrete for pile caps.

8. Rodsetters place reinforcement for piers.

9. Tops of piles are cut off.

10. Excavation is done.

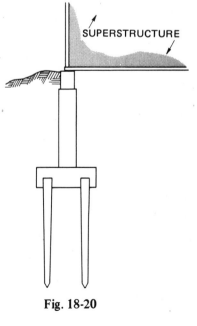

Fig. 18-20

UNIT 19.

FLOOR SYSTEMS

OBJECTIVES

After completing this unit, the student will be able to:

* describe common floor systems.
* list the major advantages and disadvantages of common floor systems.

TWO FUNCTIONS:
SUPPORT AND ENCLOSURE

Any floor system must perform two basic functions. It must provide the necessary support for any loads placed on it, and it must provide a flat surface or *deck*. The support for a floor comes from the beams, girders, columns, posts, and walls of the building. The deck is made of lumber, plywood, metal, or concrete which is supported by the structural members. The floors for all but the lowest level of the building also form the ceiling for the space below.

As with many other major parts of a structure, the floor system is designed by the architect and structural engineer who work together. The architect designs the general shape, layout, and appearance of the floor system, figure 19-1. The structural engineer calculates the load on the floor system components and designs a system that will support this load.

Fig. 19-1 The architect for this school specified a large open area. *(Portland Cement Assoc.)*

Fig. 19-2 Steel joists have prepunched holes through which utilities are run. *(United States Steel Corp.)*

Fig. 19-3 Open-web steel joists are a type of truss. *(Cargill, Wilson & Acree, Inc.)*

SUPPORTING MEMBERS

Wood and Lightweight Steel Joists

The system of floor framing used in most residential construction is also common in light commercial construction. In this system joists, which are closely spaced, rest on bearing walls or girders. The joists may be dimensional lumber or lightweight steel. Electrical and mechanical utilities are placed in the space between the joists. Steel joists have prepunched holes through which utilities are run, figure 19-2. Holes are bored through wood joists at the construction site.

Open-Web Steel Joists

Open-web steel joists are a type of truss, like roof trusses, figure 19-3. These joists consist of a top chord, bottom chord, and diagonal web members, figure 19-4. Open-web joists are supported by bearing walls and girders, as are wood joists. Utilities are run through the open webs of these joists. They can span fairly wide areas and are capable of supporting a heavier load than wood or light steel solid-web joists. Open-web joists are easy to handle and can be installed without heavy equipment. These joists are either riveted or bolted in place by ironworkers, or welded in place by welders.

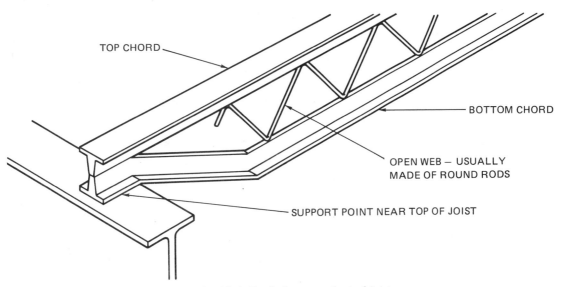

TOP CHORD

BOTTOM CHORD

OPEN WEB — USUALLY MADE OF ROUND RODS

SUPPORT POINT NEAR TOP OF JOIST

Fig. 19-4 Typical open-web steel joist

Structural Steel Floor Frames

Steel S beams and wide-flange beams are used in floor framing, figure 19-5. Although structural steel floor framing is most common with steel-frame buildings, it is sometimes used with other types of construction. With the proper decking, structural steel-framing members can be placed much farther apart than joists. Structural steel can also support much greater loads than any of the types of joists discussed. Structural steel does, however, have some disadvantages. It is heavier than wood or light metal joists. A crane is required to handle it. Also, bare metal softens when it gets hot enough. It often must be protected from overheating in case of fire, figure 19-6.

Although several workers are required to erect structural steel frames, its wide spacing makes it fast to assemble. A typical crew for erecting a structural steel floor frame consists of ironworkers, laborers, and an operating engineer to work the crane.

Concrete Floor Supports

Concrete is used in a variety of ways to support heavy loads. The use of concrete involves building forms and long waiting periods for curing, but it is capable of supporting very heavy loads.

Concrete members may be either site cast or precast. *Site casting* refers to placing concrete in forms at the construction site, figure 19-7. This requires that forms be built and reinforcement be set. Then the concrete is mixed, placed, and allowed to cure. Although this is time consuming, there is no limit to the size of members that can be cast.

A faster kind of concrete construction is through the use of *precast concrete*. Concrete is placed in reusable forms at a precast yard, figure 19-8. When the concrete has cured, the member is removed from the form and stored. Some companies specialize in manufacturing precast members.

Fig. 19-5 The floor above this manufacturing area is framed with structural steel. *(Niagara Mohawk Corp.)*

Fig. 19-6 Steel beams are protected against excess heat from fire by encasing them in concrete or gypsum.

Fig. 19-7 These cement masons are casting a concrete beam in place. *(Portland Cement Assoc.)*

Precast concrete is delivered to the construction site, ready to use. The method of assembly is similar to that for structural steel. A crew consisting of cement masons, laborers, and an operating engineer position the concrete members, figure 19-9. They fasten the concrete members with steel fittings which were cast into the members at the precast yard.

Fig. 19-8 Concrete being placed in steel forms at a precast yard *(Rotecoury-Beltcrete)*

Fig. 19-9 This mason is supervising the placing of precast concrete beams. *(Portland Cement Assoc.)*

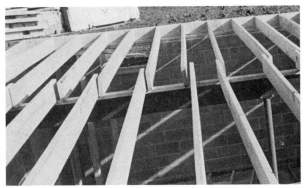

Fig. 19-10 Wood nailers are bolted to the structural steel to permit nailing the wood joists. *(Richard T. Kreh, Sr.)*

DECKING

Plywood or Timber Deck

As in light construction, wood is a popular material for floor systems in heavy construction. Most wood-frame floors have decks of plywood topped with a more durable wear surface. Wood, either plywood or timbers, is also used on other types of floor framing. When wood is to be laid over metal framing, it is either bolted to the frame or a wood nailing strip is bolted to the framing, figure 19-10. Although wood chars during fires, heavy timbers burn slowly and offer good fire protection.

Steel Deck

Sheet steel provides a rapid means of installing a deck. Steel decking is either ribbed or cellular, figure 19-11. *Ribbed-steel* decking has ribs several inches wide along its length to make it rigid. *Cellular-steel* decking is similar to ribbed steel, except both sides are enclosed forming open cells in the center. This creates several openings through which utilities may be run. Steel decks are covered with a thin layer of concrete.

Steel decks are lightweight, so the structural members of the building can also be made

Fig. 19-11 These workers are installing a ribbed-steel deck. *(Wheeling Pittsburgh Steel Corp.)*

Fig. 19-12   Flat-plate concrete floors leave a smooth ceiling below. *(Portland Cement Assoc.)*

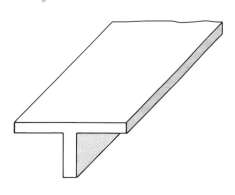

SINGLE T

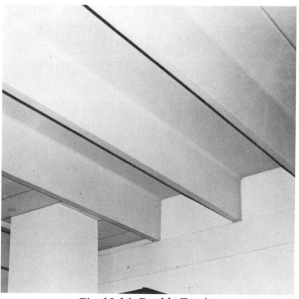

Fig. 19-14 Double-T units

DOUBLE T

Fig. 19-13 Precast single- and double-T units allow long spans.

lighter.   They are stronger than lightweight wood decks, but not as strong as some concrete decks.

The steel decking is installed by ironworkers.   The pieces of decking are fastened in place with screws or welded in place.   The concrete wear surface is placed and finished by cement masons.

Reinforced Concrete Slabs

The simplest floor to construct is a *slab on grade*.   This is a concrete slab that is reinforced with welded wire mesh and placed directly on the ground.   Concrete slabs are also used to build the floor decking in structures that are several stories high.

Some very strong floors consist of flat slabs supported by columns or beams, figure 19-12. This type of floor system provides a flat surface for the ceiling of the space below.

In order to produce a deck capable of greater spans between supports, vertical ribs are included.   A popular type of precast floor uses single-T or double-T units, figures 19-13 and 19-14.   For floors with light loads, these tees are capable of spanning as much as 100 feet between supports.   The underside of such a floor is either covered with a suspended ceiling

Fig. 19-15 This waffle-slab floor is nearly ready for the concrete. *(Portland Cement Assoc.)*

Fig. 19-16 A completed waffle-slab concrete floor *(Portland Cement Assoc.)*

or left exposed for an interesting effect. Another interesting floor construction is the waffle-slab system. In this system, reinforcing ribs are created as the floor is cast, figures 19-15 and 19-16.

ACTIVITIES

A. FLOOR SYSTEMS

Visit at least two large commercial buildings. Study the construction of the floor system in each. If the floor construction is not visible because of the finished ceiling, the building superintendent may be able to describe its construction to you. Usually there are some areas which have exposed ceilings, such as in loading and receiving areas, indoor parking areas, and mechanical rooms. Sketch a cross section of the floor construction in two buildings of different design. Be sure to include both supporting members and decks. Label the important parts.

B.   **IDENTIFICATION**

List the trades involved with the construction of the two floors sketched in Activity A.   Arrange this list in order of the work done by the various trades.

REVIEW

Matching

Choose the item in the right-hand column which is associated with each item in the left-hand column

1.   Used primarily in residential and light commercial construction
2.   Precast concrete deck unit capable of long spans
3.   Reinforced concrete floor placed directly on the ground
4.   Consists of top and bottom chords with diagonal bracing between them
5.   Heavy framing material which often must be protected from overheating in case of fire
6.   Concrete deck cast over removable pans
7.   No limit to size
8.   Decking which is later covered with a thin layer of concrete
9.   Slow-burning deck material
10.   Structural concrete which allows for rapid construction

a.   Open-web joists
b.   Wood joists
c.   Structural steel
d.   Precast concrete beams
e.   Single T
f.   Waffle slab
g.   Cellular steel
h.   Site-cast concrete
i.   Timbers
j.   Slab on grade

UNIT 20.
STRUCTURAL FRAMES AND WALLS

OBJECTIVES

After completing this unit, the student will be able to:

- describe the difference between bearing-wall construction and skeleton-frame construction.
- explain how vertical and lateral loads are supported in buildings.
- explain the principles of basic construction methods for walls.

BEARING-WALL CONSTRUCTION VERSUS SKELETON-FRAME CONSTRUCTION

The types of construction used in buildings can be classified as either bearing-wall or skeleton-frame. The basic difference between the two types is in the way the building loads are supported. In *bearing-wall construction* the walls are structural parts of the building. That means they support the structure, figure 20-1. In *skeleton-frame construction* a structural

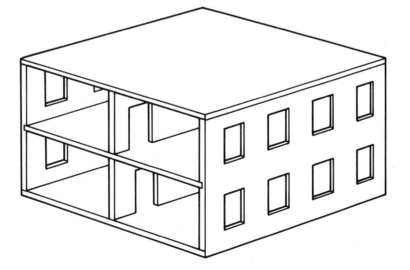

Fig. 20-1 With bearing-wall construction, the walls support the structure.

frame supports the structure, figure 20-2. In skeleton-frame construction the walls only serve to enclose a space.

Fig. 20-2   Skeleton-frame construction   *(Bethlehem Steel Corp.)*

Fig. 20-3   Masonry bearing-wall construction. *(Richard T. Kreh, Sr.)*

BEARING WALLS

Masonry

Masonry units are used extensively in bearing-wall construction up to a few stories high, figure 20-3. For very tall structures, masonry bearing walls are seldom used. By comparison with wood, the most common structural material for light construction, masonry units have very good compressive strength. However, to support the load of the skyscraper, masonry walls would have to be abnormally thick at their base. Masonry bearing walls are constructed by masons, just as are masonry foundation walls for the foundations of residences.

Precast Concrete

Precast concrete panels are very common material for bearing-wall construction, figure 20-4. Reinforced concrete provides excellent compressive strength which is necessary in bearing-wall construction. The precast method allows the walls to be assembled quickly after

Fig. 20-4   Precast concrete panels used for bearing-wall construction *(Portland Cement Assoc.)*

they are delivered to the site. The precast panels are made with steel fittings for lifting with a crane. They are lifted into position, then fastened by means of steel plates cast into them when they are made, or with steel rods called *dowels* that fit into adjoining members.

A typical construction crew for setting precast concrete members consists of the following:

- Masons fasten the members into position.
- Laborers handle materials and assist other trades.
- Riggers handle cables and pulleys and make slings to lift the members into place.
- Operating engineer operates the crane.
- Signaler directs the crane operator (operating engineer) by hand signals or two-way radio.

Tilt-up Walls

To eliminate the need for transportation, heavy precast panels may be cast at the construction site. Forms are constructed for the edges of the panels and for the window and door openings. Reinforcing steel is placed in the forms and tied or welded, then the concrete is placed. When the concrete has cured, the panels are tilted up into place, figure 20-5. Other than being cast at the construction site, tilt-up construction is very similar to precast wall construction.

SKELETON-FRAME CONSTRUCTION

Reinforced Concrete

Because of its great compressive strength, reinforced concrete is used extensively for the structural frames of buildings, figure 20-6. However, it is not practical to lift it to the tops of very tall buildings. The weight of reinforced concrete places a great load on the lower members of the structure. For these reasons, reinforced concrete frames are not often used above a few stories.

Concrete skeleton frames may be site cast, precast, or a combination of the two. It is

practical to cast vertical columns and piers on the construction site. Forms are erected by form carpenters, the rebar is set, and the concrete is placed. When the concrete is cured and the forms are removed, the finished column or pier is in place and ready for use. However, horizontal beams and girders present more of a problem. Until the concrete cures and the member can support its own weight, additional support is required. Wet concrete is very heavy

Fig. 20-5 Tilting up a concrete wall panel *(Portland Cement Assoc.)*

Fig. 20-6 Reinforced-concrete building frame *(Portland Cement Assoc.)*

and conventional forms are not strong enough to hold it up alone. For this reason horizontal members are often precast, then set in place.

Structural Steel

Structural steel provides good strength with much less weight than concrete. This makes it a common material for frames of tall structures. Steel frames can also be put up quickly, thereby saving valuable construction time.

To protect steel building frames from the weakening effects of fire, the steel members are sometimes encased in fire-resistant material. By covering the steel with a few inches of concrete or gypsum plaster, it can retain most of its strength up to four hours even in very serious fires.

The individual pieces of steel are lifted into position with a crane. They are either bolted together with high-strength steel bolts or welded. Prior to World War II, nearly all connections in structural steel were made with rivets. More recently, welding and bolts have taken the place of rivets. It is common for both methods to be used on one construction job. Often subassemblies, consisting of several pieces of steel, are welded together. These subassemblies are then bolted to the building frame. Welding has become an important trade in the construction industry. Welding is done by welders who specialize in this work and by ironworkers who

work on building frames. One of the most outstanding characteristics of ironworkers' jobs is that they work in high places under dangerous conditions, figure 20-7.

Curtain Walls

Curtain walls do not support any of the structural load. They only enclose a space. They are made of panels which are attached to the frame. These panels fill in the spaces in the frame, figure 20-8. Curtain walls can be made of masonry, precast concrete, glass, steel, or a combination of materials. Commonly, curtain-wall panels are a sandwich of insulation between a weather-resistant exterior surface and an interior finish, figure 20-9. Where windows are needed, the panels are made of glass.

Fig. 20-8 The exterior walls of this office building are of curtain-wall construction. *(Bethlehem Steel Corp.)*

Fig. 20-7 Ironworkers work in high places. *(Cargill, Wilson & Acree, Inc.)*

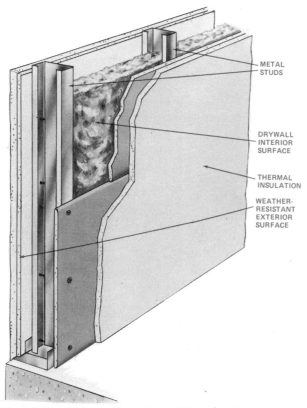

Fig. 20-9 This curtain-wall panel has metal studs and insulation. *(United States Gypsum Co.)*

Fig. 20-10 Industrial building with ribbed metal siding

ROOFING 5 LBS./SQ. FT.
ROOF DECK 2 LBS./SQ. FT.

FRAMING 4 LBS./SQ. FT.
DEAD WEIGHT = 11 LBS./SQ. FT.

Fig. 20-11 Dead weight is the weight of all building materials.

Veneer Walls

A veneer is a thin layer of facing material attached to a strong base. In construction, veneer walls are made of a durable face applied over the structural part of the wall. Veneers are usually brick, decorative concrete blocks, stone, or metals. Masonry veneers are constructed in front of the wall and fastened to it with metal wall ties.

Siding

Any of the types of siding listed for residential construction in Unit 17 can be used on nonresidential structures. Industrial buildings are often sided with ribbed metal siding, figure 20-10. This kind of siding is durable and can be applied quickly. It is either screwed or nailed to the building frame.

STRUCTURAL FUNCTIONS OF WALLS AND FRAMES

The obvious purposes of a wall are to protect the interior from the weather, provide privacy, and to divide a space into smaller rooms. However, walls and the framework which supports them also serve some important structural functions. While the architect is primarily concerned with the functions mentioned above, the structural engineer is concerned with other things.

Vertical Loads

There are two types of vertical loads which must be supported by building members. The *dead load* is the weight of all the parts of the building or structure. For example, if the roofing material, roof deck, and roof frame together weigh eleven pounds per square foot, the dead load on the roof frame is eleven pounds per square foot, figure 20-11.

Variable loads, such as people, furniture, and rain and snow are called *live loads*. If the roof in the above example is also supporting 20 pounds of snow per square foot, then the live load is 20 pounds per square foot. The total

Fig. 20-12 Diagonal bracing resists wind loads. *(Bethlehem Steel Corp.)*

load on this roof is 31 pounds per square foot. The roof frame and all the structure below must be engineered to support that load.

In shorter buildings the vertical loads are the only loads considered in the design of the structure. The vertical columns, posts, or studs support the vertical loads.

Lateral Loads

In taller buildings the wind applies considerable force to the sides of the building. In some localities, earthquakes also apply force sideways to the building. These horizontal forces are called *lateral loads*.

Lateral loads are resisted by wind bracing or shear walls. *Wind bracing* refers to diagonal members of the frame which form triangular shapes, figure 20-12. This prevents the building frame from flexing in that direction. Wind bracing may be used on exterior wall frames or it may be incorporated in interior framing. The advantage in using wind bracing in interior framing is that this does not conflict with the placement of windows.

When a building does not have a frame that can be braced with diagonal members, another method is used. *Shear walls* are substituted for diagonal braces. These shear walls are constructed of rigid material, such as precast concrete, which serves the same purpose as wind bracing, figure 20-13. Because exterior

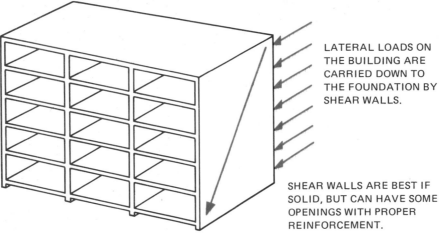

LATERAL LOADS ON THE BUILDING ARE CARRIED DOWN TO THE FOUNDATION BY SHEAR WALLS.

SHEAR WALLS ARE BEST IF SOLID, BUT CAN HAVE SOME OPENINGS WITH PROPER REINFORCEMENT.

Fig. 20-13 Shear walls

Fig. 20-14 The Marina Twin Towers use cylindrical shear walls. *(Bertrand Goldberg Associates)*

walls are often weakened by window openings, shear walls are frequently inside the structure where they serve as partitions.

An interesting example of the use of shear walls is in the Marina Twin Towers in Chicago, figure 20-14. These tall buildings have vertical columns near the all-glass outside walls for vertical support. The center of the buildings is a 32-foot diameter cylinder. This core provides lateral support for the towers.

——— ACTIVITIES ———

MODEL STRUCTURE

Construct a structural model of one of the buildings described.

Equipment and Materials

Architect's scale
Paper straws
Cardboard
Model cement

Construct a structural model of a structural steel skeleton frame for an 8-story building. Each floor is to be 40 feet by 60 feet with a rise of 10 feet between floors. Use a scale of 1/4″ = 1″-0″. Be sure to include wind bracing.

OR

Construct a structural model of a precast concrete bearing wall building for an 8-story building. Each floor is to be 40 feet by 60 feet with a rise of 10 feet between floors. Use a scale of 1/4″ = 1′-0″. Be sure to include shear walls.

REVIEW

Matching

Choose the item in the right-hand column which is associated with each item in the left-hand column.

1. Diagonal members
2. Weight of building material
3. Weight of furniture
4. Handles cables and hooks for lifting
5. Most common method for tall structures
6. Force of wind and earthquakes
7. Walls to resist horizontal force
8. Panels cast flat on the site
9. Uses walls for vertical support
10. Operates heavy equipment
11. Panels attach to building frame
12. Very strong, but too heavy for tall buildings

a. Rigger
b. Tilt-up construction
c. Shear wall
d. Wind bracing
e. Bearing-wall construction
f. Operating engineer
g. Dead load
h. Live load
i. Lateral load
j. Curtain wall
k. Concrete frame
l. Structural steel frame

UNIT **21.**
TIMBER CONSTRUCTION

OBJECTIVES

After completing this unit, the student will be able to:

• describe the major types of timber construction.

• explain how straight and curved timbers are laminated.

• discuss major advantages and disadvantages of timber construction.

TIMBER CONSTRUCTION

The terms lumber and timber are often used incorrectly. *Lumber* is the product made by sawing and planing wood. *Timber* is lumber which is 5 inches or more in thickness. *Boards* are pieces of lumber less than 2 inches in thickness. *Dimension lumber* is 2 to 5 inches in thickness. *Timber construction* is construction that uses large amounts of timber, figure 21-1. It often also involves the use of boards and dimension lumber.

Timber construction is popular in some residential architecture. However, it is introduced at this point in the text because it is most often found in heavier construction. Wood offers some advantages over other materials for construction. It is not strongly affected by acids and fumes that may be present in some industrial uses. It chars on the outside, but keeps most of its strength for a surprising length

Fig. 21-1 Timber construction *(Weyerhaeuser Co.)*

Fig. 21-2 This carpenter is joining laminated arches for a large building. *(American Institute of Timber Construction)*

Fig. 21-3 These stacks of boards will be glued together to make timbers. *(Weyerhaeuser Co.)*

Fig. 21-4 Individual boards slide past one another when loaded.

Fig. 21-5 Laminated timbers can be used to create an attractive appearance. *(Weyerhaeuser Co.)*

of time during fire. It is also very strong for its weight.

Timber does have certain disadvantages. Unless it is specially treated, it decays when in contact with the ground. There is a limit to the variety of shapes in which it can be produced. Its size is limited to that which can be sawed from a tree. However, modern technology has overcome this problem to a great extent.

Timbers are cut, erected, and fastened by carpenters. When large arches or heavy timber beams and columns are used, they are installed by a crew. A typical crew for erecting timber arches consists of a carpenter, laborer, rigger, and an operating engineer, figure 21-2.

LAMINATED TIMBERS

To overcome the limits on available sizes and shapes, timber is sometimes laminated. *Laminated timbers* are made by gluing several boards together to produce thicker pieces, figure 21-3. Timbers produced by laminating have greater strength than the total of all of the individual boards. When several boards are stacked on top of one another, then loaded like a beam, their surfaces slide past one another, figure 21-4. When they are glued together, their surfaces cannot slide, so they are more difficult to bend.

Laminated timbers are manufactured in factories. For exterior use they are glued with waterproof glue. Where their appearance is important they are made of high-grade lumber, figure 21-5. For structural use where appearance

Fig. 21-6 Where appearance is less important, low-grade timber is used. *(Weyerhaeuser Co.)*

is less important, lower grades of lumber are permitted, figure 21-6.

ARCHES

An important feature of laminated timbers is they can be produced in curved shapes. To produce curved timbers, the glued boards are clamped against a form of the desired shape. The individual boards slide over one another as workers force them into shape with clamps and air-powered tools, figure 21-7. They are left clamped in this position until the glue dries. When the clamps are removed, the glued surfaces cannot slide back to their original shape, so the timber holds its curved shape. The excess glue is cleaned from the finished laminate, it is trimmed to the proper size, then sanded and finished if appearance is important. Laminated timbers are delivered to the construction site ready for use.

Fig. 21-7 These workers are clamping boards for a laminated arch. *(American Institute of Timber Construction)*

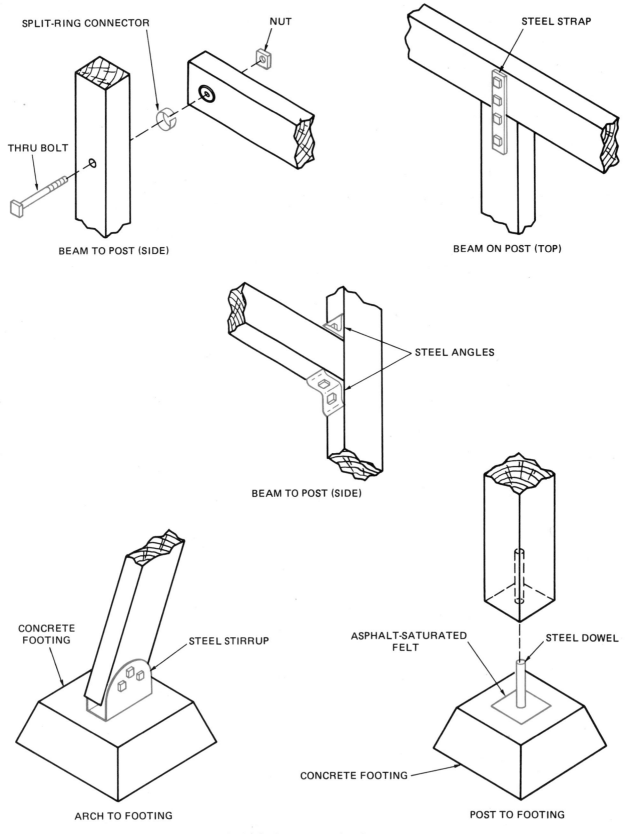

SPLIT-RING CONNECTOR

NUT

STEEL STRAP

THRU BOLT

BEAM TO POST (SIDE)

BEAM ON POST (TOP)

STEEL ANGLES

BEAM TO POST (SIDE)

CONCRETE FOOTING

STEEL STIRRUP

ASPHALT-SATURATED FELT

STEEL DOWEL

CONCRETE FOOTING

ARCH TO FOOTING

POST TO FOOTING

Fig. 21-8 Common timber fastenings

FASTENINGS

Timbers are too large to be fastened to one another and to other building materials by normal wood fastening techniques, such as nails or screws. There are, however, simple fastening devices for use with timbers, figure 21-8.

The most common devices for timber fastening are shear plates, steel angles, split rings, and lag screws. A *shear plate* is a flat steel strap that is simply screwed or bolted to both members. *Steel angles* are short lengths of angle iron used as corner brackets. *Split-ring connectors* are rings that fit into a circular groove in the face of each of the members to be connected. A bolt through the two members holds them against the split ring. *Lag screws* are large wood screws with square heads.

PLANK-AND-BEAM CONSTRUCTION

Plank-and-beam construction uses fewer structural members placed farther apart than conventional wood framing, figure 21-9. The members are heavier than those used in conventional framing. This type of construction consists of planks (dimension lumber) laid over beams which are supported by posts. Since the planks are usually 2-inch nominal thickness, they can span up to 8 feet. The beams, which are spaced 4 to 8 feet apart, range in size from 3″ x 8″ to 5″ x 10″. The beams are placed directly over the posts or columns which are 4″ x 4″ or larger.

Plank-and-beam construction requires fewer pieces of material, so it can be completed with fewer man-hours. The interior of plank-and-beam buildings can be designed to take advantage of the exposed framing, figure 21-10. This system is popular in modern homes. In nonresidential construction, the slow-burning characteristic of heavy wood allows it to be classed as slow-burning construction. This results in safer structures and lower insurance rates.

Fig 21-9 (A) Plank-and-beam framing

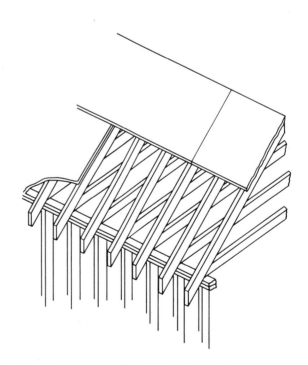

Fig. 21-9 (B) Conventional framing

Fig. 21-10   Exposed plank-and-beam construction *(Weyerhaeuser Co.)*

Fig. 21-11   Laminated arches can span great distances without support. *(Weyerhaeuser Co.)*

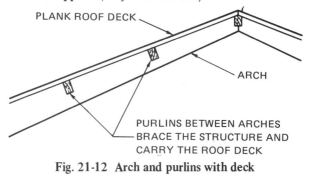

Fig. 21-12 Arch and purlins with deck

DOMED AND ARCHED ROOFS

Laminated arches are frequently used in public buildings. Because they can be produced in great lengths and are capable of long spans, arches can create a spacious interior, figure 21-11. They are also attractive when designed as part of the architecture.

When arches are used for the roof frame, intermediate members, called purlins, support the decking. *Purlins* are straight members that span the space between the arches, figure 21-12. A construction crew erects the arches, placing them on concrete footings and joining them with hardware at the top. Then, carpenters install the purlins using metal hangers, sometimes called *stirrups.* The arches and purlins make up the basic frame for this type of construction.

─── ACTIVITIES ───

A.   LAMINATING ARCHES

Equipment and Materials

    2 pieces of 1″ x 10″ x 36″ boards for forms
    1 piece of 1″ x 10″ x 36″ softwood
    4 pieces of 1/8″ x 3/4″ x 36″ softwood
    Waxed paper
    2 clamps
    Glue
    Scraper
    Block plane
    Backsaw
    Band saw

Procedure

1. Cut the forms out of 1-inch nominal thickness boards, figure 21-13.

2. Apply a uniform coat of glue to both faces of each 1/8-inch piece, except the two faces on the outside of the arch.

3. Wrap the glued stack in waxed paper to prevent the squeezed-out glue from sticking to the forms.

4. Place the laminates between the forms and clamp them securely, figure 21-14.

5. Allow 24 hours for the glue to dry, then remove the arch from the forms.

6. Scrape the excess glue from all surfaces.

7. Smooth the edges with a block plane and cut the arch to length with a backsaw.

8. Band saw a second arch of the same design from a piece of solid lumber.

9. Clamp the bottom of both arches in a vise and apply pressure downward to their top end until one arch breaks or cracks. What is the difference between the two arches?

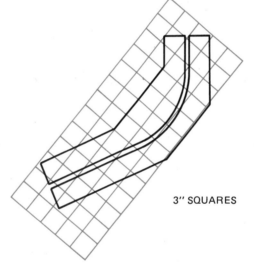

3" SQUARES

Fig. 21-13 Forms for arch (Activity A)

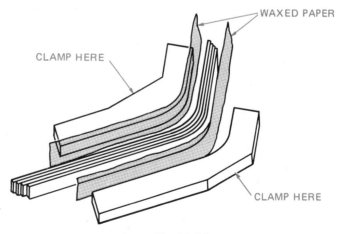

WAXED PAPER

CLAMP HERE

CLAMP HERE

Fig. 21-14

B. TIMBER CONSTRUCTION

Visit a structure that has timber construction. Study the use of timber and the kinds of fastenings used, then answer the following questions:

1. What functions do the timbers serve?

2. Is the timber construction used for appearance?

3. Is laminated timber used?

4. Why do you think timber was chosen as a building material for this structure?

5. Is pressure-treated timber used? Why?

6. Use a sketch to show at least one kind of fastening used on the timbers. Do not include nails, unless they are used with another device.

7. List the trades and occupations that were probably involved in the construction of the structural frame.

REVIEW

Multiple Choice

Select the best answer for each of the following questions.

1. Which of the following is considered a timber size?

    a. 2″ thick x 4″ wide   c. 3″ thick x 12″ wide
    b. 6″ thick x 6″ wide   d. All of the above

2. Which of the following is considered a dimension lumber size?

    a. 2″ thick x 6″ wide   c. 3″ thick x 10″ wide
    b. 2″ thick x 4″ wide   d. All of the above

3. Which of the following is considered a board size?

    a. 1″ thick x 6″ wide   c. 2″ thick x 4″ wide
    b. 3″ thick x 12″ wide   d. All of the above

4. Which of the following might be found in timber construction?

    a. Split rings   c. Pressure-treated lumber
    b. Shear plates   d. All of the above

5. Which of the following is an advantage of wood as a building material?

    a. It is slow burning.
    b. It is not affected by acids.
    c. It is very strong for its weight.
    d. All of the above

6. How are laminated timbers for exterior use different from those for interior use?

    a. They are thicker.
    b. They are made of hardwood.
    c. They are assembled with waterproof glue.
    d. All of the above

7. In what condition are laminated arches usually delivered to a construction site?

    a. Glued, sanded, and ready to be cut to length
    b. Completely finished and ready for use
    c. Glued, sanded, cut to size, and ready for finishing
    d. None of the above

8. What is the most outstanding characteristic of plank-and-beam construction?

    a. Planks and beams support the floor joists.
    b. No foundation is required.
    c. Structural members are farther apart.
    d. None of the above

9. What is a purlin?

    a. An intermediate roof support
    b. A special type of timber fastener
    c. A type of arch
    d. None of the above

10. Which of the following trades is involved in erecting arches?

    a. Masons   c. Operating engineers
    b. Ironworkers   d. None of the above

SECTION 6
SECTION 6
SECTION 6
SECTION 6

NONSTRUCTURAL SYSTEMS

LUNIT 22.
PLUMBING

OBJECTIVES

After completing this unit, the student will be able to:

- identify the common tools and materials used in plumbing.
- explain the basic principles of plumbing design.
- join plastic, copper, and cast-iron piping according to specifications.

TWO SYSTEMS

The plumbing in a residence must perform two basic functions. First, fresh water must be supplied to all points of use in the house. Second, once the water has been delivered, it must be carried away after use. To accomplish this, a plumbing system includes two basic subsystems: supply and sewage. The *supply plumbing* includes all of the pipes and fittings to carry fresh water from the municipal supply or the well to the point of use. *Sewage plumbing* includes the pipes and fittings to carry the used water and waste to the septic system or municipal sewage system. Sewage plumbing is frequently called drainage, waste, and vent plumbing, or simply DWV.

PLUMBING MATERIALS

The materials most often used for plumbing are galvanized iron, copper, plastics, and cast iron.

Galvanized Iron

Galvanized iron, once widely used, is not used as much in modern construction because it corrodes more rapidly than other materials. Galvanized-iron pipes and fittings are threaded so they can be screwed together. Two pipe wrenches are used to join galvanized-iron piping. figure 22-1. The plumber holds the pipe with one wrench and tightens the fitting with the other one.

Copper

Copper is frequently used for plumbing because it resists corrosion. However, it is relatively expensive. Copper pipes and fittings may be threaded or unthreaded for soldered joints.

The tools necessary for working with copper plumbing are a tubing cutter, steel wool or emery cloth, soldering *flux* (a very mild acid which chemically cleans the copper), solder, and

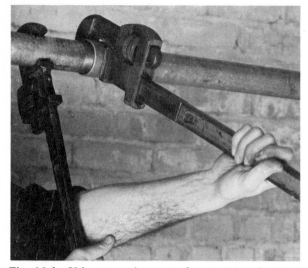

Fig. 22-1 Using two pipe wrenches to join galvanized iron piping

Fig. 22-2 Equipment for soldering copper pipe

Fig. 22-3 Apply soldering flux.

a propane torch, figure 22-2. *Solder* is a soft metal made by combining tin and lead. The percentage of each metal is specified in ordering solder. For example, 40/60 solder contains 40 percent tin and 60 percent lead. For sweating copper plumbing, 50/50 or 60/40 solder may be used. A plumber's torch consists of a propane gas cylinder, a regulator to control the working pressure of the gas coming from the cylinder, a hose, and the torch. A small propane torch with a disposable cylinder can also be used.

To sweat solder copper pipe and fittings:

1. Cut the pipe to the desired length.

2. Clean the end of the pipe and the inside of the fitting with steel wool or emery cloth.

3. Apply soldering flux to the parts to be joined, figure 22-3.

4. Assemble the pipe and fitting.

5. Heat the pipe and fitting until the solder melts when touched to the joint, figure 22-4.

6. Apply just enough solder to insure that the joint is completely soldered.

7. Clean any remaining flux from exposed surfaces with steel wool or emery cloth.

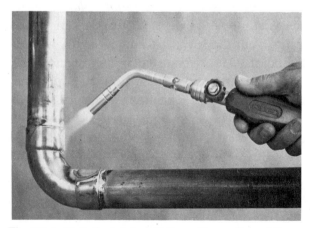

Fig. 22-4 Heat the joint until the solder melts and flows smoothly. *(The Ridge Tool Co.)*

Plastics

Plastics for use in plumbing materials are lightweight, noncorrosive, and easily joined. However, most plastic plumbing materials cannot be used around heat above 200 degrees Fahrenheit (93°C). Plastics are not suitable for some applications where high strength is required, but they are common for general supply and DWV plumbing.

Plastic pipe and fittings are joined with solvent cement. The cement is applied to the parts to be joined. The pieces are then quickly assembled and held in place for a few minutes while the cement cures. The solvent cement softens the surfaces. The softened surfaces fuse together and are held in position as the solvent evaporates.

Cast Iron

Cast iron is used extensively for DWV plumbing because of its strength and resistance to corrosion. However, it is seldom used for supply plumbing. A common type of cast-iron pipe has an enlarged end into which the straight end of the next piece fits. The joint is then packed with a fiber packing called *oakum*. Melted lead is poured over the oakum to fill the joint and make it strong, figure 22-5.

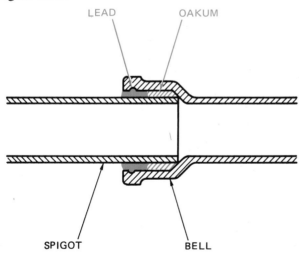

Fig. 22-5 Cast iron with a bell and spigot joint is sealed with oakum and molten lead.

FITTINGS

A wide assortment of fittings is available from manufacturers of plumbing supplies. These fittings are joined to the pipe to make turns at various angles, join additional pipes to the system, control the flow of water, gain access to the system for service, etc. Most fittings are made of the materials of which pipe is made. Plumbers must be familiar with all types of fittings so they can install their work according to the specifications of the engineer.

Couplings, figure 22-6, are used to join two pipes in a straight line. Couplings are generally used only where a single length of pipe is not long enough.

Unions, figure 22-7, allow piping to be disconnected easily. A union consists of two parts, with one part being attached to each pipe. Then the two parts of the union are screwed together. When it becomes necessary to disconnect the pipe, the two halves of the union are unscrewed.

Elbows, figure 22-8, are used to make changes in direction of the piping. Elbows turn either 90 degrees or 45 degrees. Plumbers sometimes use two 45-degree elbows to produce a more gradual turn.

Fig. 22-6 Couplings are used to permanently connect lengths of pipe.

Fig. 22-7 A union allows piping to be taken apart.

Fig. 22-8 90° elbow and 45° elbow

Tees and wyes, figure 22-9, have three openings to allow a second line to join the first from the side. Tees have a 90-degree side outlet. Wyes have a 45-degree side outlet.

Cleanouts, figure 22-10, allow access to sewage plumbing for cleaning. A cleanout consists of a threaded opening and a matching plug. When cleaning is necessary, the plug is removed and a *snake* or *auger* is run through the line. Cleanouts are installed in each straight run of DWV.

Valves, figure 22-11, are used to stop, start, or regulate the flow of water. The familiar faucets on a sink or lavatory are a type of valve.

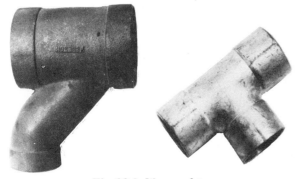

Fig. 22-9 Wyes and tees

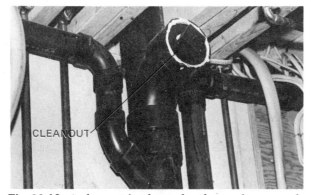

Fig. 22-10 A cleanout is a large plug that can be removed for access to the system.

Fig. 22-11 One type of water valve

DESIGN OF SUPPLY PLUMBING

In most communities water is distributed through a system of water mains under or near the street. When a new house is constructed, the municipal water department *taps* (makes an opening in) this main. The supply plumbing from the municipal tap to the house is installed by plumbers working for the plumbing contractor.

The main supply line entering the house must be larger in diameter than the individual *branches* running from the main to each point of use. There are two basic reasons for this. First, water develops friction as it flows through pipes, and the greater size reduces this friction in the long supply line. Second, when more than one fixture is used at a time, the main supply must provide adequate flow for both. Generally, the main supply for a house is 3/4-inch or 1-inch pipe.

At the point where the main supply enters the house, a water meter is installed. The water meter measures the amount of water used. The municipal water department relies on this meter to determine the proper water bill for that house.

The main water shut-off valve is located near the water meter. This is usually a *stop-and-waste valve.* A stop-and-waste valve has an

Fig. 22-12 A stop-and-waste valve is installed at a low point in plumbing.

opening in the side of the body that permits draining the system when the valve is closed, figure 22-12.

From the water meter, the main supply continues to the water heater. Somewhere between the water heater and the meter, a tee is installed to supply cold water to the house.

From the main supply, branches are run to each fixture or point of use. Generally, each branch has a shut-off valve so that the fixture can be repaired or serviced without shutting off the entire system.

When a valve is suddenly closed at a fixture, the water tends to slam into the closed valve. This causes a sudden pressure buildup in the pipes and may cause the pipes to *hammer* (a sudden shock in the supply piping). To prevent this, an air chamber is installed at or near each fixture. An *air chamber* consists of a short vertical section of pipe that is filled with trapped air, figure 22-13. When a valve is suddenly closed, the air chamber acts as a shock absorber. Although water cannot be compressed, air can be. When the pressure tends to build up suddenly, the air in this chamber compresses and cushions the resulting shock.

DESIGN OF DRAINAGE, WASTE, AND VENT PLUMBING

The main purpose of DWV, as stated earlier, is to remove water after it has been used and to carry away solid waste. To accomplish this, a branch line runs from each fixture to the main building sewer. The main building sewer carries the *effluent* (fouled water and solid waste) to the municipal sewer or septic system.

Traps

The sewer contains foul-smelling, germ-ladened gases which must be prevented from entering the house. If a pipe were simply run to the sewer, then as the effluent emptied from the pipe, sewer gas would be free to enter the building. To prevent this from happening, a trap is installed at each fixture. Another trap is installed at the point where the sewer leaves the building. A *trap* in plumbing is a point in the system that naturally fills with water to prevent sewer gas from entering the building, figure 22-14. Not all traps are easily seen.

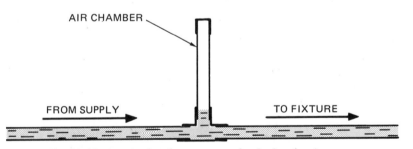

Fig. 22-13 An air chamber acts as a shock absorber in a plumbing system.

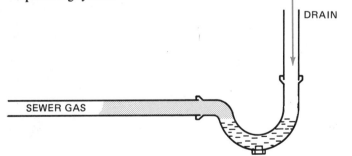

Fig. 22-14 A trap prevents sewer gas from entering the building.

Some fixtures, such as *water closets* (toilets), have built-in traps, figure 22-15.

Vents

As the water rushes through a trap it is possible for a siphoning action to be started. To illustrate this siphoning action, a piece of garden hose or tubing can be used to draw the water out of an open container, figure 22-16. By sucking water through the hose and holding

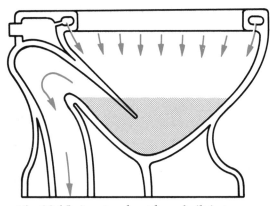

Fig. 22-15 A water closet has a built-in trap.

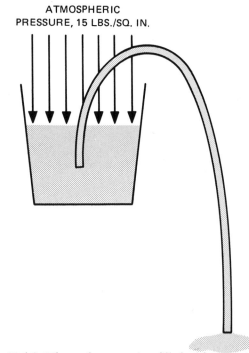

Fig. 22-16 When a hose or pipe filled with water is suspended in a container of water so that the outlet is below the inlet, atmospheric pressure forces the water from the container into the hose.

the discharge end at a point lower than the water level in the container, the water will continue to run through the hose without further sucking. This siphoning action can draw the water from the trap, leaving the sewer open to the inside of the building.

To prevent DWV traps from siphoning, a vent is installed near the outlet side of the trap. The vent is an opening that allows air pressure to enter the system and break the suction at the trap, figure 22-17. Because the vent allows sewer gas to pass freely, it must be vented to the outside of the building. Usually all of the fixtures are vented into one main vertical pipe, called a *stack*. The vent stack extends up through the roof or through an exterior wall, figure 22-18.

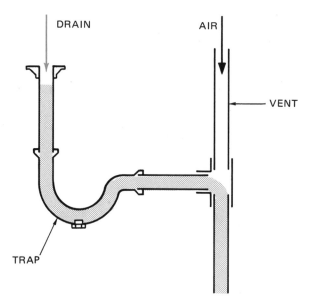

Fig. 22-17 Venting a trap allows air to enter the system and prevents siphoning.

Fig. 22-18 Plumbing vent. Notice the metal flashing to prevent leaks.

This is a simplified explanation of plumbing design. The design of a complete plumbing installation is highly technical and must meet the plumbing codes of the community. Plumbing design in new construction is usually done by a plumbing engineer. The plumbers who install the system must know basic plumbing principles to understand the specifications and drawings developed by the engineer. Since plumbers often repair or modify existing systems, they must also understand plumbing codes and plumbing design.

INSTALLATION OF PLUMBING

When the basic structure of the house is completed, the plumbing installation begins. This is done before any interior wall covering is applied. Plumbers install only the rough plumbing at this stage. *Rough plumbing* includes installation of main supply lines, main sewer lines, and all branch piping, figure 22-19. Although they are considered part of the finished plumbing, bathtubs are generally installed at this time also. This is so the interior wall covering can be finished next to the tub.

When the interior of the house nears completion, the plumbers return to install the *finish plumbing*. This includes installation of all remaining fixtures, such as sinks, lavatories, and water closets.

Fig 22-19 Rough plumbing includes all main supply drain lines and branch lines. *(Richard T. Kreh, Sr.)*

———— ACTIVITIES ————

A. JOINING COPPER OR PLASTIC PIPE

Equipment and Materials

> Two 1/2-inch valves with hose thread
> Two 1/2-inch 90-degree elbows
> Two 1/2-inch tees
> Two 1/2-inch caps
> 6 feet of 1/2-inch pipe
> Solvent cement (for plastic)
> Hacksaw (for plastic)
> Propane torch and flint lighter (for copper)
> Tubing cutter (for copper)
> Solder and flux (for copper)
> Steel wool
> Tape measure or folding rule

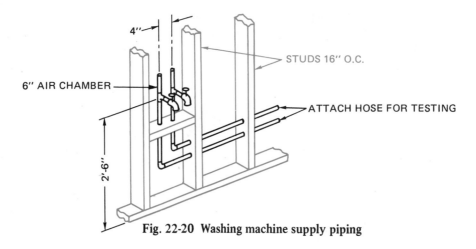

Fig. 22-20 Washing machine supply piping

Procedure

1. Cut all pipe the proper length to assemble as shown in figure 22-20. Assemble pieces without solder or cement to check the fit.

2. If using plastic pipe, clean the surfaces to be cemented with steel wool. Apply cement to both parts and immediately join the parts with a twisting motion. Hold them in place for a full minute.

3. If using copper, clean the ends of the pipe with steel wool. Apply soldering flux, join the parts, and sweat solder the joint. Using the propane torch, heat the pipe and fitting just until the solder melts when touched to the joint. Apply just enough solder so that a line of solder appears all around the joint.

CAUTION: Work on a fireproof surface. Know the location of the fire extinguisher and how to use it. Allow the joint to cool completely before handling it.

4. When soldering valves, the stem should be removed to prevent damage to the seals, figure 22-21.

5. When all fittings have been soldered, clean the excess flux from the pipe with steel wool.

6. Connect the soldered assembly to a faucet or hose bib with a hose. Turn on the water and open both valves. When water flows out of the assembly, close the outlet valve and check for leaks.

Fig. 22-21 Remove the valve stem before soldering.

REVIEW

Multiple Choice

Select the best answers for each of the following questions.

1. What does DWV mean?

   a. Drainage, waste, and vent
   b. Downward water vent
   c. Double waste vent
   d. A kind of double-weight material

2. Which of the following is part of the supply plumbing?

   a. Trap   c. Cleanout
   b. Vent   d. Air chamber

3. When do the plumbers normally begin installing piping in a house?

   a. As soon as the floor is framed
   b. As soon as the floor and walls are framed
   c. When the structure is enclosed, but before interior wall covering is applied
   d. When the house is nearly completed

4. What is a typical size pipe for a main house supply?

   a. 1/2 inch   c. 2 inches
   b. 3/4 inch   d. 4 inches

5. Which of the following materials is most apt to corrode?

   a. Copper   c. Cast iron
   b. Galvanized iron   d. Plastics

6. What is the purpose of soldering flux?

   a. To act as an adhesive in the joint
   b. To protect the joint from corrosion
   c. To help transfer the heat into the joint
   d. To chemically clean the joint

7. What is the purpose of a trap?

   a. To allow atmospheric pressure to enter the system
   b. To prevent sewer gas from entering the building
   c. To collect solid waste
   d. To create a siphoning action

8. What is the purpose of a vent?

   a. To allow atmospheric pressure to enter the system
   b. To prevent sewer gas from entering the building
   c. To prevent pressure buildup
   d. To act as an overflow in case of stoppage

9.   Where is a stop and waste valve most apt to be located?

   a. At the inlet to the water heater
   b. At the inlet to the water closet
   c. In the waste plumbing
   d. At the lowest point in the supply plumbing

10.   When do the plumbers install lavatories, sinks, and water closets?

   a. As soon as the floor is framed
   b. As soon as the floor and walls are framed
   c. When the structure is enclosed, but before interior wall covering is applied
   d. When the house is nearly completed

LUNIT 23.
CLIMATE CONTROL

OBJECTIVES

After completing this unit, the student will be able to:

- describe the operating principles of common heating and air-conditioning systems.

- explain the importance of thermal insulation.

- calculate simple heating loads.

Buildings of all types, especially buildings where people live, work, and play, use climate control systems. In nearly all parts of the country some means of heating is required in the winter. In most parts of the country cooling has become a necessity in the summer.

Heating, ventilating, and air conditioning (HVAC) is an important part of the construction industry. The services of mechanical engineers, electrical engineers, and heating and air-conditioning engineers are used to design the systems in most buildings. Electricians, plumbers, and HVAC technicians install the systems. All of these occupations require some knowledge of the principles of climate control.

HEAT TRANSFER

Controlling air temperature is a process of transferring heat into or out of a building space. This heat transfer can be accomplished by convection, radiation, evaporation, or gravity flow.

- *Convection:* Heat flows from a warm surface to a cold surface. For example, heat flows from warm air to a cold wall.

- *Radiation:* The movement of heat by heat rays. This does not require air or other medium. The sun's heat travels through space by radiation.

- *Evaporation:* As moisture evaporates it uses heat, thereby cooling the surface from which it evaporated. This is how perspiration cools the body.

- *Gravity flow:* Cool air is more dense than warm air. Therefore, warm air rises and cool air settles. Due to gravity flow, the air near a ceiling is warmer than the air at the floor.

279

AIR CYCLE

One of the most common systems for climate control circulates the air from the living spaces through or around heating or cooling devices.   A fan forces the air into large sheet metal or plastic pipes called *ducts*. These ducts, which are installed by sheet metal technicians, connect to openings in the room. The air enters the room and either heats it or cools it as needed.

Air then flows from the room through another opening into the *return duct*.   The return duct directs the air from the room over a heating or cooling device, depending on which is needed.   If cool air is required, the return air passes over the surface of a cooling coil.   If warm air is required, the return air is either passed over the surface of a *combustion chamber* (the part of a furnace where fuel is burned) or a heating coil.   Finally, the conditioned air is picked up again by the fan and the air cycle is repeated, figure 23-1.

Furnace

If the air cycle described above is used for heating the air, the heat is generated in a furnace.   Furnaces for residential heating produce heat by burning fuel oil or natural gas, or from electric heating coils.   If the heat comes from burning fuel oil or natural gas, the *combustion* (burning) takes place inside a combustion chamber.   The air to be heated does not enter the combustion chamber, but absorbs heat from the chamber's outer surface.   The gases given off by the combustion are vented through a chimney.   In an electric furnace the air to be heated is passed directly over the heating coils.   This type of furnace does not require a chimney.

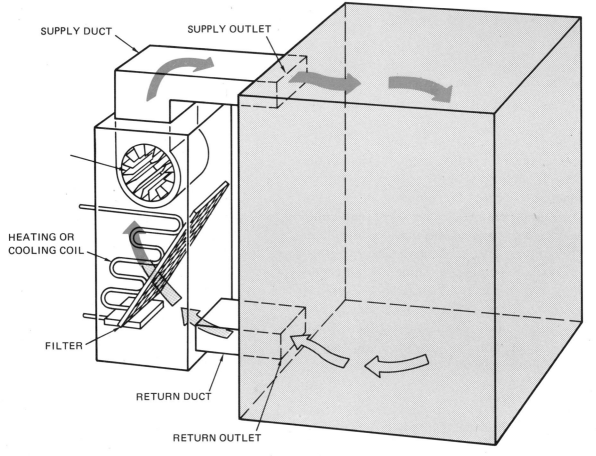

Fig. 23-1 The air cycle

A *thermostat* senses the temperature at some point in the house. When the temperature drops below a preset level, the thermostat, which is an automatic switch, starts the furnace.

Refrigeration Cycle

If the air from the room is to be cooled, it is passed over a cooling coil. The most common type of residential cooling system is based on the following two principles:

- As liquid changes to vapor it absorbs large amounts of heat.

- The boiling point of a liquid can be changed by changing the pressure applied to the liquid. This is the same as saying that the temperature of a liquid can be raised by increasing its pressure, and lowered by reducing its pressure.

The principal parts of a refrigeration system are the cooling coil (*evaporator*), *compressor* (an air pump), the *condenser*, and the *expansion valve*, figure 23-2.

Keep in mind that common refrigerants can boil (change to a vapor) at very low

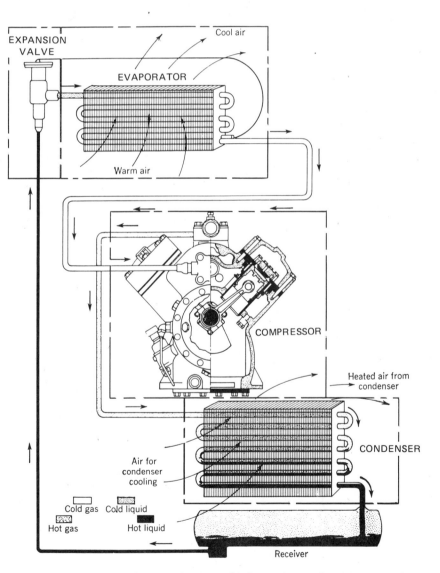

Fig. 23-2 Schematic diagram of refrigeration cycle

temperatures – some as low as minus 21 degrees Fahrenheit (-29°C). Also remember that a liquid boils at a higher temperature when it is under pressure.

The warm air from the ducts is passed over the evaporator. As the cold refrigerant liquid moves through the evaporator coil, it picks up heat from the warm air. As the liquid picks up heat, it changes to a vapor.

The heated refrigerant vapor is then drawn into the compressor where it is put under high pressure. This causes the temperature of the vapor to rise even more.

Next, the high-temperature, high-pressure vapor passes to the condenser where the heat is removed. In residential systems this is done by blowing air over the coils of the condenser. As the condenser removes heat, the vapor changes to a liquid. It is still under high pressure, however.

From the condenser, the refrigerant flows to the expansion valve. As the liquid refrigerant passes through the valve, the pressure is reduced. This lowers the temperature of the liquid still further, so that it is ready to pick up more heat.

The cold, low-pressure liquid then moves to the evaporator. The pressure in the evaporator is low enough to allow the refrigerant to boil again and absorb more heat from the air passing over the coil of the evaporator.

HOT-WATER BOILER SYSTEM

Many buildings are heated by hot-water systems. In a hot-water boiler system the water is heated in an oil or gas-fired boiler, then circulated through pipes to radiators or convectors in the rooms. The boiler is supplied with water from the freshwater supply for the house. The water is circulated around the combustion chamber where it absorbs heat, figure 23-3.

In some systems, one pipe leaves the boiler and runs through the building and back to the boiler. In this type, called a *one-pipe system*, the heated water leaves the supply, is circulated through the outlet, and is returned to the same pipe, figure 23-4. Another type, the *two-pipe system*, uses two pipes running throughout the building. One pipe supplies heated water to all of the outlets. The other is a return pipe which carries the water back to the boiler for reheating, figure 23-5.

Although several designs are used for hot-water heat outlets, most rely on convection

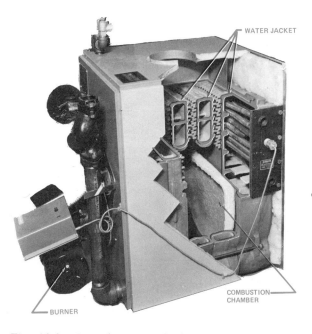

Fig. 23-3 In a hot-water boiler, water is circulated around the combustion chamber. *(Burnham Corp.)*

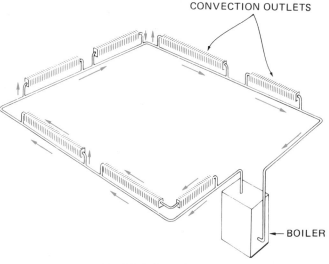

Fig. 23-4 One-pipe system

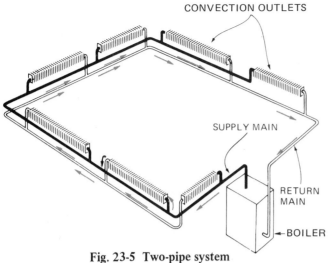

Fig. 23-5 Two-pipe system

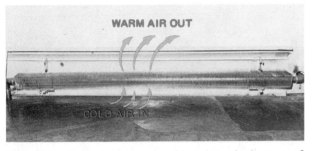

Fig. 23-6 Convection draws cold air into the bottom of the outlet and forces heated air out the top. Front cover has been removed to show operations. *(Richard T. Kreh, Sr.)*

for heat transfer, figure 23-6. Cold air enters the bottom of the outlet. As it rises past the hot-water-filled pipes, it picks up heat. The heated air exits near the top of the outlet.

Hot-water systems use a pump, called a *circulator*, to force the water through the system. The water is kept at a temperature of 150 to 180 degrees Fahrenheit (66°C to 82°C) in the boiler. When heat is needed, the thermostat starts the circulator.

ELECTRIC RESISTANCE HEAT

There are a number of heating system designs that rely on electric heating elements located in each room. Some such systems have electric heating elements imbedded in the floor or ceiling. In these systems the surface of the room is heated. The main method of heat transfer is radiation.

Another kind of electric heat has heating outlets similar to those described for hot-water heat. Heat transfer is by convection as the cool air passes the heating element.

SOLAR HEAT

In recent years there has been a growing concern about shortages of energy supplies. Each day it becomes more important to use the tremendous supply of energy available from the sun.

Greenhouse Effect

The simplest form of solar heating can be observed in greenhouses. Glass has a characteristic that is useful in solar heating. It allows the sun's radiant heat to pass through easily, but does not allow reflected heat to pass. This is the principle that allows the sun's energy to warm a greenhouse. If the reflected heat passed through glass as easily as the incoming radiant heat, most of the heat that entered through the windows would be reflected back out. This use of solar heat is called the *greenhouse effect*.

Just as windows admit heat to a greenhouse, windows also admit heat to houses and other buildings. By planning the sizes and location of windows, this heat can be used to warm a building in the winter and shade it in the summer. In the winter the sun is closer to the horizon for most of the day than it is in summer. By placing large window areas on the south side of the building, the winter sun shines through the windows, figure 23-7. Because the sun is higher in the sky during the summer, it can be kept off the windows through most of the day by building a large overhang on the south side of the roof, figure 23-8.

Solar Collectors

Solar energy can also be used as a source of heat for a hot-water system. All that must be done is to concentrate the sun's heat on pipes carrying water to the heating system. *Solar collectors* direct the sun's energy onto the heating system pipes.

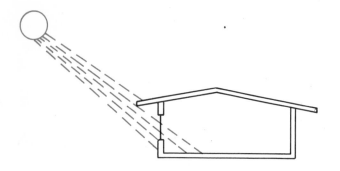

Fig. 23-7 In the winter, the sun is close to the horizon and shines in the windows.

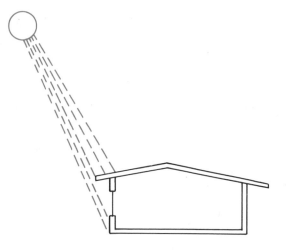

Fig. 23-8 Because the sun is higher in the sky in the summer, windows can be shaded by the roof overhang.

A flat-plate solar collector is basically a box containing several pipes and having a light-transmitting top. The basic box can be of any material. Sheet metal is the most common, but wood is perfectly suitable. The pipes are connected to the heating system at each end by a manifold. The *manifold* is a large pipe with fittings to connect all of the smaller pipes. The top surface is made up of a layer of glass and a layer of plastic. The glass takes advantage of the greenhouse effect. The transparent plastic covers the glass to protect it. A layer of dull black or dark green sheet metal is placed between the glass and the pipes. This surface absorbs a large amount of radiant heat, figure 23-9.

In operation, solar flat-plate collectors are placed where the sun's rays strike their surface in the winter, figure 23-10. The sun's energy heats an antifreeze solution in the collector's pipes. This warmed liquid is pumped to a large tank near the regular boiler. The water entering the boiler is circulated through a coil in the tank. This preheats the water going into the boiler, figure 23-11. Solar collectors do not provide 100 percent of the heat needed to heat a residence, but the use of solar collectors can reduce the fuel consumption of a boiler by as much as 60 percent.

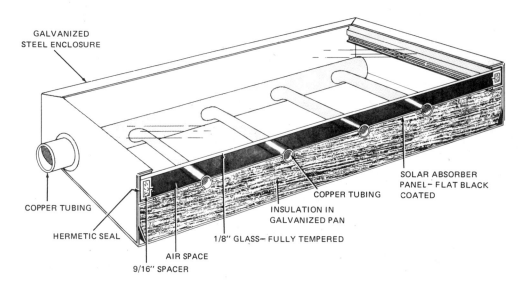

GALVANIZED
STEEL ENCLOSURE

SOLAR ABSORBER
PANEL— FLAT BLACK
COATED

COPPER TUBING

COPPER TUBING

INSULATION IN
GALVANIZED PAN

HERMETIC SEAL

1/8" GLASS— FULLY TEMPERED

AIR SPACE

9/16" SPACER

Fig. 23-9 A commercially-made solar collector

Fig. 23-10 Flat-plate collectors are positioned where they get direct sunlight.

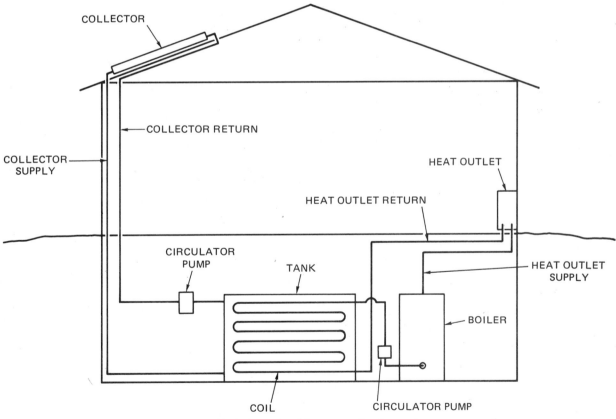

Fig. 23-11 Solar-assisted hot-water heating system

THERMAL INSULATION

So far, the methods of supplying heated or cooled air to a building have been discussed. It is equally important to prevent heat from entering a cooled building in the summer and from leaving a heated building in the winter.

Architects and heating engineers measure heat by *Btu* (British thermal units). A Btu is the amount of heat required to raise one pound of water one degree Fahrenheit. The rate of heat transfer is expressed at *Btuh* (British thermal units per hour).

All materials conduct heat. The rate at which a material conducts heat is its *K factor*. This is the number of Btuh that is conducted by one square foot of the material one inch thick with a difference of one degree Fahrenheit on each side. For example, consider a one inch thick piece of wood with one side being one degree colder than the other. If one Btu passes through one square foot of this wood every hour, its K factor is 1.

Since buildings are composed of an assortment of materials, the K factor is not a practical way to measure the amount of heat that is lost through a floor, ceiling, or wall. The combination of all of the K factors in a building section is the *U factor* for that section. Figure 23-12 lists the approximate U factors for some common types of construction.

The purpose of thermal insulation is to resist the flow of heat. The resistance of a material to the flow of heat is its *R value*. The R value is the reciprocal of the U factor (R=1/U). In other words, by including thermal insulation with a high R value in a building section, the U factor, or ability to conduct heat, of that section is reduced.

The most common insulating materials for buildings are fiberglass, foamed polystyrene (Styrofoam^R), and urethane foam. Fiberglass insulation is manufactured in rolls and batts (pieces a few feet long), figure 23-13. Foamed-polystrene insulation is usually manufactured in sheets from 1 to 4 feet wide

and 4 to 8 feet long. Urethane foam may be available in sheets or it may be sprayed onto the surface to be insulated, figure 23-14.

Type of Building Section	U Value
Wood frame with plywood sheathing wood siding, and 1/2-inch drywall no insulation.	0.24
Wood frame with plywood sheathing wood siding, and 1/2-inch drywall 3 1/2-inch (R-11) insulation.	0.07
8-inch concrete block	0.25
Single-glazed window	1.1
Double-glazed window	0.6

Fig. 23-12 U factors for some typical building sections

Fig. 23-13 Fiberglass insulation is available in rolls or batts. Batts are short pieces of this material.

Fig. 23-14 Foamed-in-place polyurethane is used for insulation. *(Upjohn Co.)*

The thermal insulation is installed in a building before the inside walls are covered. It is carefully fitted between the framing members, so that there are no openings through which heat can pass easily, figure 23-15.

ESTIMATING HEATING REQUIREMENTS

Design Temperature Difference

The difference between the inside and outside temperatures greatly affects the amount of heat that is lost through the shell of a building. The difference between the lowest probable outside temperature and the desired inside temperature *(design temperature)* is called the *design temperature difference*. The design temperature difference must be known in order to determine the heating requirements of the building.

Determining Thermal Resistance of a Building

Properly installed insulation is important to comfortable, economical heating. Although it is impossible to completely stop the flow of heat through a building section, insulation can greatly reduce it. Insulating materials vary in their ability to restrict the flow of heat, depending on their type density and other characteristics. For this reason, insulation is specified according to its R value, rather than thickness.

A building section consists of the materials supporting the structure, the inside and outside surface coverings, and whatever material is used to minimize heat transfer. Figure 23-16 shows a building section and the thermal resistance of each part. Notice that the total R value for the section is 4.59. Fiberglass insulation has a thermal resistance of approximately 3.7 resistance units per inch of thickness. If all 3 1/2 inches of available stud space were insulated with fiberglass, 12.95 resistance units would be substituted for the .95 units provided by the air space (3.7 x 3 1/2"). This would increase the total R value to 16.59 (12.95 – .95 + 4.59).

Notice that the original resistance is less than one quarter of the insulated resistance. With good insulation, slight variations in the resistance of the structural and finish components of the building have a minor effect on the overall resistance. In wall sections, the total resistance is the resistance of the insulation plus three units for the structural and finish components. Similar reasoning can be applied to the floor and ceiling to arrive at values for

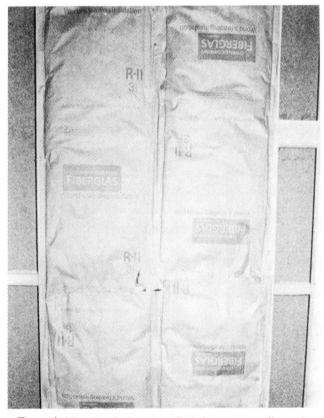

Fig. 23-15 Insulation installed between wall studs *(Richard T. Kreh, Sr.)*

FLOW OF HEAT

	RESISTANCE UNITS
INSIDE AIR FILM	0.68
1/2 INCH DRYWALL	0.40
AIR SPACE BETWEEN STUDS	0.95
FIBERBOARD SHEATHING 1/2 INCH THICK	1.52
BUILDING PAPER	0.06
WOOD BEVEL SIDING	0.81
OUTSIDE AIR FILM	0.17
TOTAL (R)	4.59

Fig. 23-16 A typical building section showing thermal resistance without insulation

Type of Building Section	R Value
Wood frame walls	3 plus the R value of the insulation used
Floors above unheated spaces	2 plus the R value of the insulation used
Ceilings	1 1/2 plus the R value of the insulation
Single-glazed windows	0.88
Double-glazed windows	1.67
Doors with glass	Use R value of the glass for the entire door
Doors without glass	1.67

Fig. 23-17 R values for common building sections

these sections. Uninsulated floors have a resistance of approximately 2 units. Uninsulated ceilings have a resistance of approximately 1 1/2 units.

Windows and doors offer much less resistance to the flow of heat than do other building sections, so the values mentioned above do not apply to them. A single layer of window glass has an R value of approximately 0.88. However, trapped air offers good resistance to heat flow, therefore double glazing increases the R value to approximately 1.67. The resistance values of several common building sections is shown in figure 23-17.

The amount of heat lost through the various sections of the entire building can be found from the R value for each section and the exposed area of each section. By dividing the resistance (R) into the area, the heat transmission load is found in Btuh per degree Fahrenheit

of design temperature difference. The *heat transmission load* is the amount of heat that is lost through the building materials.

The following four steps are used to find the transmission load:

1. Find the square-foot area of each outside section by multiplying its height by its length.

2. Divide the R value listed in figure 23-17 into the section area to find the heat transmission per degree difference for that section.

3. Add the transmission load per degree difference for all sections.

4. Multiply the total transmission load per degree difference by the number of degrees of design temperature difference. This is the total heat transmission load for the building.

——— ACTIVITIES ———

A. SOLAR WATER HEATER

Equipment and Materials

    8 linear feet of 1″ x 4″ lumber
    8 linear feet of 1″ x 1″ lumber
    1′ x 3′ plywood or hardboard (any thickness)
    1′ x 3′ glass

1′ x 3′ sheet metal
11 feet of 3/8-inch plastic pipe
6 feet of 1/2-inch plastic pipe
6 plastic tees, 1/2″ x 3/8″
6 plastic 90-degree elbows, 1/2″ x 3/8″
Small water pump (the type that can be powered by an electric drill is suitable)
4 feet of 1/2-inch hose
3 hose clamps
Saw
Hammer
Supply of 4d common nails
Tape measure or folding rule
Drill and 3/4-inch bit
Thermometer
3 square feet of fiberglass insulation

Procedure

1. Construct the solar collector as shown in figure 23-18.

2. Position the collector where the glass surface gets direct sunlight. The collector should be tilted to face directly into the sun.

3. Connect the pump with a piece of the hose so that it pumps water into the collector.

4. Fill the pail with room-temperature water. Record the temperature.

5. Attach a short piece of hose to the pump inlet and another to the collector outlet. These hoses are to be kept in the pail of water.

6. Run the pump for 15 minutes and record the water temperature.

7. Try running the pump slower for 15 minutes and record the temperature. Experiment with different pump speeds to get the highest water temperature.

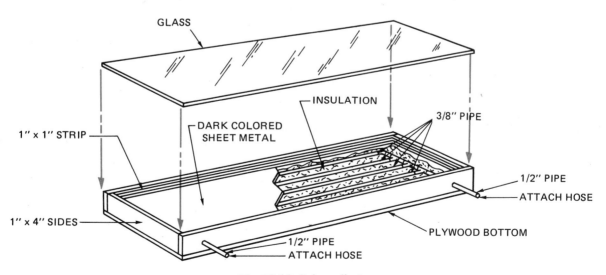

Fig. 23-18 Solar collector

B.   ESTIMATING TRANSMISSION LOADS

No special equipment or material needed.

Procedure

Find the total transmission load for a building with the following description:

24' x 40' frame construction with 8-foot ceilings
R-9 insulation in walls
R-21 insulation in floors and ceilings
2 doors, 3' x 7' each (no glass)
7 windows, 2' x 4' each (single glass)
1 window, 6' x 4' (single glass)
70°F design temperature/10°F outside temperature

1.   Find the area of the floor in square feet.

2.   Divide the R value shown in figure 23-17 into the area of the floor. This is the transmission load per degree for the floor.

3.   The area of the ceiling is the same as the area of the floor, but its R value is different. Use the R value shown for ceilings to find the transmission through the ceiling.

4.   Find the total area of all outside walls by multiplying the perimeter by the height of the ceilings.

5.   Find the total area of all windows.

6.   Find the total area of all doors.

7.   Subtract the total area of the windows and doors from the total wall area.

8.   Using figure 23-17, find the transmission per degree Fahrenheit of the walls minus windows and doors.

9.   Using figure 23-17, find the transmission through the windows.

10.   Using figure 23-17, find the transmission through the doors.

11.   Add the transmission of all individual building sections (steps 2, 3, 8, 9, and 10) to find the building transmission per degree Fahrenheit.

12.   Multiply the transmission per degree Fahrenheit by the number of degrees of design temperature difference. This is the total amount of heat that will be lost through the surfaces of the building per hour.

REVIEW

A.   Questions

Give a brief answer for each question.

1.   List three methods of heat transfer.

2.   What is the duct that carries cool air from a room to the furnace called?

3. What device starts and stops the circulator in a hot-water system?

4. Which method of heat transfer does not require air or other medium?

5. What heat transfer method is used when heat is absorbed by boiling water?

B.   Matching

Choose the item in the right-hand column associated with each item in the left-hand column.

1. Cools warm air   a. Evaporator
2. Heated vapor is put under pressure   b. Expansion valve
3. Heat is removed from refrigerant   c. Condenser
4. Refrigerant picks up heat   d. Compressor
5. Pressure of refrigerant is reduced

UNIT 24.
ELECTRICAL WIRING

OBJECTIVES

After completing this unit, the student will be able to:

- describe the relationship between voltage, current, and resistance.
- identify common electrical equipment.

To fully understand the wiring system that provides electrical power throughout a building, it is necessary to know how electricity flows. Electricity is a form of energy that cannot be seen or touched. However, its principles can be demonstrated.

CURRENT, VOLTAGE, AND RESISTANCE

In order to do work, electric current must be made to flow through a device, such as a motor or lamp. *Current* is the movement of tiny particles called electrons. An electric generator provides a force which pushes the electrons through a wire. When more electrons flow, more work is done. The amount of current flowing through a device or wires is measured in *amperes*, sometimes called *amps*.

If no force is applied by a generator, battery, or some other source, no current flows through the wires. The force that causes the current to flow is called *voltage*. The more

voltage applied to a wire, the more current (amps) flows through it. Voltage and amperage (current flow) can be compared to a water system – the greater the water pressure, the more water flows through it, figures 24-1 and 24-2.

There is one other factor that affects the amount of current flowing through a system. If the current must do a great amount of work to flow through the system, less current will flow. If the current can flow without doing much work, more current will flow. This principle is easily observed in a water system. When the water must flow through a small nozzle, relatively little water flows. When the nozzle is opened, more water flows. The force that slows the flow of electric current is called *resistance*.

Some resistance is present in any electrical system. If only the wires (*conductors*) made up the system, there would be very little resistance. In this case a low voltage would cause high

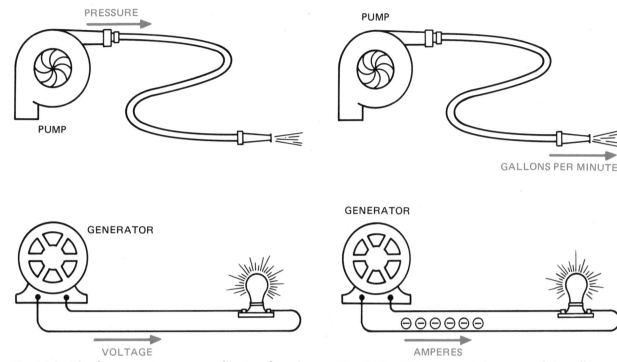

Fig. 24-1 The force a water pump applies to a hose is called pressure. The force a generator applies to a lamp is called voltage.

Fig. 24-2   Water current is measured in gallons per minute. Electrical current is measured in amperes.

current flow. If the resistance is high, such as when the current flows through a heater, the same voltage is able to make less current flow.

The amount of work done by electric current depends on the amount of current flowing and the voltage causing it to flow. Electrical work is measured in units called *watts*. One watt is the amount of work done by one ampere with a force of one volt. The utility company's electrical meter on the outside of a house measures the number of watts used and the number of hours for which they were used.

CIRCUITS

A *circuit* is an arrangement of materials that allows current to flow. It must include an energy source, a device that makes use of the current, connecting wires, and a switch to stop and start the flow of current, figure 24-3.

A complete circuit must provide a path for current to flow from the power source, through

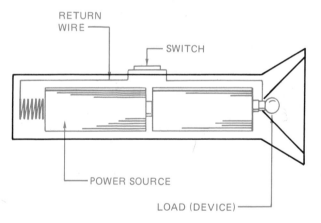

Fig. 24-3 A flashlight is an example of a simple circuit.

the device, and back to the power source. If current does not return to the source, the circuit will be unable to allow more electrons to pass and no current will flow. This is called an *open circuit*. When a switch is turned off, the circuit is opened.

If current is allowed to flow back to the source without overcoming the resistance of the device, an excess of current will flow. This condition is known as a *short circuit*. A short

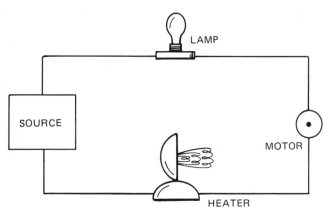

Fig. 24-4   In a series circuit the current must flow through all devices to return to the source.

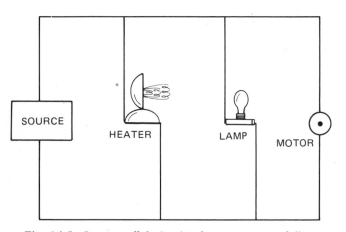

Fig. 24-5   In a parallel circuit, the current can follow one of two or more paths to return to the source.

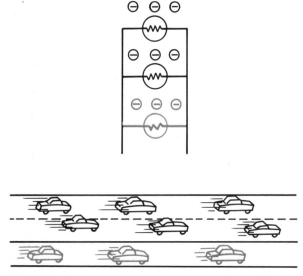

Fig. 24-6   A parallel circuit is like a multilane highway; as more branches are added, it is easier for electrons to get through.

circuit overloads the circuit wires and can either melt the conductors (wires) or start a fire in the insulation on the wires.

There are two basic kinds of circuits – series and parallel. In a *series circuit,* devices are wired in line with one another so that current must flow through each device to return to the source, figure 24-4. In a *parallel circuit,* the current can take one of two or more paths to return to the source, figure 24-5. Most wiring in buildings is parallel.

Every time a new device is added in a parallel circuit, the current has another path to return to the source. The effect of this is to lower the circuit resistance and allow more current to flow. A parallel circuit can be compared with a highway. Every time a new lane is added it is easier for electrons to get through, figure 24-6. When too many devices are added the current becomes excessive and the wires overheat, as with a short circuit.

To prevent overloading a circuit, a fuse or circuit breaker is installed. These *overcurrent-protection devices* automatically stop the current flow when a certain level is reached.

POWER DISTRIBUTION

Electrical power often must be transported great distances from the generating plant to the user. Due to the resistance of the miles of wire required for distribution, electricity is transported at as much as 600,000 volts. The voltage is reduced to 13,000 volts by transformers at substations. These substations supply distribution stations where the voltage is further stepped down to 2,200 volts. From the distribution station it is transported only a few miles to homes, businesses, and factories where it is stepped down to a more manageable voltage. Some industries use 480-volt electricity, but homes use 240 and 120 volts. From the last transformer a cable, called a *service drop,* carries the current to the KWH meter, figure 24-7. This is where the utility company's responsibility ends and the customer's starts.

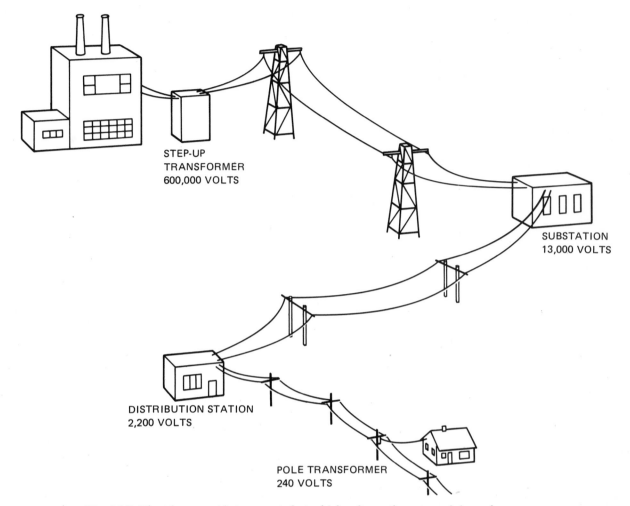

STEP-UP
TRANSFORMER
600,000 VOLTS

SUBSTATION
13,000 VOLTS

DISTRIBUTION STATION
2,200 VOLTS

POLE TRANSFORMER
240 VOLTS

Fig. 24-7 Electric current is transported at a high voltage, then stepped down for use.

GROUNDING

Large power generating plants are connected to the ground by means of a metal rod driven into the ground. Each user of electrical energy is also grounded, figure 24-8. In this manner, the earth provides a path for current to return to the source. Most electrical devices have a means for connecting to this ground system. If a live conductor accidentally comes in contact with the frame of the device, the current is directed through the ground rather than through the user. Some devices are grounded by attaching a ground wire to a water pipe, figure 24-9. Water pipes run through the earth and provide an excellent ground. The 3-prong plug on most small appliances provides grounding

Fig. 24-8 Electrical system grounded through a ground rod

Fig. 24-9 Electrical system grounded through a water pipe

CONVENIENCE OUTLETS
WATERPROOF CONVENIENCE OUTLETS
LIGHT FIXTURES
FURNACE FAN
BURNER
ELECTRIC WATER HEATER
GARBAGE DISPOSAL
DISHWASHER
KITCHEN RANGE
CLOTHES DRYER
EXHAUST FAN

Fig. 24-10 Electrical outlets commonly used in residences

Fig. 24-11 Convenience outlets are common outlets for plugging in various equipment.

through a ground rod or water pipe where the electrical service enters the building.

ELECTRICAL MATERIALS

The electrical system in a house is made up of the service drop and service panel, circuit wiring, and outlets. An *outlet* is a point in the system where equipment can be plugged in or permanently wired into the system, figure 24-10. The most common outlets in a house are light fixtures, switches, and convenience outlets. Switches are commonly referred to as outlets because they are installed in electrical boxes as are other devices used at outlets. However, since they do not draw current, engineers do not count them to determine the circuit load. *Convenience outlets* are the common outlets for plugging in various equipment, figure 24-11.

All connections in the wiring must be made inside a box. This includes connections with convenience outlets, switches, light fixtures, permanently connected appliances, and connections with other cables. Electrical boxes are made of steel or high-impact plastic. They protect the structure from fire in the event that an electrical spark occurs at the connection. Electrical boxes are made in many shapes and sizes for various uses, figure 24-12.

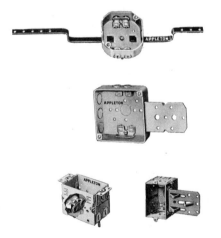

Fig. 24-12 Electrical boxes come in a variety of shapes and sizes.

TYPES OF WIRING

There are three types of wiring commonly used in electrical systems, figure 24-13:

- Nonmetallic sheathed cable
- Armored cable
- Conduit

Nonmetallic sheathed cable, commonly called *romex*, is made of copper or aluminum conductors covered with plastic or fabric insulation. It is lightweight, inexpensive, and easy to install.

Armored cable, commonly called *BX*, is made of separately insulated conductors encased in a spiral wound steel covering. It is flexible and easy to install. It provides more physical protection than romex, but cannot be used where moisture is present.

Conduit is a metal tubing with conductors running inside of it. The conduit is installed first, then the electricians pull the wires through it. Although conduit is more expensive and takes longer to install, it is the type of wiring used in most nonresidential construction.

Electrical cable is manufactured in a range of sizes and with 2, 3, or 4 conductors. The size of the conductor is specified by American Wire Gauge (AWG). The higher the AWG number, the smaller the conductor. General purpose wiring in residences is generally 14 or 12 gauge. Cable is specified by gauge and number of conductors. For example, "14-3 w/ ground" indicates a cable with three 14-gauge insulated conductors and one uninsulated ground wire.

DESIGNING AN ELECTRICAL SYSTEM

Engineers consider many factors in designing the electrical system for a house. The system must provide electrical power for fixed appliances, such as electric heating systems, furnaces, and water heaters. It must also provide outlets at convenient locations for small appliances and lighting. It must be the proper size to be safe and to prevent overloading.

The National Fire Protection Association publishes the *National Electrical Code* which specifies the design of safe electrical systems. Electrical engineers and electricians must know this code which is accepted as the standard for all installations. Among the things it covers are:

- Kinds and sizes of conductors
- Locations of outlets and devices
- Overcurrent protection (fuses and circuit breakers)
- Number of conductors allowed in a box
- Safe construction of devices
- Grounding
- Switches

The specifications for the structure indicates such things as the type and quality of the equipment to be used, the kind of wiring, and any other information that is not given on the drawings. However, electricians must know the *National Electrical Code* and any state or local codes that apply because specifications sometimes refer to these codes.

From the service entrance large cables carry electricity to the service panel. The service or distribution panel contains a main disconnect

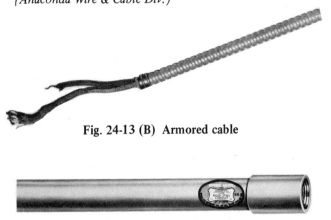

Fig. 24-13 (A) Type NM nonmetallic sheathed cable *(Anaconda Wire & Cable Div.)*

Fig. 24-13 (B) Armored cable

Fig. 24-13 (C) Rigid steel conduit *(Republic Steel Corp.)*

and overcurrent-protection devices, figure 24-14. Usually the overcurrent-protection devices are circuit breakers. The *main disconnect* is actually a large switch that allows all of the electrical power to the building to be disconnected. A *circuit breaker* is an automatic switch which opens the circuit if an excess of current tries to flow.

The service panel also splits the current up into several branch circuits. Each branch circuit

has a circuit breaker or fuse. Branch circuits distribute the current to the various devices in the system. The designer of the electrical system must determine the expected load on each branch. The size of the conductors and the rating of the overcurrent protection depend on the expected load.

The set of working drawings for a building includes an electrical plan. The electrical plans for many single-family houses are included on the floor plans. On larger construction jobs there may be several pages of electrical plans. The plans include symbols to indicate where devices are to be located, figure 24-15. Electricians must be able to read these plans. Figure 24-16 shows some of the most common electrical symbols.

ROUGHING-IN WIRING

After the building is framed and enclosed, and before the interior wall covering is applied, the wiring is roughed in. The electricians check the plans and specifications to determine the type and location of all materials.

The service panel is installed first. Then the locations of all devices are marked on the studs and joists. At each point where an outlet or switch is to be installed, a box is fastened to the building frame, figure 24-17.

When all of the boxes are installed, the electricians drill holes through the framing members and install the cables, figure 24-18.

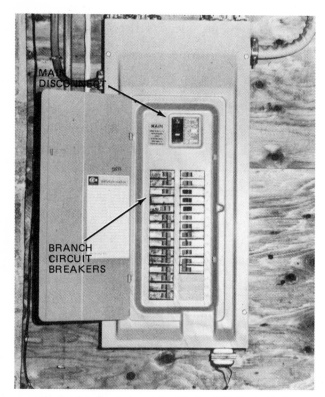

Fig. 24-14 Service panel *(Richard T. Kreh, Sr.)*

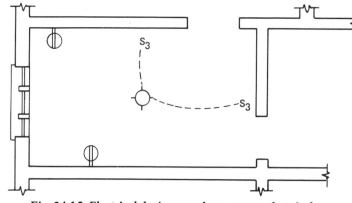

Fig. 24-15 Electrical devices are shown on an electrical plan by the use of symbols.

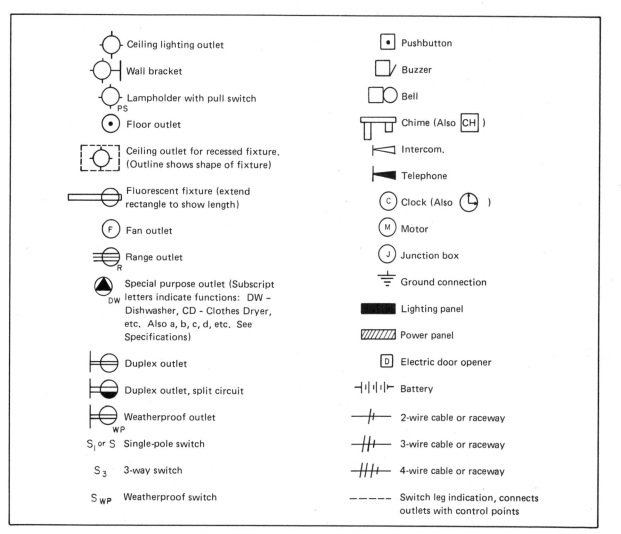

Ceiling lighting outlet	Pushbutton
Wall bracket	Buzzer
Lampholder with pull switch	Bell
Floor outlet	Chime (Also CH)
Ceiling outlet for recessed fixture. (Outline shows shape of fixture)	Intercom.
Fluorescent fixture (extend rectangle to show length)	Telephone
F Fan outlet	C Clock (Also ⏰)
Range outlet	M Motor
Special purpose outlet (Subscript letters indicate functions: DW – Dishwasher, CD - Clothes Dryer, etc. Also a, b, c, d, etc. See Specifications)	J Junction box
	Ground connection
Duplex outlet	Lighting panel
Duplex outlet, split circuit	Power panel
Weatherproof outlet	D Electric door opener
S_1 or S Single-pole switch	Battery
S_3 3-way switch	2-wire cable or raceway
S_{WP} Weatherproof switch	3-wire cable or raceway
	4-wire cable or raceway
	Switch leg indication, connects outlets with control points

Fig. 24-16 Common electrical symbols

Fig. 24-17 Electrical boxes are fastened to the building frame wherever switches and outlets are to be located.

Fig. 24-18 Electricians install electrical cable before the wall covering is applied. *(Richard T. Kreh, Sr.)*

Fig. 24-19 Bending conduit with a tubing bender *(The Ridge Tool Co.)*

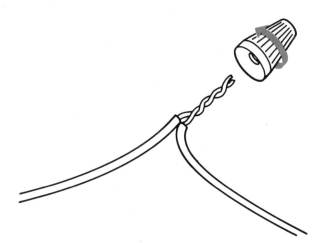

Fig. 24-20 Two or more conductors are connected by holding them together, sometimes slightly twisted, and screwing on a wire nut. The wire nut should cover the bare conductors completely.

Where metal framing is used, the manufacturer provides holes through which wiring can be run. If romex or BX cable is used, it is stapled to the framing members. If rigid conduit is used, it is attached to the boxes with threaded connectors. Conduit is cut to length, then bent with a tubing bender to fit the installation, figure 24-19. Wires are then pulled through the conduit and into the boxes. The conductors are connected to one another with *wire nuts,* figure 24-20. These are threaded plastic fittings which are screwed on to the bare ends of the conductors to make a connection.

Before the wall covering is applied, the wiring is inspected to make sure it meets the code requirements. Government agencies employ a large number of electrical inspectors.

ACTIVITIES

A. WIRING BRANCH CIRCUITS

Construction electricians install electrical systems before the interior wall covering is applied. They consult working drawings and specifications, plan the layout, then install the electrical apparatus and wiring. When the system is completed, they test the circuits for proper connections and grounding. An electrical inspector also checks the electrician's work to see that it meets all regulations.

Equipment and Materials

2 electrical boxes, 2″ x 3″
1 octagon box
Nonmetallic sheathed cable, 14-2 and 14-3
Duplex receptacle
2-way switch
Two 3-way switches
Light fixture

Procedure

Wire the circuits for a convenience outlet and a light fixture, figure 24-21; and wire the circuits for a light fixture controlled from two places, figure 24-22.

CAUTION: Have the circuit checked by the instructor before connecting it to a power source.

1. Cut the cable to the proper length, allowing approximately 6 inches inside each box.

2. Strip 6 inches of sheathing from each end of the cable before inserting it in the boxes.

3. Strip approximately 5/8 inch of insulation from the end of each conductor.

4. Conductors that are to be connected to one another are connected with wire nuts.

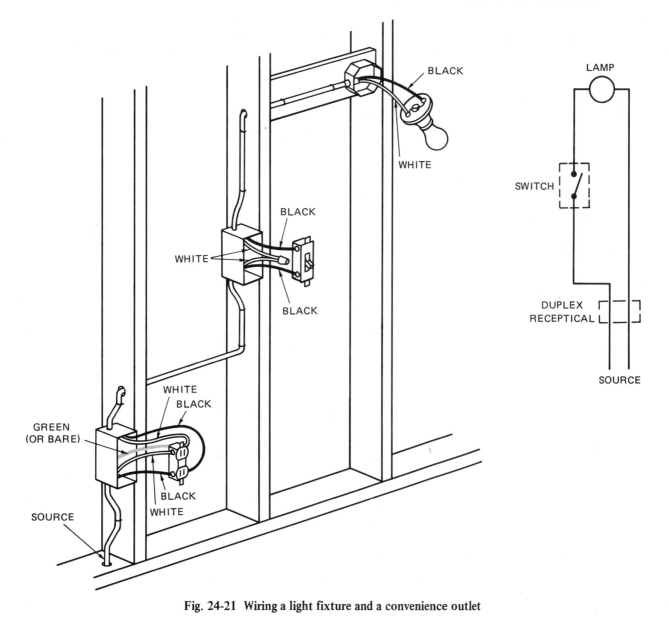

Fig. 24-21 **Wiring a light fixture and a convenience outlet**

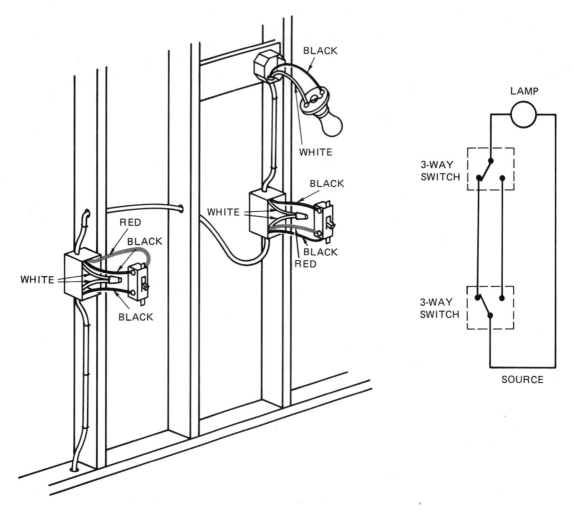

Fig. 24-22 Wiring a light fixture controlled by two 3-way switches

5. To attach a conductor to a device, clamp it under the head of a terminal screw, figure 24-23.

6. Be sure the wires are not kinked as the device is mounted in the box.

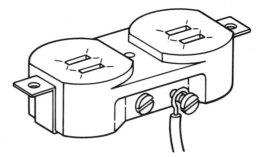

Fig. 24-23 The conductor should be wrapped around the terminal screw in a clockwise direction to prevent it from slipping out.

REVIEW

Questions

Give a brief answer for each question.

1. How does adding devices in parallel affect the resistance of a circuit?

2. How does adding devices in parallel affect the current flowing in the circuit?

3. Are switches wired in parallel or series with the device they control?

4. How does adding devices in parallel affect the voltage on a circuit?

5. What publication discusses the requirements for safe wiring?

6. What is the purpose of an electrical box?

7. What is the proper name of the electrical cable commonly called romex?

8. What is the proper name of the rigid metal tubing sometimes used in electrical wiring?

9. At what stage during the construction of a residence do the electricians rough in electrical wiring?

10. While referring to figure 24-24, answer the following:

    a. How many convenience outlets are there?
    b. How many 3-way switches are there?
    c. How many light fixtures are there?
    d. Where is the service panel located?

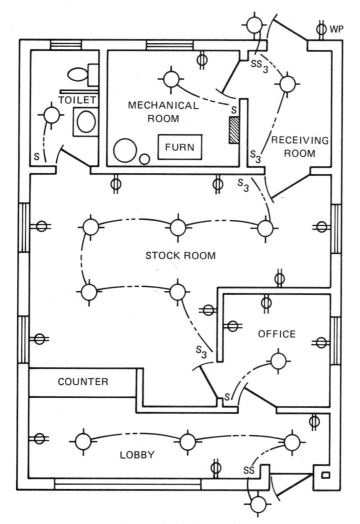

Fig. 24-24 Electrical plan for an auto parts store

UNIT 25.
INTERIOR FINISHING

OBJECTIVES

After completing this unit, the student will be able to:

- use common interior finishing materials.
- consider the factors in finishing the interior of a residence.

When all of the mechanical and electrical systems rough-in work has been completed and inspected, the interior finish work is begun. This includes installing the following:

- Ceilings
- Wall coverings
- Flooring or carpeting
- Molding and trim
- Cabinets and countertops
- Plumbing fixtures
- Electrical fixtures

Most of the interior finish is included in the subcontracts for the rough work. However, some trades are primarily concerned with finish work and others have specialists for this phase of construction. In general, workers who specialize in finish work must work to more precise dimensions and use more caution to protect surrounding work.

CEILINGS

The ceilings are usually the first interior surface to be covered. The ceiling material is either attached to the ceiling joists or hung from the joists on steel wires. The most common type of ceiling consists of gypsum wallboard nailed to the ceiling joists, figure 25-1.

Fig. 25-1 Nailing gypsum wallboard to the ceiling joists

Fig. 25-2 Drywall nail

Fig. 25-3 The dent caused by the hammer will be filled with joint compound.

Fig. 25-4 Applying bedding coat *(United States Gypsum Co.)*

Fig. 25-5 Placing reinforcing tape *(United States Gypsum Co.)*

Fig. 25-6 Applying a second coat *(United States Gypsum Co.)*

Fig. 25-7 Applying third coat

Gypsum wallboard is made of a plaster core 3/8, 1/2, or 5/8 inch thick with a strong paper covering. Its name comes from the fact that gypsum rock is used to make the plaster. It is manufactured in sheets four feet wide and eight to sixteen feet long. The long edges are tapered to permit concealing the joints.

Gypsum wallboard is usually installed by drywall mechanics who specialize in this work. However, it may be installed by carpenters in smaller construction companies. The wallboard is nailed to the joists with special nails. These nails have large flatheads and a ringed shank to prevent them from pulling out, figure 25-2. The nail heads are driven slightly beyond the surface of the wallboard. This leaves a shallow dent which is filled with joint compound, figure 25-3.

The edges of the wallboard are concealed with paper tape and joint compound. A layer of joint compound is applied with a joint knife or trowel, then the tape is pressed into it. This first coat is covered with a second coat of compound. When the second coat is dry, a finish coat is applied over a wider area, figures 25-4 through 25-7. When the completed joints are dry, the surface is lightly sanded to remove any imperfections.

A *suspended ceiling* consists of a metal framework hung on wires from the ceiling joists and fiber panels which fit into the framework, figure 25-8. Drywall mechanics or carpenters

Fig. 25-8 Suspended ceiling *(Celotex Corp.)*

attach the wires to the overhead framing, then hang the framework on these wires checking to see that it is level. The entire framework is installed first, then the panels are set in place.

WALLS

Gypsum wallboard is also a common wall covering material. It provides a sound surface for painting or papering and resists the spread of fire. On walls, gypsum wallboard is usually applied horizontally so that only one horizontal joint results, figure 25-9. When gypsum wallboard is used on the ceilings and walls, it is nailed to all surfaces first. Then the joints and nail heads are treated.

Another common wall covering is plywood or hardboard paneling. These materials consist of sheets, usually 4 feet by 8 feet, of plywood or hardboard with a decorative face. The decorative face may be hardwood veneer, wood grain printed on vinyl, or any attractive pattern on plastics. Wood-grained paneling creates a warm, natural atmosphere in dens, family rooms, living rooms, offices, and kitchens. Plastic-faced paneling provides an easy-to-clean, water-resistant surface in bathrooms and laundry rooms.

Wall paneling can be nailed to the wall framing, glued to the framing, or cemented to gypsum wallboard. Special colored nails are available for nailing wood-grained paneling and its trim. Water-resistant, plastic-faced paneling is usually cemented in place with special adhesives, figure 25-10.

Wall paneling is cut and installed by finish carpenters. They carefully measure the location of windows, doors, and electrical outlets and cut the pieces with common woodworking tools.

FLOORS

Hardwood flooring is laid by finish carpenters. Some carpenters specialize in laying flooring.

Hardwood flooring is generally made of narrow strips of oak or maple wood. These strips have tongue-and-groove joints, figure 25-11. As each piece is installed over the

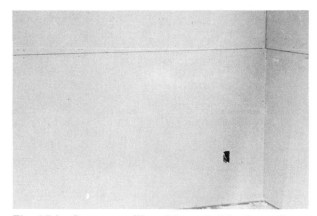

Fig. 25-9 Gypsum wallboard is applied horizontally so that only one joint results.

Fig. 25-10 Plastic-faced panels are cemented in place with special adhesive. *(Masonite Corp.)*

Fig. 25-11 Hardwood strip flooring

subfloor, it is driven up tight against the preceding one. It is nailed through the tongue. The completed floor is sanded with a floor sander to prepare it for varnishing.

When the thickness of the floor will not be built up by applying wood flooring, underlayment is applied over the subfloor, figure 25-12. Floor underlayment is either plywood or particleboard. It strengthens the floor as it builds areas up to the thickness of the hardwood floors.

Carpeting is also a common floor covering. Carpeting and the pad used under it are purchased by the square yard. Floor covering installers stretch the carpet to the edge of the

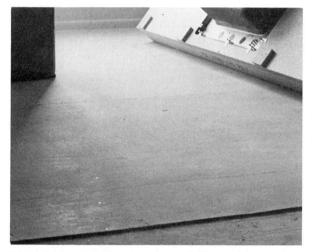

Fig. 25-12 Underlayment is applied over the subfloor when the thickness of the floor is not built up by hardwood flooring.

Fig. 25-13 Floor covering installers stretch the carpet to the edge of the room where it is held in place by carpet grippers.

room where it is held in place by carpet grippers, figure 25-13.

Seamless vinyl and vinyl tiles are often used where floors might be wet. Seamless vinyl (sometimes incorrectly called linoleum) is measured and cut much like carpeting, then cemented to underlayment with a special adhesive. Vinyl tiles are cemented individually.

Ceramic tile is also popular for use on bathroom floors. Ceramic tiles are manufactured in a variety of sizes and colors. They are cemented to the floor, then the joints between the tiles are filled with a mortarlike material called *grout*. Ceramic tile is usually installed by a tile setter.

MOLDING

Wood is machined into a variety of shapes, called *molding*, for use as trim. Molding is used to create special effects on paneling, to cover joints between building parts, and to protect areas. When the interior walls are covered with wood-grained paneling, special colored molding is used to match the paneling. Molding is installed by finish carpenters.

Window and door frames are trimmed with molding called *casing*, figure 25-14. The casing is mitered (cut at a 45-degree angle) at the corners and nailed through the wall covering into the wall framing. Windows also frequently have a stool and apron at the bottom.

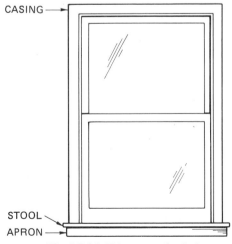

Fig. 25-14 Trim around window

To protect the walls from floor cleaning equipment and furniture legs, base molding is installed. Base molding is similar in shape to casing, but wider.

Corners of molding are mitered or coped to present a neat appearance. *Coping* means to cut the end of one piece so that it can be butted against the face of the other, figure 25-15. A miter box is used to cut accurate miters. The molding is fastened in place with finishing nails which are set and covered with wood putty.

CABINETS

Cabinetmaking is a specialized field. Some custom cabinetmaking is done by independent cabinetmakers, but most cabinets are mass-produced by large companies. Engineers and designers develop various styles and include special features, such as revolving shelves, special drawers, and attractive door designs. Drafters make working drawings from which the production department produces hundreds of cabinets. The completed cabinets are delivered to the construction site ready for installation by the finish carpenters.

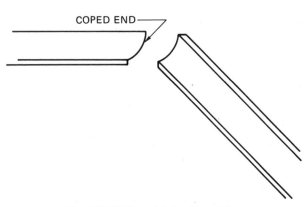

Fig. 25-15 Coped joint in molding

The specifications for a residence indicate the brand and style of the cabinets, figure 25-16. The working drawings indicate where the cabinets are to be installed, figure 25-17. Cabinets may be included in several rooms, but most are used in kitchens. The kitchen cabinet layout is carefully planned for convenience. The cabinets and appliances used for food preparation are close to one another and allow for easy serving. Usually the kitchen includes base cabinets with a countertop and wall cabinets above.

DIVISION 10

C.   CABINETS

1.   Kitchen cabinets shall be Kingswood Oakmont, as manufactured by the B. J. Sutherland Company of Louisville, Kentucky, or equal. Sizes and styles are to be as shown on the special detail drawings.

2.   Bathroom vanity shall be RV-48 Moonlight, as manufactured by the B. J. Sutherland Company of Louisville, Kentucky, or equal.

3.   Kitchen cabinet and vanity countertops shall be 1/16" laminated plastic bonded to 3/4" plywood. Countertops shall be of one-piece molded construction, with 4-inch backsplash and no back seams. The color and pattern are to be selected by the owner.

Fig. 25-16 Cabinet specifications

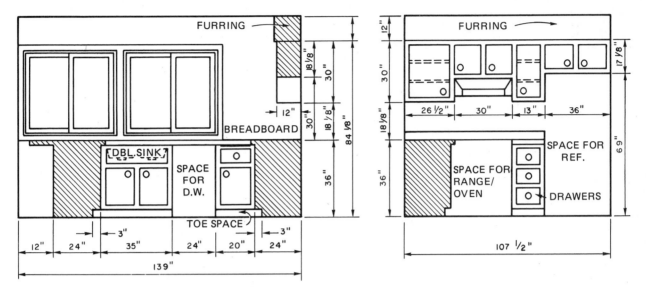

KITCHEN CABINET ELEVATIONS

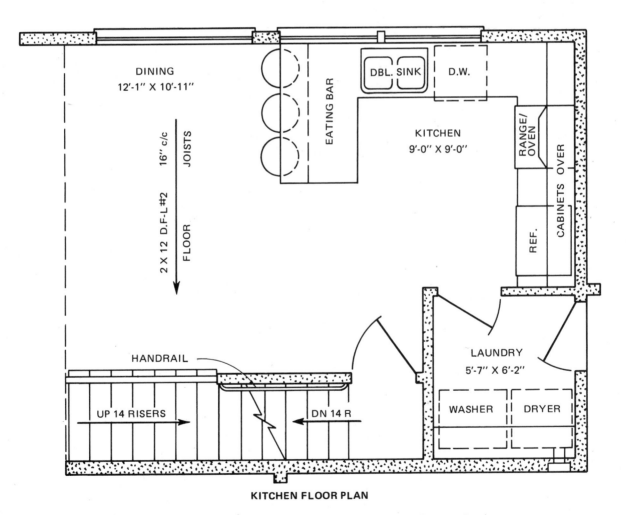

KITCHEN FLOOR PLAN

Fig. 25-17 Kitchen floor and elevation plans *(Home Planners, Inc.)*

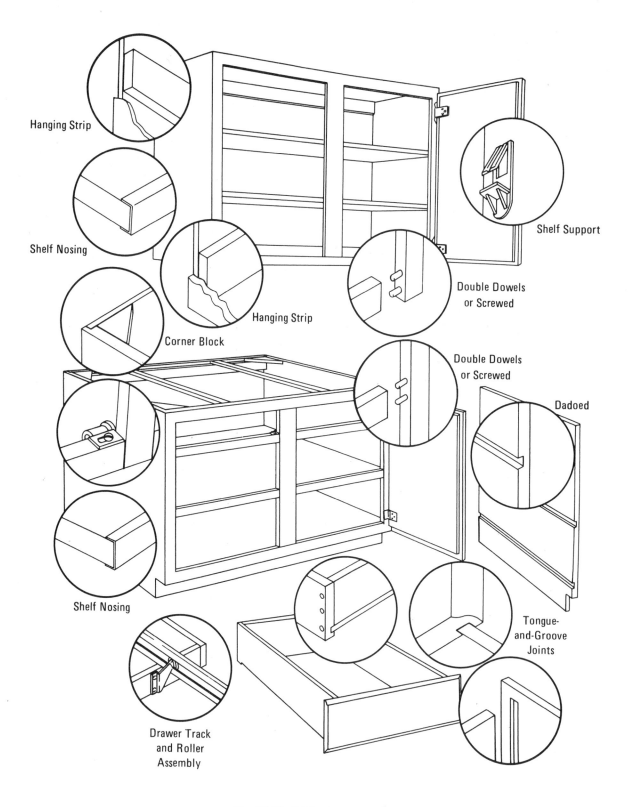

Hanging Strip

Shelf Nosing

Corner Block

Hanging Strip

Shelf Support

Double Dowels
or Screwed

Double Dowels
or Screwed

Dadoed

Shelf Nosing

Drawer Track
and Roller
Assembly

Tongue-
and-Groove
Joints

Fig. 25-18 Cabinet construction.

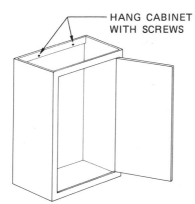

HANG CABINET
WITH SCREWS

Fig. 25-19 A hanging strip of solid wood is provided in the back of the cabinet.

Good quality cabinets have strong, glued joints, figure 25-18. Although most cabinets are factory made, good quality cabinets can be constructed using carpentry tools.

The cabinets are carefully uncrated, set in place, and shimmed with thin pieces of wood to level them. The backs of the cabinets are often made of thin hardboard with one solid wood crosspiece included to screw the cabinet to the wall framing, figure 25-19. The base cabinets rest on the floor and the wall cabinets are hung 14 to 24 inches above the base cabinets.

Countertops are made of particleboard or plywood covered with plastic laminate. Countertops for most kitchen base cabinets are 25 inches wide with a 3- or 4-inch *backsplash* to protect the wall. Preformed countertops are available with the plastic laminate molded over the edge and the backsplash, figure 25-20. This type of countertop is simply cut to length and attached to the cabinets with screws.

Countertops can also be constructed by the carpenter. The plywood or particleboard is fastened in place. Then the plastic laminate is cut slightly larger than the countertop. Contact cement is applied to the plywood or particleboard and the back of the plastic laminate. When the contact cement is dry to touch the plastic laminate is pressed into place. When properly used, contact cement bonds immediately on contact. After the edge has been covered

Fig. 25-20 Preformed plastic countertop

Fig. 25-21 Laminate is trimmed with an electric router.

in the same manner, the laminate is trimmed with a special bit in an electric router, figure 25-21. Carbide-tipped bits are used for trimming plastic laminates. Either a bit with a ball-bearing pilot is used, or a special guide is attached to the router base. All adjustments must be made carefully to regulate the amount that is trimmed.

The final important step in interior finishing is cleaning. After the finish work has been completed by each trade, all debris must be removed. This step is important enough that it is sometimes included in the specifications.

—— ACTIVITIES ——

A.   GYPSUM WALLBOARD APPLICATION

Installing drywall panels and preparing them for painting may seem easy. However, small defects on the finished surface will greatly affect the final appearance of the wall or ceiling. Drywall mechanics and finishers must work carefully to insure a smooth surface.

Equipment and Materials

4-foot section of wall frame with one opening
3/8- or 1/2-inch gypsum wallboard to cover wall frame
Supply of ring-shank drywall nails
1/4-gallon wallboard joint compound
100-grit abrasive paper
Perforated tape
Steel square
Utility knife
Tape measure or folding rule
Hammer
Joint knife

Procedure

1. Measure the area to be covered and the exact location of any openings.

2. With a pencil, lay out any necessary cuts on the best face of the wallboard.

3. Straight cuts are made in wallboard by first cutting the paper on the face, folding it to break the gypsum core, then cutting the paper on the back, figure 25-22.

4. Nail the wallboard to each stud, using drywall nails spaced approximately 10 to 12 inches apart. Nails should be driven just far enough to create a slight dent without tearing the paper on the face of the sheet.

5. Use a joint knife to apply a thin coat of joint compound to fill each nail dimple. Apply a thin (approximately 1/8 inch thick by 4 to 5 inches wide) coat of joint compound to all joints.

6. Embed perforated paper tape in the fresh compound at the joints.

7. Apply a second thin coat of joint compound over the perforated tape. Feather the edges out to approximately 8 inches wide.

8. After the compound is completely dry, remove any large bumps with abrasive paper.

9. Apply a finish coat of compound to all joints and nail heads. Feather the edges at the joints 12 to 15 inches wide.

10. After all compound is dry, smooth all surfaces with abrasive paper.

Fig. 25-22 (A) The paper on the face of the wallboard is cut with a knife.

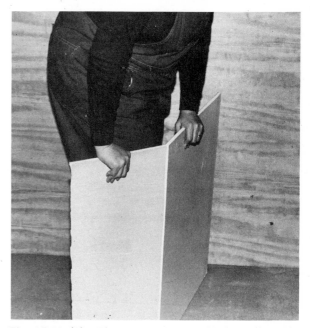

Fig. 25-22 (B) The gypsum core is broken where the paper was cut.

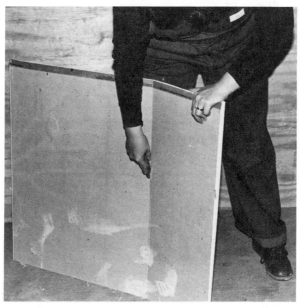

Fig. 25-22 (C) The paper on the back is cut.

B. BUILDING COUNTERTOPS

Equipment and Materials

Plywood or particleboard, 2 feet square
1″ x 1″ x 24″ piece of lumber
Three 1 1/4 x 8 flathead steel screws
Electric or hand drill and selection of
   bits
Screwdriver

Contact cement
Plastic laminate to cover surface
Plastic laminate edge banding
Electric router and laminate trimmer
   bit
Waxed paper

Procedure

1. To create an edge with the appearance of thicker material, attach a piece of solid wood to the underside of the surface at the edge, figure 25-23.

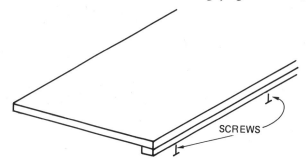

SCREWS

Fig. 25-23 Attach a piece of solid wood to build up
the edge of the counter.

2. Brush a uniform coat of contact cement on the back of the laminate and on the surface to be covered.

CAUTION: Some contact cement is highly flammable. Do not use contact cement near an open flame. Use adequate ventilation.

3. When the contact cement is no longer sticky to touch, cover the surface with two pieces of waxed paper, overlapping them near the center. The waxed paper prevents the laminate from sticking until it is in position.

4. Position the laminate on top of the waxed paper, allowing a slight overhang at the edges. Raise one side of the laminate enough to remove one piece of waxed paper. Raise the other side and remove the remaining piece of waxed paper, figure 25-24.

5. Apply pressure all over the surface to insure good contact at all points. This may by done with a soft-rubber mallet or by rubbing the surface with the corner of a piece of soft pine. Be careful not to break the overhanging edges.

6. Cement the edge banding to the counter edge in the same way. It is not necessary to use waxed paper with the edge banding. Be sure the top edge of the edge banding is against the underside of the top laminate before allowing the cemented surfaces to touch.

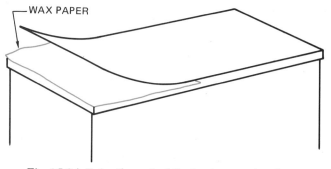

WAX PAPER

Fig. 25-24 Raise the end of the laminate and pull out
the second piece of waxed paper.

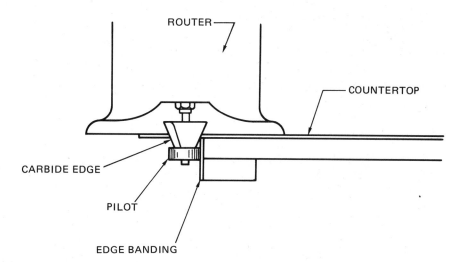

Fig. 25-25 Adjust the router depth of cut so that the countertop will be flush with the edge banding.

7. Insert the laminate trimmer bit in the router and adjust the depth of cut as shown in figure 25-25. To begin with, it is best to adjust the depth of cut slightly high. Then make a trial cut and readjust the depth.

8. Trim the overhang from the top laminate with the router base on the countertop and the trimmer-bit pilot against the edge banding.

REVIEW

A. Identification

Identify the trade or profession that performs the interior finishing jobs listed:

1. Installs window casing
2. Installs carpeting
3. Installs ceramic tile floors
4. Applies gypsum wallboard
5. Installs plumbing fixtures
6. Installs suspended ceilings
7. Installs kitchen cabinets
8. Plans the kitchen layout
9. Installs base molding
10. Installs lighting fixtures

B. Identification

List the items used for interior finish in figure 25-26, page 316.

Fig. 25-26

L UNIT 26.
PAINTING

OBJECTIVES

After completing this unit, the student will be able to:

- explain the purposes of paint and clear wood finishes.
- describe the differences between the various kinds of paint and finishing materials.
- prepare surfaces for paint or clear finish.
- apply paint and varnish.

Surfaces are painted for several reasons. Decoration is only the most obvious. Paint also provides protection from the sun, wind, and rain, figure 26-1. Steel and iron rust unless they are protected from moisture by paint or some other coating. Wood warps, cracks, and decays if allowed to absorb too much moisture. Painted surfaces are also easier to clean than unpainted surfaces.

There are several kinds of paint for interior and exterior uses, figure 26-2. Painters must know their differences and how to use each. Painters must also know how to use wood stains and several kinds of clear coating materials.

PAINT

Paint consists of solid pigments ground into a fine powder, a vehicle or liquid to hold the pigment, driers, and thinners. The *pigment* is

Fig. 26-1 **Paint provides protection and improves appearance.** *(Weyerhaeuser Co.)*

Fig. 26-2 Painters must be familiar with a wide range of products.

COMPOSITION OF PAINT BY WEIGHT

PIGMENT 35%

Black Iron Oxide.	57.2%
Barium Sulfate	36.5%
Silica and Silicates	6.3%

VEHICLE 65%

Nonvolatile	
Plasticized	
Acrylic Resin	34.8%
Volatile	
Water	65.2%

Fig. 26-3 Ingredients of typical water-base paint

COMPOSITION OF PAINT BY WEIGHT

PIGMENT 34%

Titanium Dioxide	11.4%
Calcium Carbonate	85.0%
Silicates.	3.6%

VEHICLE 66%

Nonvolatile	
Soya Alkyd Resin	42.2%
Volatile	
Mineral Spirits	57.4%
Driers	0.4%

Fig. 26-4 Ingredients of typical alkyd-resin paint

the coloring material in paint. White lead, zinc oxide, and titanium dioxide are common pigments. The *vehicle* is the liquid in which the other ingredients are mixed. The kind of vehicle used depends on the kind of paint. *Driers* are substances added to paint to speed its drying. Without driers, paint would dry very slowly, if at all. *Thinners* are chemical solvents added to make the paint more liquid and easier to apply. The thinner evaporates from the paint after it is applied to a surface.

Water-Base Paint

Water-base paint has a water-soluble, synthetic-resin vehicle. The most common synthetic resin in this type of paint is acrylic latex, often called *acrylic latex paint*, figure 26-3. The thinner for water-base paint is water. This paint dries quickly (usually within 30 minutes) and covers well.

Alkyd-Resin Paint

Alkyd-resin paints have a vehicle of oil and alkyd resin (a type of plastic), figure 26-4. Alkyd resin is made by combining alcohol and acid. Alkyd-resin paints produce an exceptionally hard surface which is very water resistant. Although it is not a true enamel, alkyd-resin paint is sometimes called enamel because its hard surface resembles that of enamel. These paints are thinned with mineral spirits or turpentine.

Interior Paints

Paint which is used on interior surfaces must be easily cleaned; produce a smooth, uniform surface; and have good covering ability. Oil-base and alkyd-resin paints for interior use are available in gloss, semi-gloss, and flat paint. Water-base paint is available in semi-gloss and flat. Most interior walls and ceilings are painted with flat paint. A *flat* paint is one which has no gloss when dry. Kitchen and bathroom walls are sometimes painted with semi-gloss paint. Woodwork is usually painted with gloss or semi-gloss paint.

Exterior Paint

Paint for the outside of a building requires different properties than that intended for indoor use. Exterior paint provides greater protection from sun, snow, sleet, and rain. Some white exterior house paint also has a self-cleaning property. This paint is chalky so that the surface cleans itself when it rains. Colored paints must be nonchalking to resist fading. Paint for exterior trim is usually glossy and nonchalking.

PAINTING

To get good results from any paint job, the surface to be painted must be properly prepared. The surface should be clean, dry, and free of old loose paint, figure 26-5. Wood surfaces should be sanded where necessary to smooth rough spots. Sanding is especially important on interior woodwork. Any defects, such as split boards, rusty metal, and loose fasteners, must be repaired before painting begins. Nail heads should be set and puttied. When painting the exterior of a building, painters protect nearby shrubs from dropped paint. When painting the interior, plumbing fixtures, finished floors, and other unpainted work are protected with drop cloths, figure 26-6.

Most paint manufacturers recommend applying one coat of primer before the regular paint. *Primer* is a special paint that adheres to the surface better than regular paint. The primer should be the one recommended by the paint manufacturer.

In general, painting should proceed from top to bottom and from large areas to trim. In painting the exterior, painters complete the siding from the roof to the foundation, then paint the windows, doors, and other trim. If the structure is made of masonry or masonry veneer, the painters are particularly careful not to drop paint on the masonry work. When painting the interior, the ceilings are painted first, then the walls, then the windows, doors, and trim.

Even though the paint may have been mixed when it was purchased, it should be stirred before it is used, figure 26-7. It can be applied with a brush, roller, or sprayer.

To brush paint on, use a good quality brush as wide as is convenient on the surface being

Fig. 26-5 To get good results from any paint job, the surface should be clean, dry, and free of old loose paint.

Fig. 26-6 A drop cloth protects fixtures and finished surfaces from paint spills.

Fig. 26-7 Always stir paint before using.

Fig. 26-8 Tap the bristles of the brush on the inside of the can to remove excess paint.

Fig. 26-9 Large surfaces are often painted with a roller.

painted. Dip the brush about one-third the length of the bristles into the paint. Remove the excess by tapping the bristles against the inside of the can, figure 26-8. Flow the paint on with long, full strokes.

To use a paint roller, pour a little paint into a roller pan. Work the roller back and forth in the pan until the roller cover is evenly saturated with paint. Roll the paint in several directions on the surface, then finish by rolling in one direction, figure 26-9.

Regardless of whether painting with a brush or roller, paint an area 2 or 3 feet wide across the ceiling or down the wall. Before the paint in that area dries, paint another area, overlapping the first slightly. If paint is allowed to overlap an area that is already dry, a line may show.

When the job is finished, or at the end of the day, the painters clean their equipment. Brushes and paint rollers are first cleaned

Fig. 26-10 Clean painting equipment with the thinner for the paint used.

with the thinner for the paint being used, figure 26-10. The thinner and any remaining traces of paint are washed out with soap and water, figure 26-11. Rollers are hung to dry. Brushes are wrapped in paper to protect the bristles, figure 26-12. Store paint burshes flat so the bristles will not be bent.

Fig. 26-11 Clean all traces of thinner out of the equipment with soap and water.

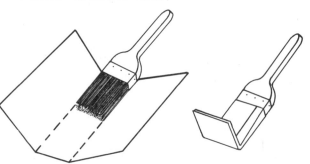

Fig. 26-12 After the brush is thoroughly cleaned, it is wrapped in paper and stored.

CAUTION: It is dangerous to use gasoline or kerosene to clean painting equipment. These fuels present a fire hazard and may cause severe skin irritation.

STAINS AND PENETRATING FINISHES

Some surfaces are not painted. Instead the grain figure of the wood is used for a decorative effect. These surfaces still need protection from the weather. A *penetrating finish* is one which is absorbed into the surface of the wood. The wood is protected while retaining the appearance of natural wood.

Often it is desirable to darken or change the color of wood. *Wood stain* is made from natural colors mixed with a penetrating vehicle and drier. Exterior stains provide a penetrating finish and stain in one operation. *Exterior stain* is applied in the same way as exterior paint.

Stains for interior uses are similar to exterior stains, but they generally do not have as much body and do not protect the wood. On interior trim and cabinetwork, stain is used to change the color of the wood before a clear finish is applied. There are several kinds of stain for interior use. One of the most common is pigmented oil stain. In use, pigmented oil stain is applied to the surface, then any stain which is not absorbed by the wood is wiped up with a rag. Stained surfaces should be allowed to dry before a clear finish is applied. Follow the manufacturer's instructions for drying times.

CLEAR FINISHES

There are a great number of clear finishing materials available. Each has different properties and is used in a different way. Only a few of the most common types of clear coatings for wood are discussed here. In selecting and using any paint or finishing material, it is always wise to ask for the assistance of the paint dealer and follow the manufacturer's instructions.

Shellac

Shellac is one of the oldest finishing materials in use. The basic ingredient in shellac

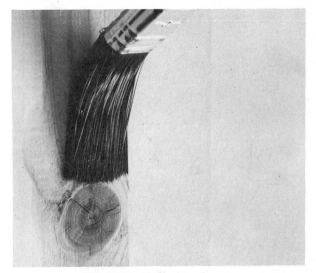

Fig. 26-13 Shellacking knots

is the secretion of an insect which is found in India. This solid material is dissolved in denatured alcohol to make shellac finishing material.

Shellac produces a very fine finish on wood. However, it does not withstand heat, direct sunlight, or water spills well. An important use of shellac is for sealing knots in pine and other resinous woods before painting, figure 26-13. The shellac prevents the resin in the knot from discoloring the paint.

Lacquer

True lacquer has a nitrocellulose base in some kind of fast-drying vehicle. However, it is common to refer to any finishing material that dries very quickly through evaporation as lacquer. Many of the modern coatings in this category produce very tough, water-resistant, alcohol-resistant surfaces. They are excellent for spray application because of their very short drying time, figure 26-14. Brushing lacquers are specially formulated to dry more slowly.

Varnish

Varnish consists of natural or synthetic resins in an oil base. Varnish also contains driers and thinners, much like paint. There are several kinds of varnish, depending on the resin used, the kind of oil, and other ingredients. Varnish

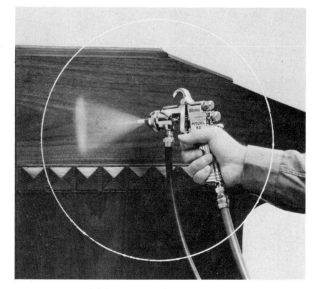

Fig. 26-14 Spraying lacquer on cabinets

Fig. 26-15 Sand woodwork before varnishing.

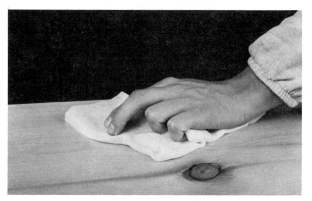

Fig. 26-16 Clean surface with a tack rag.

Fig. 26-17 Flow the finish on with long strokes and in the direction of the grain.

Fig. 26-18 Brush across the grain to spread the finishing material.

produces an exceptionally tough, clear finish.

A disadvantage of varnish is its slow drying time and tackiness (sticky quality). Varnish is difficult to apply without getting dust bubbles in its surface. However, the tough, durable surface produced by varnish makes it a popular finishing material.

Applying Clear Finishes

As there are a wide range of products available, no one set of instructions applies to all clear finishing materials. All manufacturers print instructions on their labels. However, the general procedure is the same for many of these products.

As with painting, the surface should be dry, clean, and smooth. The finish can only be as smooth as the surface on which it is applied. Surfaces should be thoroughly sanded with 150 to 180-grit abrasive paper, figure 26-15. Any scratches will show more clearly after the finish is applied. The surface should be dusted with a tack rag. A *tack rag* can be made by working a small amount of mineral spirits and a few drops of varnish into a clean, dust-free rag. This will remove all traces of dust, figure 26-16.

Before applying a clear finish, clean up all dust and, if possible, mop the floor. Do not shake or stir varnish as this will introduce bubbles. Dip the bristles of a good-quality brush one-third their length into the finishing material. Remove the excess by tapping the bristles against the inside of the can. Flow the finish on with long strokes in the direction of the grain, figure 26-17. Before the finish begins to dry, brush across the grain to spread the finishing material, figure 26-18. Finally, brush in the direction of the grain using only the tips of the bristles to remove brush marks, figure 26-19. Allow the finish to dry thoroughly, then lightly sand with fine abrasive to remove any imperfections.

Fig. 26-19 Brush in the direction of the grain using only the tips of the bristles to remove brush marks.

Apply a second and third coat following the same procedure. Generally, at least three coats are recommended for brushed-on finishes. Equipment should be cleaned using the recommended thinner and soap and water. The final coat may be rubbed with fine steel wool, pumice and water, or rubbing compound when completely dry.

WOOD PRESERVATIVES

Although they are not coatings like paint and clear finishes, wood preservatives are another important wood treatment. Wood that is exposed to water and certain insects and fungi decays very quickly unless it is treated. Wood preservatives prevent the decay which would otherwise ruin the wood.

Preservatives can be applied by dipping or brushing, but only a thin surface layer is treated in this way. A more effective treatment results from pressure treating the wood. The wood is loaded into large chambers where the preservative is forced into the cells of the wood under pressure, figure 26-20. Utility poles, bridge timbers, and piers are examples of the uses of pressure-treated timbers.

Fig. 26-20 Lumber being loaded into a pressure-treating chamber *(Koppers)*

—— ACTIVITIES ——————————————————————————

A.   PAINTING

Select a small project and apply either one coat of primer and two coats of paint or three coats of paint. Be prepared to explain why you chose the particular coating.

B.   IDENTIFICATION

Study the labels on three different types of paint and two types of clear finishing materials. Give the following information about each:

1. Brand name

2. Type of paint or clear finish

3. Percent of pigment

4. How much new wood will one gallon cover?

5. Is primer or sealer recommended? If so, what kind?

6. What thinner should be used?

7. How many coats are recommended?

8. Drying time

REVIEW

Multiple Choice

Select the best answer for each of the following questions.

1. Why are surfaces painted?

   a. To prevent decay
   b. For protection from the weather
   c. To prevent rusting
   d. All of the above

2. Which of the following is not used in paint?

   a. Oil
   b. Nitrocellulose
   c. Titanium dioxide
   d. Mineral spirits

3. What is an advantage of alkyd paints?

   a. They can be thinned and cleaned up with water.
   b. They produce a very hard surface.
   c. They can be applied by brushing or spraying.
   d. They have an oil vehicle.

4. What should be used to thin water-base paint?

   a. Gasoline
   b. Mineral spirits
   c. Turpentine
   d. None of the above

5. What is the purpose of pigment in paint?

   a. It makes the paint more durable.
   b. It makes the paint easier to apply.
   c. It gives the paint color.
   d. None of the above.

6. Which of the following surfaces would probably be painted with semi-gloss paint?

   a. Living room ceiling   c. Bedroom walls
   b. Living room walls   d. Kitchen walls

7. What is the purpose of pigmented oil stain?

   a. To protect the wood from water
   b. To color the wood
   c. To prevent scratches
   d. All of the above

8. Which of the following is an ingredient in shellac?

   a. Nitrocellulose   c. Denatured alcohol
   b. Tung oil   d. Acrylic resin

9. What is the greatest disadvantage of varnish?

   a. It is difficult to apply without picking up dust.
   b. It is not water resistant.
   c. It is not durable.
   d. It deteriorates with age.

10. What is the most effective way to apply wood preservative?

   a. Pressure treating   c. Brushing
   b. Spraying   d. Dipping

L UNIT 27.
LANDSCAPING

OBJECTIVES

After completing this unit, the student will be able to:

- list the important considerations in landscape design.
- outline the procedure for landscaping a typical building site.

DESIGNING THE LANDSCAPE

One of the final steps in completing any construction project is landscaping. This may be the simple grading and planting of a roadside, figure 27-1, or it may involve elaborate gardens and constructed features, figure 27-2.

Landscaping improves appearance, holds the soil in place, and provides access to structures.

The landscape design begins early in the planning of the project. On small residential jobs the architect for the building designs the landscaping. On larger projects the planners rely on a landscape architect for this part of the design. Four or five years of college preparation are required to become a landscape architect.

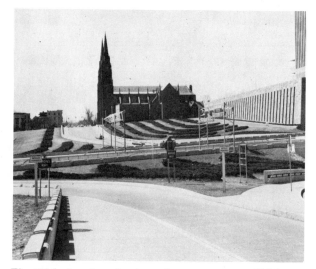

Fig. 27-1 Landscaping is an important part of highway construction.

Fig. 27-2 Landscapes may include elaborate gardens.

Environmental Design For:
SCHOHARIE BOCES CENTER
Schoharie, New York

Fig. 27-3 Completed landscape plan

Fig. 27-4 This landscape design includes many constructed features.

Fig. 27-5 These lamps are part of the landscape of a pedestrian mall.

Fig. 27-6 Patios are constructed landscape features. *(Bethlehem Steel Co.)*

The landscape architect considers the needs of the people served by the structure, the environmental surroundings, and advice from other professionals and experts in designing the landscape.

All of the features of the design are included on a working drawing called a *landscape plan*, figure 27-3. This plan shows the location of buildings; the locations and designs of driveways, parking lots, patios, and walks; and the kind and location of all vegetation.

When the structure is completed, the landscape constructor begins work on the landscape. Landscape contractors sometimes design the landscape for smaller projects. On larger projects the contractor is usually selected by competitive bidding in the same manner as other subcontractors. Workers who are employed by landscape contractors are called *landscapers*.

CONSTRUCTED FEATURES

The first step in landscaping the site is to complete constructed features. These include such things as driveways, parking lots, patios, and fountains. Most of these features are constructed of materials which might also be used in a building. For example, driveways and walks may be concrete and patios may be stone, wood, or brick. The details of such features are shown on drawings like those used for the main structure. Where an extensive amount of construction is included in the landscape, the landscape contractor works with contractors from the appropriate trade to complete the work. Figures 27-4 through 27-6 show examples of constructed landscape features.

Fig. 27-7   Rough grading is done with earth-moving equipment.

Fig. 27-8 Rake the top soil to the finished grade.

GRADING

The contour of an area is basic to the overall landscape. Not only does *grading* (shaping the contour of the site) affect the appearance, but it controls the runoff of water. Rain and melting snow run downhill. Eventually this *surface water* finds it way to the sea. On a properly graded site, water runoff is gradual until it reaches storm drains or streams. If low spots remain on the site, water will collect in these spots until it seeps through the soil. If the land is contoured too steeply, or if there are gullies, the runoff is fast. This can result in soil erosion.

Earth-moving equipment is used where large amounts of earth must be rearranged, figure 27-7. This operation is done when the initial site work is completed. Most of the earth's surface has a thin layer of topsoil. Where the topsoil must be scraped away, it is piled up so that it can be spread over the contoured site later.

Rough grading does not prepare the site for planting. It simply contours the site. *Finished grading* often involves a great amount of hand work. Large stones and debris can be removed from the topsoil by rakes mounted on tractors. However, to prepare the soil for a fine lawn, landscapers hand rake the topsoil, figure 27-8. The raked surface must be smooth and completely free of unwanted stones.

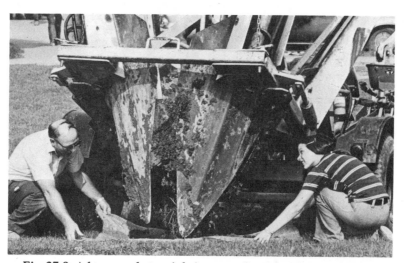

Fig. 27-9 A large maple tree is being transplanted with a tree spade.

Fig. 27-10 Shrubs are effective for stopping people from cutting across the corners of lawns.

Fig. 27-11 The roots of this tree are balled in burlap.

PLANTINGS

Trees

Trees are a valuable part of a landscape design. They provide shade, break the force of harsh wind, and create a natural, attractive appearance. Their roots are also valuable in controlling soil erosion. Landscape designers try to include existing trees in their plans. Many of the trees used are grown in nurseries and transplanted on the site, figure 27-9. The landscape architect specifies the kind of trees to be planted. Landscape gardeners must know how to transplant all of the trees commonly grown in their area.

Shrubs

Shrubs are smaller than trees and usually have several woody stems. They are attractive when used as part of a total design. They are also valuable for controlling traffic. A row of shrubs (*hedge*) planted near a walkway keeps people from straying off the walk, figure 27-10.

Shrubs, like trees, are grown in nurseries. The landscape contractor buys shrubs from the nursery. Shrubs and trees are sold in pots or with their roots balled and wrapped in burlap, figure 27-11.

Grass

Large areas of landscape are usually covered with grass. This provides an attractive, easily maintained ground cover and prevents soil erosion. The most familiar use of grass is around homes, but it is also valuable for roadsides, parks, and lawns around commercial buildings. The landscape designer specifies the type of grass that is suited to the particular site.

Before grass is planted, the topsoil is prepared. If the soil is compacted, it is cultivated to break it up. The soil is analyzed to determine what fertilizer is needed. Fertilizer is spread with a lawn spreader, figure 27-12.

There are three methods of planting grass: sodding, plugging, and seeding. *Sod* is a blanket of existing grass that is grown on a sod farm. A

Fig. 27-12 Fertilizer is spread with a lawn spreader.

Fig. 27-13 Placing sod

sod cutter removes the growing grass along with a thin layer of soil. The rolled up strips of sod are transported to the site where they are carefully placed on the prepared topsoil, figure 27-13. In some parts of the country, *plugging* is a common method for planting grass. With this method, small plugs of grass are inserted into holes in the topsoil. Most grass, however, is planted by *seeding*. Grass seed is spread evenly over the topsoil, then rolled to force the seeds into the soil.

Freshly planted grass must be treated with care until it is well established. Lawns near walks and buildings are roped off to stop people from walking on them. A *mulch* of clean straw or hay is spread over the surface. Mulching protects the new grass from direct sunlight and

helps the soil hold its moisture. Later, the mulch decays and provides organic fertilizer. On steep slopes netting is used to hold the soil and grass seed in place, figure 27-14.

LANDSCAPE MAINTENANCE

Landscaping involves the planting and growing of many living plants. Like any living thing, the landscape requires care. Landscape gardeners mow lawns, prune trees and shrubs, and care for gardens. From time to time these plants require fertilizing and other special care. Landscape gardeners analyze the needs of this expensive part of the owner's investment and provide the necessary care.

Fig. 27-14 Erosion netting is used to hold grass seed and soil in place until the grass is established.

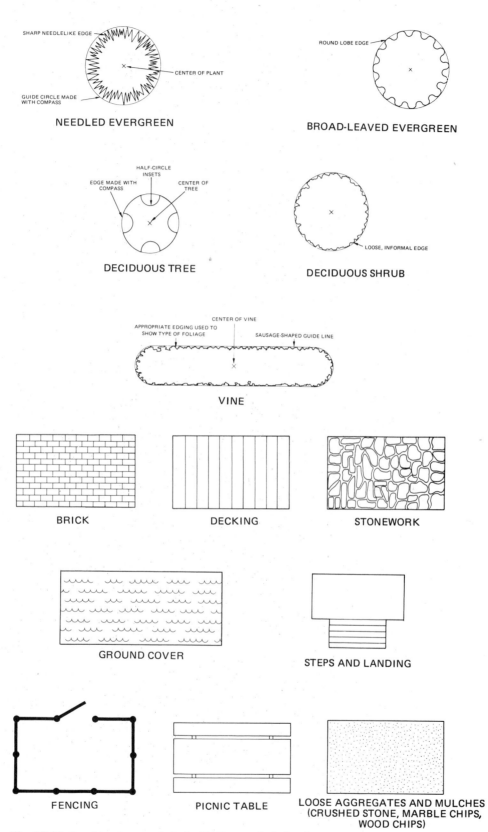

Fig. 27-15 Landscaping symbols (guide lines and circles do not appear on final plan)

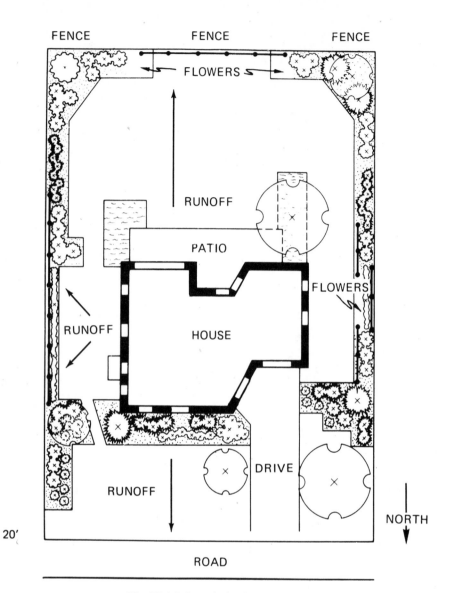

Fig. 27-16 Sample landscaping plan

───── ACTIVITIES ─────────────────────────────────

A. DESIGNING LANDSCAPE

Landscape architects arrange trees and shrubs with such constructed features as walkways, patios, terraces, and fences. They often supervise the necessary grading, construction, and planting. In order to do this, landscape architects must study construction techniques as well as horticulture and art.

Equipment and Materials

Architect's scale
Pencils and paper
Straightedge
Compass

Procedure

Using the symbols shown in figure 27-15, draw a landscape design for your home. You may draw a plan of the existing landscape, figure 27-16, or completely redesign it. Your design should include the following:

1. General shape and location of buildings

2. Approximate size and shape of the area to be landscaped

3. Constructed features

4. Trees

5. Shrubs

6. Lawn

7. At least one ornamental garden

8. It is not necessary to include contour lines on this drawing. Indicate the direction of water runoff by arrows labeled "runoff".

B. LANDSCAPING PROCEDURES

Study the landscape around your school or another commercial structure and list all of the features of the landscape. Make an outline of the tasks involved in producing that landscape.

REVIEW

1. When is the landscape designed?

   a. Before the main structure is designed
   b. Before construction begins
   c. When construction is nearly finished
   d. As soon as construction of the main structure is completed

2. What professional usually designs the landscape for a major project?

   a. Landscaper   c. Landscape architect
   b. Civil engineer   d. Landscape contractor

3. Which of the following steps is normally done first?

   a. Finished grading   c. Transplant trees
   b. Construct patio   d. Seeding

4. Who would normally construct a concrete driveway?

   a. General contractor   c. Landscaper
   b. Road builder   d. Cement mason

5. What might result from improper grading?

   a. Water collects in puddles   c. Unsightly appearance
   b. Soil erosion   d. All of the above

6. Which operation is usually done with machines?

   a. Rough grading
   b. Seeding
   c. Planting shrubs
   d. Finished grading

7. Which of the following is not a method of planting grass?

   a. Seeding
   b. Sodding
   c. Spraying
   d. Plugging

8. What is the minimum education required to become a landscape architect?

   a. High school
   b. 2-year college
   c. 4-year college
   d. No minimum requirement

SECTION 7
SECTION 7
SECTION 7
SECTION 7

MANUFACTURED
CONSTRUCTION

LUNIT 28.
MANUFACTURED CONSTRUCTION

OBJECTIVES

After completing this unit, the student will be able to:

- describe various manufacturing systems used in construction.

- compare manufactured construction with conventional construction.

DEVELOPMENT OF MANUFACTURED CONSTRUCTION

The American manufacturing industry is world famous for its efficient use of personnel and materials. In manufacturing, assemblies are put together on an assembly line by workers who specialize in a particular part of the total job. Manufactured goods are produced in controlled shops using special tools. Therefore, parts can be interchanged, quality is carefully controlled, and time is saved.

Until the middle of the twentieth century, nearly all construction was done using the same methods that had been used for centuries. Each piece of a structure was delivered to the construction site and installed separately. In the 1950s, lumber dealers devised a system to save valuable time. Roof trusses were assembled quickly on special fixtures, figure 28-1. A construction crew that would normally have spent an entire day framing a roof could set roof trusses in two or three hours. Soon after the introduction of prefabricated trusses, similar methods were used to manufacture prehung doors, prefabricated wall panels, and other items.

Fig. 28-1 These workers are assembling roof trusses with automatic machines. *(Bostitch Division of Textron, Inc.)*

337

PANELIZED HOUSING

Major home builders were quick to recognize the advantages possible with the use of manufactured building components. By the 1960s, houses could be enclosed in a few days with *panelized construction*. Using this method the excavation and foundation are completed, then the panelized components are delivered to the site. These components include factory-assembled floor, wall, and roof panels with exterior sheathing in place, figure 28-2. Panelized construction results in an enclosed shell ready for installation of utilities and finishing.

SECTIONAL AND MODULAR HOUSING

Panelized construction reduces the time it takes to erect the basic shell of a house. However, the shell only accounts for approximately one-third the cost of a house. To further take advantage of the benefits of manufactured housing requires more complete finishing and installation of utilities.

Two systems are used to manufacture completed building units. *Sectional houses* are completely built on assembly lines, figure 28-3. They are constructed with the same materials and types of construction as site-constructed houses. A completed house consists of two or more sections which are placed together on the foundation. These sections require only a small amount of exterior finishing where they are joined and hook up to water, sewage, and electrical service. A sectional home can be ready for occupation the day after it is delivered to the site, figure 28-4.

Modular construction allows more flexibility than sectional construction. A *module* is a boxlike unit that includes several rooms. Modules are combined to make homes, motels, and office buildings, figure 28-5.

A special type of module, called a *core unit*, contains most of the utilities for the finished building. By making three connections (water, sewage, and electrical), the core unit provides complete utilities for the structure.

Fig. 28-2 Panelized house being erected *(Northern Homes)*

Fig. 28-3 Sectional house on an assembly line *(Cardinal Industries, Inc.)*

Fig. 28-4 Completed sectional house *(Cardinal Industries, Inc.)*

Fig. 28-5 A completely finished motel unit being set in place *(Cardinal Industries, Inc.)*

Fig. 28-6 Precut materials are stored near where they will be used. *(Cardinal Industries, Inc.)*

Fig. 28-7 Carpenters use pneumatic nailers to assemble the units. *(Cardinal Industries, Inc.)*

This greatly reduces the time required for many of the subcontractors to complete the house on the site.

MANUFACTURING CORE UNITS

This discussion of how core units are manufactured by a typical company is representative of how much manufactured construction is done. The main parts of the core are constructed at the same time in different parts of the factory. Materials are cut to size for the various assemblies, then stockpiled near where they will be used, figure 28-6.

The floor is framed using conventional design with joists and headers. To save time and insure greater accuracy, jigs are used to position the members. A *jig* is any simple device to position parts for assembly. Jigs for construction may consist of blocks of wood nailed to a work surface. Carpenters nail the members with pneumatic (air-powered) nailing machines, figure 28-7. The sections are mounted on wheels so they can be moved along the assembly floor. The subfloor and finished flooring are installed before the unit goes to the final assembly area.

Walls are framed in a similar manner. Most walls have 2" x 4" or 2" x 6" studs spaced 16 inches or 24 inches on centers. Bathroom walls are framed with 2" x 6" to provide room for plumbing. The walls are assembled on a raised work surface, so the carpenters work in a comfortable upright position, figure 28-8.

Fig. 28-8 Walls are assembled on a raised surface. *(Cardinal Industries, Inc.)*

Fig. 28-9 The partially completed walls are stored on carts, then lifted into place with a crane. *(Cardinal Industries Inc.)*

Fig. 28-10 A completely assembled plumbing drainage system ready for installation

Fig. 28-11 Final assembly of a unit *(Cardinal Industries, Inc.)*

Electric hoists are used to turn framed components over. One surface is covered with wallboard or prefinished paneling. The partially completed walls are stored on rolling carts, figure 28-9.

The ceiling is built in the same way as the floor and walls. The ceiling, which is a single panel, may be painted prior to installing on the core unit.

As the structural parts of the core unit are being built, the plumbing shop assembles *plumbing trees*, figure 28-10. These assemblies of pipes and fittings include nearly all of the piping for the unit. The plumbers do not have to work around framing members, and jigs are used to assist in making the trees. This means that accurately constructed plumbing is ready for installation in very little time.

In the final assembly area, carpenters nail the walls to the floor assembly and to one another, figure 28-11. Next the ceiling is nailed on. Plumbers install the plumbing tree and fixtures. Electricians install the wiring and electrical fixtures, figure 28-12. Insulation is placed between the framing members of exterior surfaces. Finally, the interior is painted and trimmed according to specifications and cabinets are installed. Each core unit is hooked up and tested before it leaves the factory, figure 28-13.

Fig. 28-12 As the unit nears completion, electricians, plumbers, and painters finish their work. *(Cardinal Industries, Inc.)*

Fig. 28-13 Core units complete with kitchen and bath-room fixtures and cabinets *(Cardinal Industries, Inc.)*

Fig. 28-14 These manufactured houses are ready for trans-porting to their foundations. *(Cardinal Industries, Inc.)*

TRANSPORTATION AND PLACEMENT

The greatest restriction on manufactured construction is the size that can be transported, figure 28-14. In most states, objects over 12 feet wide are not allowed on the highways. This means that sections and modules cannot exceed this size.

When the manufactured building components arrive at the site, they are lifted from the truck to the foundation with a crane, figure 28-15. The foundation has anchor bolts that fit into predrilled holes in the house frame. A sectional house can easily be installed on a foundation by a crew consisting of:

- An operating engineer

- A rigger who also functions as a signaler

- An electrician to make the electrical hookup

- A plumber to make water and sewage connections

Fig. 28-15 Lifting a manufactured house to its founda-tion *(Cardinal Industries, Inc.)*

These persons may be regular employees of a manufactured housing contractor. Their skills and training are similar to those required in traditional construction.

───── ACTIVITIES ─────

A. MODEL SECTIONAL HOUSE

Draw a floor plan for a three-bedroom house to be constructed in two or three sections. On a scale of 3/8″ = 1′-0″, construct a simple cardboard model of the floor and walls of that house. Do not fasten the section together. Remember that sections over 12 feet wide cannot be transported.

B. WORKING CONDITIONS IN MANUFACTURED HOUSING

Make a list of all of the trades involved in the construction of a typical residence. For each of the trades listed, compare the working conditions for site-constructed and manufactured housing. List everything that helps describe the nature of the work performed by each of the trades on each type of construction. It may be easier to make the comparisons under two columns: one for site-constructed and one for manufactured construction.

REVIEW

Questions

Give a brief answer for each question.

1. What is the name for an assembly of pipes and fittings to be installed in a manufactured house?

2. What were the first building components to be prefabricated?

3. Give two advantages of manufactured construction over traditional construction.

4. What kind of construction uses factory-built panels for floors, walls, and roofs which are erected at the construction site?

5. What portion of the total cost of a typical house is spent on the shell?

6. What kind of manufactured construction is used when several identical units are put together for a motel?

7. What is the name of a module containing plumbing, wiring, and heating equipment?

8. Why are manufactured homes built in two or three sections instead of one large unit?

9. What construction must be completed at the site before a manufactured house is delivered?

10. How many connections must be made to hook up the utilities in a core unit? What are they?

LACKNOWLEDGMENTS

Reviewers

James E. Good, Consulting Editor
American Industrial Arts Association,
    President
James P. Gorham
Industrial Arts Teacher
Frank Hoffman
F.L. Hoffman Construction Corporation
Robert C. Kurzon, AIA
Architect
Russell Miller
Industrial Arts Teacher

Classroom Testing

This text was classroom tested by the construction classes at Ravena-Coeymans-Selkirk Central High School.

**Contributors of Photographs and
    Technical Material**

Acme-Cleveland Company
Adjustable Clamp Company
American Institute of Architects
American Institute of Timber Construc-
    tion
American Plywood Association
Anaconda Wire & Cable Division
Andersen Corporation
ARB, Inc.

Bethlehem Steel Corporation
Bostitch Division of Textron, Inc.
Bucyrus-Erie Company
Burnham Corporation
Cardinal Industries, Inc.
Cargill, Wilson & Acree, Inc.
C-E Morgan
Celotex Corporation
Cem-Fill Corporation
Chrysler Corporation
Cleveland Twist Drill
Community College of the Finger Lakes
Construction Specifications Institute
Deere & Company
Dow Corning Corporation
Engineering Graphics
Bertrand Goldberg Associates
Gold Bond Building Products
Gypsum Association
Home Planners, Inc.
International Conference of Building
    Officials
Keuffel & Esser Company
Koppers
Martin Marietta Corporation
Masonite Corporation
National Concrete Masonry Association
Niagara Mohawk Power Corporation
Northern Homes
Northwestern Mutual Life Insurance
    Company
Portland Cement Association

Powell & Minnock Brick Works, Inc.
PPG Industries
Republic Steel Corporation
Richard T. Kreh, Sr.
Rockwell International
Rohm & Haas Company
Rotec/oury-Beltcrete
Schroeder Brothers Corporation
Snap On Tool Corporation
The Blacker & Decker Manufacturing
    Company
The Boeing Company
The L.S. Starrett Company
The Ridge Tool Company
The Stanley Tool Division
Cortland Community College
U.S. Department of Agriculture
USDA Soil Conservation Service
U.S. Forest Products Laboratory
United States Steel Corporation
Upjohn Company
Western Wood Products Association
Weyerhaeuser Company
Wheeling Pittsburgh Steel Corporation

Delmar Staff

Kathleen E. Beiswenger – Associate
    Editor

Barbara A. Brown – Copy Editor

CAREER INDEX

ACTIVITIES INDEX

INDEX